Beginning F# 4.0

Second Edition

Robert Pickering
Kit Eason

Apress®

Beginning F# 4.0

Robert Pickering   Kit Eason
St. Germain-En-Laye
France

ISBN-13 (pbk): 978-1-4842-1375-9   ISBN-13 (electronic): 978-1-4842-1374-2
DOI 10.1007/978-1-4842-1374-2

Distributed to the book trade worldwide by Springer Science+Business Media New York, 233 Spring Street, 6th Floor, New York, NY 10013. Phone 1-800-SPRINGER, fax (201) 348-4505, e-mail orders-ny@springer-sbm.com, or visit www.springer.com. Apress Media, LLC is a California LLC and the sole member (owner) is Springer Science + Business Media Finance Inc (SSBM Finance Inc). SSBM Finance Inc is a Delaware corporation.

For information on translations, please e-mail rights@apress.com, or visit www.apress.com.

Apress and friends of ED books may be purchased in bulk for academic, corporate, or promotional use. eBook versions and licenses are also available for most titles. For more information, reference our Special Bulk Sales–eBook Licensing web page at www.apress.com/bulk-sales.

Any source code or other supplementary material referenced by the author in this text is available to readers at www.apress.com. For detailed information about how to locate your book's source code, go to www.apress.com/source-code/.

Printed on acid-free paper

For Noah and Darwin.

Contents at a Glance

About the Authors xv

About the Technical Reviewer xvii

Acknowledgments xix

Foreword xxi

■Chapter 1: Getting Started 1

■Chapter 2: How to Obtain, Install, and Use F# 7

■Chapter 3: Functional Programming 19

■Chapter 4: Imperative Programming 65

■Chapter 5: Object-Oriented Programming 93

■Chapter 6: Organizing, Annotating, and Quoting Code 125

■Chapter 7: The F# Libraries 147

■Chapter 8: Data Access 167

■Chapter 9: Parallel Programming 197

■Chapter 10: Distributed Applications 223

■Chapter 11: Language-Oriented Programming 241

■Chapter 12: Compatibility and Advanced Interoperation 265

■Chapter 13: Type Providers 285

Index 303

Contents

About the Authors xv

About the Technical Reviewer xvii

Acknowledgments xix

Foreword xxi

■Chapter 1: Getting Started 1

What Is Functional Programming? 1

Why Is Functional Programming Important? 2

What Is F#? 2

Who Is Using F#? 3

Who Is This Book For? 4

What's Next? 5

■Chapter 2: How to Obtain, Install, and Use F# 7

Obtaining F# on Microsoft Windows 7

Obtaining F# on Apple OS X 10

Obtaining F# on Linux 12

The Examples in This Book 14

Summary 18

■Chapter 3: Functional Programming 19

Literals 19

Anonymous Functions 21

Identifiers and let Bindings 21

    Identifier Names 23

    Scope 23

    Capturing Identifiers 27

    The use Binding 28

Recursion 28

Operators 29

Function Application 31

Partial Application of Functions 32

Pattern Matching 33

Control Flow 37

Lists 38

    Pattern Matching Against Lists 40

    List Comprehensions 42

Types and Type Inference 44

Defining Types 47

    Tuple and Record Types 47

    Union or Sum Types (Discriminated Unions) 50

    Type Definitions with Type Parameters 53

    Recursive Type Definitions 55

Active Patterns 56

    Complete Active Patterns 56

    Partial Active Patterns 57

Units of Measure 58

Exceptions and Exception Handling 60

Lazy Evaluation 62

Summary 64

■Chapter 4: Imperative Programming **65**

The Unit Type 65

The Mutable Keyword 67

Defining Mutable Records 69

The Reference Type 70

Arrays 73

Array Comprehensions 76

Array Slicing 77

Control Flow 77

Calling Static Methods and Properties from .NET Libraries 80

Using Objects and Instance Members from .NET Libraries 82

Using Indexers from .NET Libraries 85

Working with Events from .NET Libraries 85

Pattern Matching over .NET Types 88

The I > Operator 90

Summary 91

■Chapter 5: Object-Oriented Programming **93**

Records As Objects 94

F# Types with Members 98

Object Expressions 100

Defining Classes 104

Optional Parameters 107

Additional Constructors 108

Defining Interfaces 109

Implementing Interfaces 110

Classes and Inheritance 112

Methods and Inheritance 112

Accessing the Base Class 114

Properties and Indexers 115

Autoproperties 117

Overriding Methods from Non-F# Libraries 118

Abstract Classes 118

Classes and Static Methods 119

Casting 120

Type Tests 122

Defining Delegates 122

Structs 123

Enums 123

Summary 124

■Chapter 6: Organizing, Annotating, and Quoting Code 125

Modules 125

Namespaces 127

Opening Namespaces and Modules 128

Giving Modules Aliases 130

Signature Files 131

Private and Internal let Bindings and Members 131

Module Scope 132

Module Execution 134

Optional Compilation 136

Comments 138

Doc Comments 138

Comments for Cross-Compilation 140

Custom Attributes 141

Quoted Code 143

Summary 146

■Chapter 7: The F# Libraries 147

The Native F# Library FSharp.Core.dll 147

The FSharp.Core.Operators Module 147

The FSharp.Reflection Module 152

The FSharp.Collections.Seq Module 154

The FSharp.Text.Printf Module 160

The FSharp.Control.Event Module 163

Summary 166

■Chapter 8: Data Access 167

The System.Configuration Namespace 167

The System.IO Namespace 170

Using Sequences with System.IO 172

The System.Xml Namespace 173

ADO.NET 176

Data Binding 182

Data Binding and the DataGridView Control 185

Using Dapper to Access Relational Data 186

ADO.NET Extensions 189

Introducing LINQ 190

Using LINQ to XML 193

Summary 195

■Chapter 9: Parallel Programming 197

Threads, Memory, Locking, and Blocking 198

Reactive Programming 201

Data Parallelism 207

The Array.Parallel Module 207

The FSharp.Collections.ParallelSeq Module 209

Asynchronous Programming 209

Message Passing 213

Summary 222

■Chapter 10: Distributed Applications 223

Networking Overview 223

Using HTTP 224

Using HTTP with Google Spreadsheets 226

Using Suave.io 229

Creating Web Services 235

Summary 240

■Chapter 11: Language-Oriented Programming 241

What Is Language-Oriented Programming? 241

Data Structures as Little Languages 241

A Data Structure–Based Language Implementation 245

Metaprogramming with Quotations 252

Implementing a Compiler and an Interpreter for an Arithmetic Language 254

The Abstract Syntax Tree 255

Interpreting the AST 255

Compiling the AST 257

Compilation vs. Interpretation 261

Summary 264

■Chapter 12: Compatibility and Advanced Interoperation 265

Calling F# Libraries from C# 265

Returning Tuples 266

Exposing Functions That Take Functions As Parameters 267

Using Union Types 269

Using F# Lists 272

Defining Types in a Namespace 273

Defining Classes and Interfaces 274

Calling Using COM Objects 276

Using COM-Style APIs 277

Using P/Invoke 279

Using F# from Native Code via COM 281

Summary 283

■Chapter 13: Type Providers 285

What Are Type Providers? 285

Using the CSV Type Provider 286

Using the HTML Type Provider 291

Answering Some Questions with the HTML Type Provider 293

Rank the Stations by Traffic 293

Finding All of the Stations on the Northern Line 294

Which Station Has the Most Distinct Letters in Its Name? 294

Using the SQL Client Type Provider 294

Joining Datasets from Differing Data Sources 298

Summary 302

Index 303

About the Authors

Robert Pickering is a Microsoft MVP acknowledged as a community leader and a world class expert on F#. In his ten year career as a software engineer he has participated in a wide range of projects building large, scalable, and fault tolerant systems on the Microsoft .NET platform. He has experience in both consulting and working as an engineer for a software house. He has been invited to speak at prestigious events such as Microsoft TechEd, JAOO, and TechDays Paris. He has been involved in organizing conferences as track lead for events such as Functional Programming eXchange, London, and he organizes the ALT.NET community meetings in Paris. He has also appeared in podcast and screen casts such as dnrtv.com and hanselminutes.com.

Kit Eason is a software developer and educator with 30 years of experience in industries from automotive engineering through university supercomputing to energy trading. He currently works as a senior developer at Adbrain (www.adbrain.com), a leading data intelligence company that empowers marketers to regain control of their customer relationships in today's hyperconnected yet highly fragmented world. Kit also works as an author for Pluralsight: his courses there include "F# Jumpstart" and "F# Functional Data Structures." He has also appeared on the ".NET Rocks!" podcast.

About the Technical Reviewer

Fabio Claudio Ferracchiati is a senior consultant and a senior analyst/developer using Microsoft technologies. He works for Blu Arancio (`www.bluarancio.com`). He is a Microsoft Certified Solution Developer for .NET, a Microsoft Certified Application Developer for .NET, a Microsoft Certified Professional, and a prolific author and technical reviewer. Over the past ten years, he's written articles for Italian and international magazines and coauthored more than ten books on a variety of computer topics.

Acknowledgments

The first vote of thanks must go to the person who changed my professional life, and those of many others: Don Syme, the "father of F#." Don does invaluable work in mentoring and encouraging me and the whole F# community. He sets a positive tone that is reflected in everything the community does.

Huge thanks also to Fabio Claudio Ferracchiati, our technical reviewer, who has turned around reams of material in what seems like record time.

Thanks also to the various employers who have supported me (admittedly with varying degrees of scepticism!) during my journey into F#. Extra special thanks to Edoardo Turelli and all the team at Adbrain, who have somehow unlocked the secret of having the right people working on the right problems in the right way.

I'm deeply indebted to the many members of the F# community (both open source and within Microsoft) who have grown F# from an academic project to a thriving commercial and scientific language with a broad-based ecosystem. Every commit counts!

I'd like to thank everyone at Apress who contributed to this book, notably James DeWolf, Melissa Maldonado, and Douglas Pundick. Thank you for your patience, professionalism, and support.

Finally, huge appreciation to my wife, Val, for her unstinting support in everything I do; and to my children, Matt and Kate, both of them frankly more talented developers than I, for keeping me on my toes.

Foreword

That moment. That secret weapon moment. That I-got-lucky-and-came-across-something-that-helped-me-win-the-game moment. This might just be it.

This book teaches you all you need to know to get going with F#, an open source, cross-platform programming language suitable for just about every kind of programming and data processing task. And yes, learning F# is like learning a secret weapon. Wielding it, you will find yourself doing things previously beyond your limits: it will empower you, and with it you will do great things.

Why do I know this? Because I have seen the authors of this book, Kit Eason and Robert Pickering, learn F# and wield it powerfully and effectively in job after job. I've seen how it has changed the way they think about programming. In this book, they share what they have learned with you, and they want to help you learn and use this secret weapon too.

No programming language is a "silver bullet;" F# won't magically slay dragons in and of itself. However, F# does an excellent job of removing the incidental complexity that bedevils so much of programming. Take one example: the pervasive use of "null" values in languages such as C# and Java. In one real-world case study by Simon Cousins, using F# reduced the incidence of null checks by 200x in a transaction processing engine, with over 3,000 extra null checks in the fully object-oriented application in question. This is no minor thing: to continue the secret weapon analogy, a null check is like a potential weapon failure at a critical moment, a gun-jam. At any one of these 3,000 code points, that application was at risk of failing. It is simply better–and less risky–to fight your battles with a weapon that doesn't jam. F# reduces the number of potential failure points, and does so systematically. Some argue that incidental complexity is not important. This is wrong: removing incidental complexity is the first and most essential step you can take to becoming a more productive programmer, since it liberates you to address the real heart of programming. Learning F# will help you do this.

F# is known as a "functional-first" programming language, meaning you use simple functional programming as the first way to solve most problems. This is simple and easy, and lets you solve most programming problems with ease. F# programming is, however, pragmatic. Good software engineering really matters in F#: we care about code quality, naming, documentation, and good design. This book will show you all of these things. It will also teach you how to use F# for data access, web programming, parallel programming, and a myriad of other practical tasks. Finally, it will show you how to contribute back to the F# community through open source packages.

Take the moment and learn F#, and don't look back. Thousands of people are enjoying this language daily, and with more efficient, expressive coding, and higher productivity. And not just productivity, but delight and happiness in craftsmanship as well.

—Don Syme
F# Language Designer and F# Community Contributor

CHAPTER 1

■ ■ ■

Getting Started

This introductory chapter will address some of the major questions you may have about F# and functional programming.

What Is Functional Programming?

Functional programming (FP) is the oldest of the three major programming paradigms. The first FP language, IPL, was invented in 1955, about a year before FORTRAN. The second, Lisp, was invented in 1958, a year before COBOL. Both Fortran and Cobol are imperative (or procedural) languages, and their immediate success in scientific and business computing made imperative programming the dominant paradigm for more than 30 years. The rise of the object-oriented (OO) paradigm in the 1970s and the gradual maturing of OO languages ever since have made OO programming the most popular paradigm today.

Since the 1950s there has been vigorous and continual development of powerful FP languages—SML, Objective Caml (OCaml), APL, and Clean, among others—and FP-like languages—Erlang, Lisp, and Haskell being the most successful for real-world applications. However, FP remained a primarily academic pursuit until recently. The early commercial success of imperative languages made it the dominant paradigm for decades. Object-oriented languages gained broad acceptance only when enterprises recognized the need for more sophisticated computing solutions. Today, the promise of FP is finally being realized to solve even more complex problems—as well as the simpler ones.

Pure functional programming views all programs as collections of functions that accept arguments and return values. Unlike imperative and object-oriented programming, it allows no side effects and uses recursion instead of loops for iteration. The functions in a functional program are very much like mathematical functions because they do not change the state of the program. In the simplest terms, once a value is assigned to an identifier, it never changes; functions do not alter parameter values; and the results that functions return are completely new values. In typical underlying implementations, once a value is assigned to an area in memory, it does not change. To create results, functions copy values and then change the copies, leaving the original values free to be used by other functions and eventually to be thrown away when no longer needed. (This is where the idea of garbage collection originated.)

The mathematical basis for pure functional programming is elegant, and FP therefore provides beautiful, succinct solutions for many computing problems. That said, the stateless and recursive nature of FP can make it seem harder to apply for many common programming tasks. However, one of F#'s great strengths is that you can use multiple paradigms and mix them to solve problems in the way you find most convenient.

Electronic supplementary material The online version of this chapter (doi:10.1007/978-1-4842-1374-2_1) contains supplementary material, which is available to authorized users.

R. Pickering and K. Eason, *Beginning F# 4.0*, DOI 10.1007/978-1-4842-1374-2_1

Why Is Functional Programming Important?

When people think of functional programming, they often view its statelessness as a fatal flaw without considering its advantages. One could argue that since an imperative program is often 90 percent assignment and since a functional program has no assignment, a functional program could be 90 percent shorter. However, not many people are convinced by such arguments or attracted to the ascetic world of stateless recursive programming, as John Hughes pointed out in his classic paper "Why Functional Programming Matters."

> *The functional programmer sounds rather like a medieval monk, denying himself the pleasures of life in the hope that it will make him virtuous.*

John Hughes, Chalmers University of Technology
(`www.cse.chalmers.se/~rjmh/Papers/whyfp.html`)

To see the advantages of functional programming, you must look at what FP permits rather than what it prohibits. For example, functional programming allows you to treat functions themselves as values and pass them to other functions. This might not seem all that important at first glance, but its implications are extraordinary. Eliminating the distinction between data and functions means that many problems can be more naturally solved. Functional programs can be shorter and more modular than corresponding imperative and object-oriented programs.

In addition to treating functions as values, functional languages offer other features that borrow from mathematics and are not commonly found in imperative languages. For example, functional programming languages often offer curried functions, where arguments can be passed to a function one at a time and, if all arguments are not given, the result is a residual function waiting for the rest of its parameters. It's also common for functional languages to offer type systems with much better power-to-weight ratios, providing more performance and correctness for less effort.

Further, a function might return multiple values, and the calling function is free to consume them as it likes. We'll discuss these ideas, along with many more, in detail and with plenty of examples in Chapter 3.

What Is F#?

Functional programming is the best approach to solving many thorny computing problems, but pure FP isn't suitable for general-purpose programming. So FP languages have gradually embraced aspects of the imperative and OO paradigms, remaining true to the FP model but incorporating features needed to easily write any kind of program. F# is a natural successor on this path. It is also much more than just an FP language.

Some of the most popular functional languages, including OCaml, Haskell, Lisp, and Scheme, have traditionally been implemented using custom runtimes, which leads to problems such as lack of interoperability. F# is a general-purpose programming language for .NET (a general-purpose runtime) and for .NET's open source counterparts. It smoothly integrates all three major programming paradigms. With F#, you can choose whichever approach works best to solve problems in the most effective way. You can do pure FP if you're a purist, but you can easily combine functional, imperative, and object-oriented styles in the same program and exploit the strengths of each. Like other typed functional languages, F# is strongly typed but also uses inferred typing, so programmers don't need to spend time explicitly specifying types unless an ambiguity exists. Further, F# seamlessly integrates with the .NET Framework Base Class Library (BCL). Using the BCL in F# is as simple as using it in C# or Visual Basic (and maybe even simpler).

F# was modelled on OCaml, a successful object-oriented FP language, and then tweaked and extended to mesh well technically and philosophically with .NET. It fully embraces .NET and enables users to do everything that .NET allows. The F# compiler can compile for all implementations of the Common Language Infrastructure (CLI) and it supports .NET generics without changing any code. The F# compiler not only produces executables for any CLI but can also run on any environment that has a CLI, which means F# is not limited to Windows but can run on Linux, Apple Mac OS X, Apple iOS, FreeBSD, and Android. (Chapter 2 covers some routes to using F# on these diverse platforms.)

The F# compiler is distributed with Visual Studio 2015: you simply need to select the F# option during installation. It is also available in Xamarin Studio (`http://xamarin.com/studio`). Although there are commercial versions of Visual Studio and Xamarin Studio, in both cases the free edition fully supports F#. Alternatively, Ionide (`http://ionide.io`) provides an F# IDE for the Atom and Visual Studio Code editors. You can also download and integrate F# with other editors and IDEs such as Emacs and Vim. F# supports IntelliSense expression completion and automatic expression checking. It also gives tool tips to show what types have been inferred for expressions. Programmers often comment that this really helps bring the language to life.

F# was first implemented by Dr. Don Syme at Microsoft Research (MSR) in Cambridge. There is an F# team within Microsoft, but the F# compiler itself and most of the tools in its ecosystem are open source, and there is a very vibrant and friendly open source community around the language. Generally, the term "Visual F#" is used when referring to the Microsoft implementation of F# and its integration with Microsoft Visual Studio. The wider term "F#" refers both to the Microsoft implementation and related activity, and to the wide variety of open implementations and tools.

Although other FP languages run on .NET, F# has established itself as the de facto .NET functional programming language because of the quality of its implementation and its superb integration with .NET and Visual Studio.

No other .NET language is as easy to use and as flexible as F#!

Who Is Using F#?

F# was initially marketed by Microsoft as a language for use in mathematics and the more math-oriented aspects of finance. Unfortunately, the legacy of this initial perception persists today. The reality is that developers are using F# in a remarkable variety of arenas, from quantum computing to scientific instrument control to music. Here, for example, is a testimonial from Tachyus, a startup that creates technology to optimize energy production for the oil and gas industry:

> *F# has allowed us to deliver enterprise-grade software on a rapid, start-up cadence. The F# type system makes it not just a great language for implementation, but also for design: once you've built a domain model with F# types, you've got the compiler's guarantee your model is consistent. Strong typing and functional-first programming have eliminated huge classes of runtime bugs, whereas most languages require voluminous test suites to catch them. The ability to write concise, expressive, and safe code has allowed us to break into a competitive enterprise software market faster than we'd ever expected.*

> Paul Orland, Tachyus
> (`http://fsharp.org/testimonials/#kaggle-1`)

Meanwhile Rachel Reese, at jet.com, a US-based online retail startup, explains their rationale for using F#:

We started building two solutions, a C# solution and an F# solution, to see where they would take us. In the end, we chose to stick with the F# path. The main reason: we were able to deliver the same functionality with far less code. This clearly eases maintainability and reduces bugs. If you've been part of the F# community for any length of time, you know that this is a very well known feature of the language and a commonly cited reason to switch to F#.

Rachel Reese, jet.com
(http://techgroup.jet.com/blog/2015/03-22-on-how-jet-chose/)

In a very different application area, Anton Tcholakov uses F# to control scientific equipment:

Over the past few years, I have worked in a research lab at the University of Warwick where we often develop custom instrumentation for our experiments. Along the way, I've found that good experiment control software presents many interesting challenges: it requires a combination of concurrent control of several external devices and real-time data charting. Cancellation support is essential because experiments can be long-running and you may want to stop them part way through without losing your data. Good error handling and logging are needed to find the causes of failure when it occurs. Sometimes it's necessary to implement computationally demanding signal processing in software as well. Fortunately, I discovered F#, which is the perfect Swiss army knife for many of these problems.

Anton Tcholakov, University of Warwick
(https://medium.com/@ant_pt/using-f-for-scientific-instrument-control-b1ef04d20da0#.nokyfi865)

The common thread for almost all F# adoptions is not that the applications are mathematical or functional: it's that the developers wanted to concentrate on the problem to be solved, not on the noise or patterns imposed by any particular language. F# has a great habit of "getting out of the way," as you'll soon discover.

Who Is This Book For?

This book is aimed primarily at IT professionals who want to get up to speed quickly on F#. A working knowledge of the .NET Framework and some knowledge of either C# or Visual Basic would be nice, but it's not necessary. To be comfortable learning F#, all you really need is some experience programming in any language.

Even complete beginners who've never programmed before and are learning F# as their first computer language should find this book very readable. Though it doesn't attempt to teach introductory programming per se, it does carefully present all the important details of F#.

What's Next?

Chapter 2 gives you just enough knowledge about setting up an F# development environment to get you going. Chapters 3, 4, 5, and 6 cover the core F# syntax. I deliberately keep the code simple, because this will give you a better introduction to how the syntax works. Chapter 7 looks at the core libraries distributed with F# to introduce you to their flavor and power, rather than to describe each function in detail.

Then you'll dive into how to use F# for the bread-and-butter problems of the working programmer. Chapter 8 covers data access, Chapter 9 covers concurrency and parallelism, and Chapter 10 covers how applications can take advantage of a network.

The final chapters take you through the topics you really need to know to master F#. Chapter 11 looks at support for creating little languages or domain-specific languages (DSLs), a powerful and very common programming pattern in F#. Chapter 12 explores advanced interoperation issues. Finally, Chapter 13 shows how to use F# type providers to access external data sources in a beautifully fluent way.

CHAPTER 2

■ ■ ■

How to Obtain, Install, and Use F#

This chapter is designed to get you up and running with F# as quickly as possible. You'll learn how to obtain F#, and how to install it on Windows, Apple OS X, and Linux. There are many ways to edit and build F# projects on the various supported platforms. Rather than cover every permutation, I'll concentrate on the most straightforward route to get you up and running with an IDE on each platform. If you have a favorite editor that I don't cover, such as Emacs, Vim, or Visual Studio Code, rest assured that these programs have bindings to let you use F# effectively. The F# website, fsharp.org, has up-to-date information on the various options.

Obtaining F# on Microsoft Windows

The most common IDE in use for Windows .NET projects is Visual Studio. Visual Studio comes in many editions depending on your requirements (and budget!), but all of them from the free Community edition upwards support F#. (F# is not supported by Visual Studio Express.) Search on www.visualstudio.com and download the edition that suits you. During the install you can select F# as one of the languages you want to work with. However, if you do not do this, or if you already had Visual Studio installed without having selected F#, don't worry. As soon as you create or open an F# project, an on-demand install will occur.

The next step is to install the Visual F# Power Tools. This is a suite of enhancements for Visual Studio that make it much easier to work with F# code. Although it's sometimes treated as an optional extra, you should definitely install Visual F# Power Tools. Without it you won't have basics such as "Go to definition" and "Refactor Rename." To install Power Tools, run Visual Studio and go to Tools ➤ Extensions and Updates ➤ Online, then search for FSharp Power Tools. You can also find the Power Tools in the Visual Studio Gallery. Once Power Tools is installed, exit from Visual Studio and rerun it as Administrator. You can do so by right-clicking the Visual Studio icon while holding down the Shift key, and selecting "Run as administrator" (see Figure 2-1).

© Robert Pickering and Kit Eason 2016
R. Pickering and K. Eason, *Beginning F# 4.0*, DOI 10.1007/978-1-4842-1374-2_2

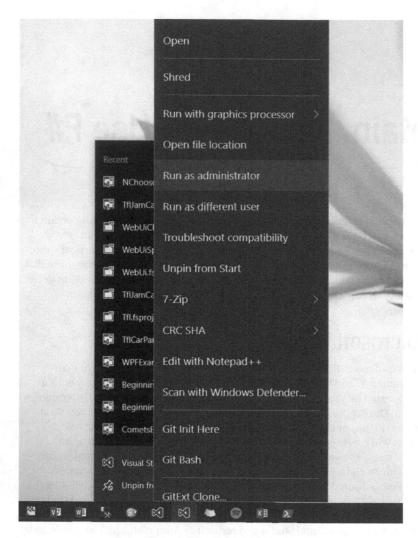

Figure 2-1. *Running Visual Studio as Administrator*

Once Visual Studio is running as Administrator, go to Tools ➤ Options ➤ F# Power Tools ➤ General and turn on all the options (see Figure 2-2). Restart Visual Studio so that the changes come into effect. If any of the Power Tools behaviors aren't compatible with your workflow, you can always come back to this dialogue and turn them off, but most of them are stable, useful, and unobtrusive.

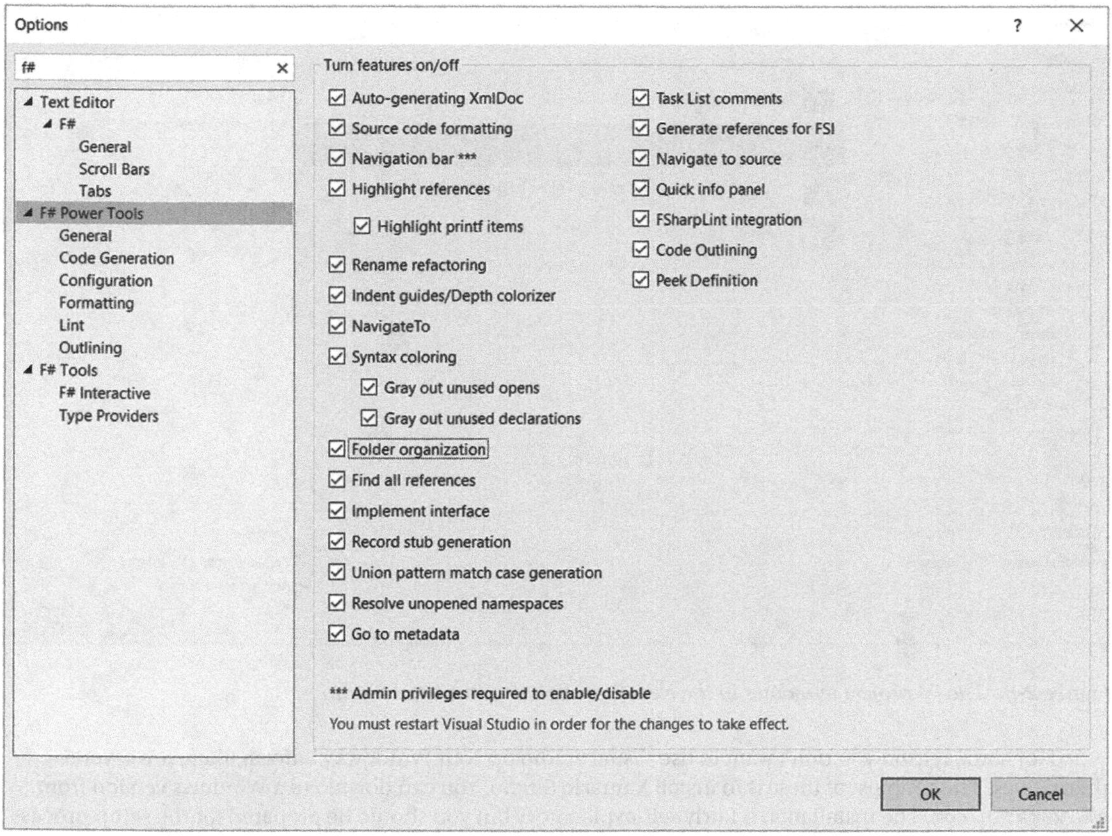

Figure 2-2. *Configuring Visual F# Power Tools*

Verify your setup by going into Visual Studio and selecting File ➤ New ➤ Project. You should be able to find a number of F# project templates under Installed ➤ Templates ➤ Visual F# or Installed ➤ Templates ➤ Other Languages ➤ F# (Figure 2-3).

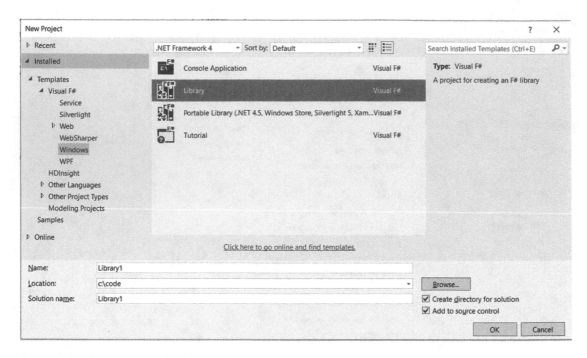

Figure 2-3. *The F# project templates in the New Project dialog in Visual Studio*

If for some reason you don't want to use Visual Studio on your Windows platform, there are several alternatives. The simplest of these is to install Xamarin Studio. You can download a Windows version from www.xamarin.com. The installation is fairly self-explanatory but you should be prepared for the setup process to download and install a number of other dependences such as the Android SDK and GTK#. You can also set up Emacs or Vim to work nicely with F#.

Obtaining F# on Apple OS X

The most straightforward way to start working with F# on Apple OS X (including targeting other platforms such as iOS and Android) is to install Xamarin Studio. Note that Xamarin Studio currently requires you to be running at least version 10.10 of OS X.

To install Xamarin Studio, go to www.xamarin.com and download Xamarin Studio for OS X. Run the installation and follow the prompts.

If you want to target iOS (Apple iPhone) applications, you also need to set up an Apple Developer Account and install the Apple IDE XCode. The Xamarin Studio install will prompt you about this but you can safely continue and add XCode and a developer account later if necessary (Figure 2-4).

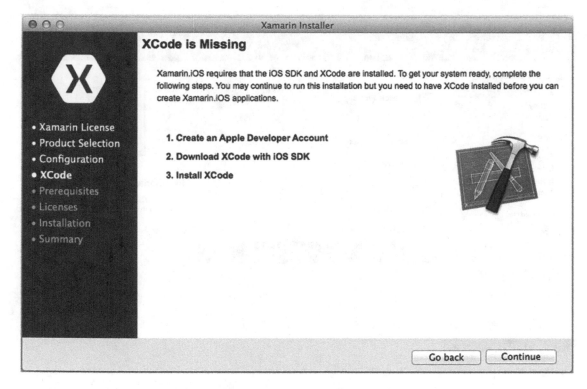

Figure 2-4. XCode is required by Xamarin Studio to create iOS apps

Verify your installation by going to File ➤ New ➤ Solution. Under Other ➤ .NET ➤ and Other ➤ Miscellaneous you should see a number of F# project types including Console Project and Library (see Figure 2-5).

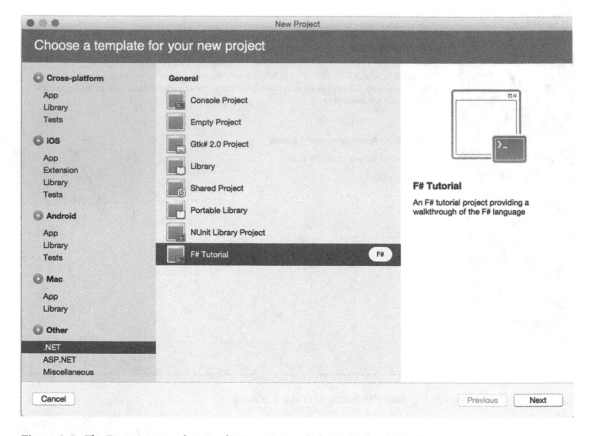

Figure 2-5. *The F# project templates in the New Project dialog in Xamarin Studio*

Obtaining F# on Linux

The choice of development environment on Linux is less straightforward than for Windows and Mac. In fact, you're spoilt for choice. Most professional Linux-based developers wanting to use F# and C# tend to gravitate towards one of the long-established editors such as Emacs and Vim, both of which can be set up to work with the F# language and compiler. A further complication is the variety of existing Linux distributions; the steps you need to follow to get F# installed vary between distributions. You can find a certain amount of getting-started information for various distributions and editors on the F# web site, fsharp.org.

To keep things simple for this beginners guide, I'm going to focus on one Linux distribution, Ubuntu, and one environment, MonoDevelop. MonoDevelop provides a very pleasant development environment including code editing, compilation, debugging, and interactive evaluation through F# Interactive. Another advantage, from the point of view of the material in this book, is that MonoDevelop's command tree is very similar to those of Visual Studio on Windows and Xamarin Studio on Windows and OS X.

To install F# with MonoDevelop on Ubuntu, enter the following commands into the console, entering your password when prompted. (These commands are listed on fsharp.org if you want to save yourself some typing.)

```
sudo apt-key adv --keyserver keyserver.ubuntu.com --recv-keys
3FA7E0328081BFF6A14DA29AA6A19B38D3D831EF
echo "deb http://download.mono-project.com/repo/debian wheezy main" | sudo tee /etc/apt/
sources.list.d/mono-xamarin.list
sudo apt-get update
sudo apt-get install mono-complete fsharp
sudo apt-get install monodevelop
```

Now run MonoDevelop:

```
monodevelop
```

When MonoDevelop has started up, go to Tools ➤ Add-in Manager ➤ Gallery, and enter "F#" into the search box at the top right (see Figure 2-6). In the results you should see an item called F# Language Binding. Select this and click the Install button. When the installation finishes, close the Add-in Manager. Now close MonoDevelop and start it again.

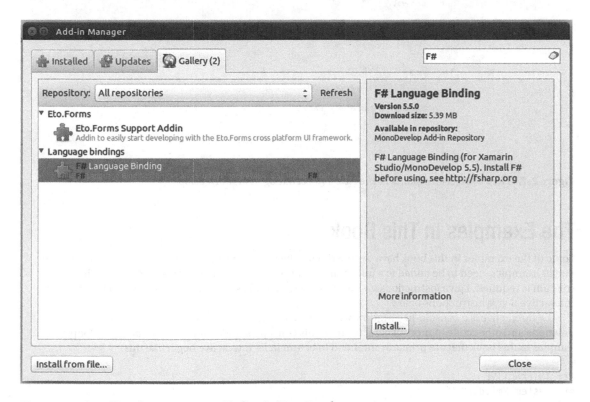

Figure 2-6. *Installing the F# Language Binding in MonoDevelop*

Verify your installation by going to File ➤ New ➤ Solution. Under Other ➤ Miscellaneous ➤ General you should see a number of F# project types including F# Console Application and F# Library (see Figure 2-7).

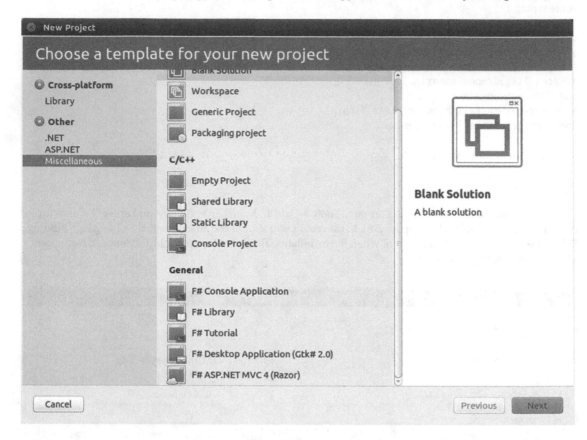

Figure 2-7. *The F# project templates in the New Project dialog in MonoDevelop*

The Examples in This Book

Some of the examples in this book have been written to be run in F# Interactive, and others, generally the longer examples, need to be added to a full solution and compiled and executed accordingly. Where a solution is required, I give instructions on how to set it up. For the shorter examples that can be run in F# Interactive, I give instructions below.

F# Interactive is a console-like window where you can send or type code to define and evaluate functions and other code. A more general term for this concept is REPL, or read-evaluate-print loop. Code samples in this book that are primarily intended to be run in F# Interactive begin like this:

```
#if INTERACTIVE
#r "System.Xml.dll"
#else
module Rss
#endif
```

This has the effect of including a reference to one or more DLLs (files containing other functions you want to use) when the code is run in F# Interactive. (When the code is compiled as part of a project, the reference is included at the project level). On the other hand, the module declaration is only included when the code is compiled, since a module declaration isn't supported in F# Interactive. So if you do want to include the sample in a compiled project, you should be able to do so without change.

If your project includes references that you have added via NuGet or another package manager, and you want to execute code that depends on them in F# Interactive, you need to reference the DLLs using their paths, thus:

```
#if INTERACTIVE
// You may have to alter this path depending on the version
// of FSharp.Data downloaded and on you project structure
#r @"../packages/FSharp.Data.2.2.5/lib/net40/FSharp.Data.dll"
#else
module UndergroundHTML
#endif
```

In the examples I use forward slashes in the paths. This works on either Windows or Mono platforms, whereas backslashes will work only on Windows.

To run an example in F# Interactive, take the following steps. (The screenshots shown are for Visual Studio but for Xamarin and MonoDevelop you should see very similar screens.)

- Create a new file in your IDE (Visual Studio, Xamarin Studio, MonoDevelop, or another editor configured to use F#). If your IDE supports the concept of projects, you may want to create a project of type F# Library, in which case a file called something like Library.fs will be created for you (Figure 2-8).

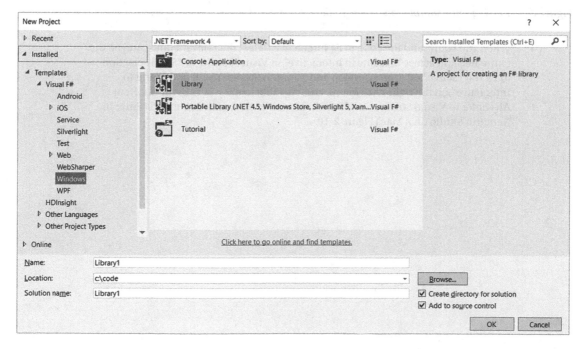

Figure 2-8. *Creating a new project*

- Paste the code for the example, including the #if INTERACTIVE construct describe above, into the code file, completely replacing its contents (Figure 2-9).

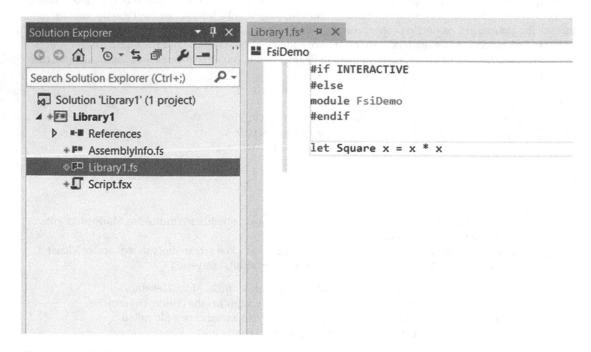

Figure 2-9. *Placing some sample code in an .fs file*

- When you want send the code to F# Interactive, select the relevant lines, maybe the entire file, and select "Execute in Interactive" in Visual Studio, or "Send selection to F# Interactive" on MonoDevelop and Xamarin Studio. You'll find "Send to Interactive" on the right-click menu, and on a shortcut. By default the shortcut is Alt+Enter in Visual Studio, Ctrl+Enter in MonoDevelop, and Command+Enter in Xamarin Studio on a Mac (Figure 2-10).

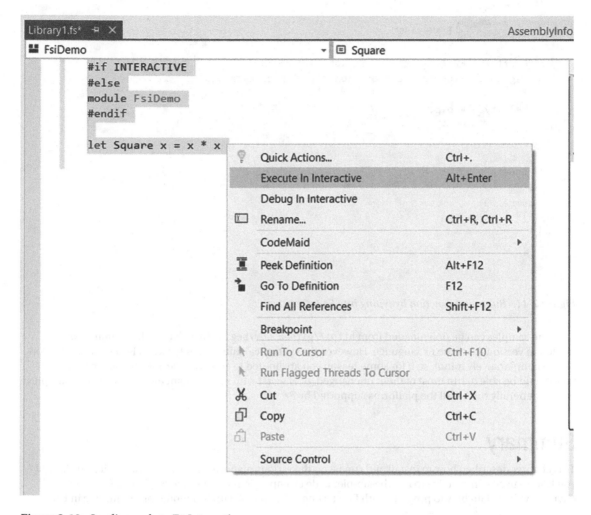

Figure 2-10. *Sending code to F# Interactive*

> *Note that sending code to F# Interactive doesn't necessarily make the F# Interactive*
> *window visible or even give it focus. If you can't see it, you need to find the menu*
> *option to view it. In Visual Studio, this is View ➤ F# Interactive, or View ➤ Other*
> *Windows F# ➤Interactive. In MonoDevelop and Xamarin Studio, it is View ➤*
> *Pads ➤ F# Interactive.*

- If your code just defines a function and doesn't call it, you can call the function by typing its name and any arguments directly into F# Interactive and following them with *two semi-colons* (Figure 2-11).

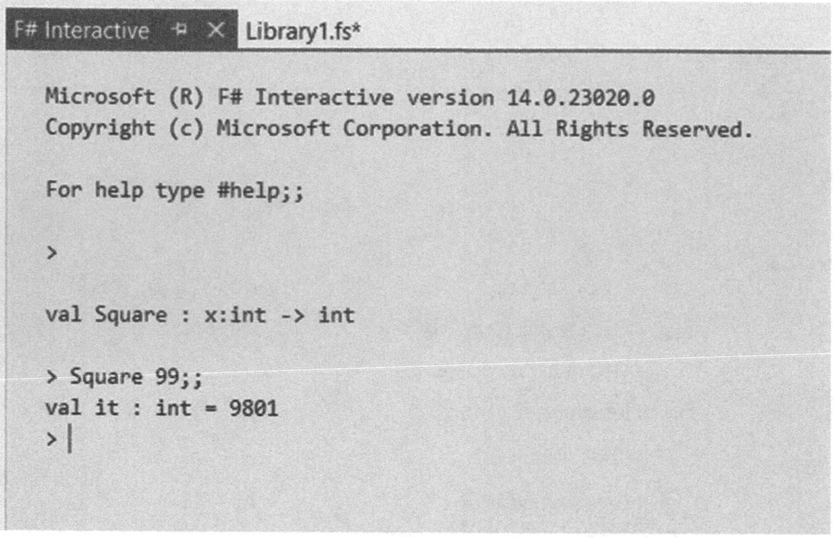

```
F# Interactive  ⚲ ✕  Library1.fs*

Microsoft (R) F# Interactive version 14.0.23020.0
Copyright (c) Microsoft Corporation. All Rights Reserved.

For help type #help;;

>

val Square : x:int -> int

> Square 99;;
val it : int = 9801
>
```

Figure 2-11. Running a function by typing into F# Interactive

The samples can be downloaded from http://github.com/beginningfsharp. The examples were written in version 4.0 of the F# language. However, the syntactical differences between F# 4.0 and F# 3.0 and 3.1 are comparatively minor, so if for some reason you are limited to an earlier version of the language, you should be able to run most of them unchanged, or at worst with minor changes,. Likewise, the examples should generally run on all the platforms supported by F#.

Summary

This chapter described how to install and run F# on the various platforms that are available. It also showed you how to use F# Interactive to run the simpler code examples in the rest of the book. The following chapters will explain how to program with F#, starting in Chapter 3 with functional programming in F#.

CHAPTER 3

■ ■ ■

Functional Programming

You saw in Chapter 1 that pure functional programming treats everything as a value, including functions. Although F# is not a pure functional language, it does encourage you to program in the functional style; that is, it encourages you to use expressions and computations that return a result, rather than statements that result in some side effect. In this chapter, you'll survey the major language constructs of F# that support the functional programming paradigm and learn how they make it easier to program in the functional style.

Literals

Literals represent constant values and are useful building blocks for computations. F# has a rich set of literals, summarized in Table 3-1.

Table 3-1. *F# Literals*

Example	F# Type	.NET Type	Description
"Hello\t ", "World\n"	string	System.String	A string in which a backslash (\) is an escape character.
@"c:\dir\fs", @""""	string	System.String	A verbatim string where a backslash (\) is a regular character.
"""She said "Hello""""	string	System.String	Like a verbatim string except you don't have to use pairs of " to represent double-quotes. Instead, the entire string is enclosed in triple double-quotes.
"bytesbytesbytes"B	byte array	System.Byte[]	A string that will be stored as a byte array.
'c'	char	System.Char	A character.
true, false	bool	System.Boolean	A Boolean.
0x22	int/int32	System.Int32	An integer as a hexadecimal.
0o42	int/int32	System.Int32	An integer as an octal.
0b10010	int/ int32	System.Int32	An integer as a binary.
34y	sbyte	System.SByte	A signed byte.
34uy	byte	System.Byte	An unsigned byte.

(*continued*)

© Robert Pickering and Kit Eason 2016
R. Pickering and K. Eason, *Beginning F# 4.0*, DOI 10.1007/978-1-4842-1374-2_3

Table 3-1. (*continued*)

Example	F# Type	.NET Type	Description
34s	int16	System.Int16	A 16-bit integer.
34us	uint16	System.UInt16	An unsigned 16-bit integer.
34l	int/int32	System.Int32	A 32-bit integer.
34ul	uint32	System.UInt32	An unsigned 32-bit integer.
34n	nativeint	System.IntPtr	A native-sized integer.
34un	unativeint	System.UIntPtr	An unsigned native-sized integer.
34L	int64	System.Int64	A 32-bit integer.
34UL	uint64	System.Int64	An unsigned 32-bit integer.
3.0F, 3.0f	float32	System.Single	A 32-bit IEEE floating-point number.
3.0	float	System.Double	A 64-bit IEEE floating-point number.
3474262622571I	bigint	Microsoft.FSharp. Math.BigInt	An arbitrary large integer.
474262612536171N	bignum	Microsoft.FSharp. Math.BigNum	An arbitrary large number.

In F#, string literals can contain newline characters, and regular string literals can contain standard escape codes. Verbatim string literals use a backslash (\) as a regular character, and two double quotes ("") are the escape for a quote. You can define all integer types using hexadecimal and octal by using the appropriate prefix and postfix indicator.

The following example shows some of these literals in action, along with how to use the F# printf function with a %A pattern to output them to the console. The printf function interprets the %A format pattern using a combination of F#'s reflection (covered in Chapter 7) and the .NET ToString method, which is available for every type, to output values in a human-readable way.

```
#if INTERACTIVE
#else
module Examples
#endif

// some strings
let message = "Hello
World\r\n\t!"
let dir = @"c:\projects"

// a byte array
let bytes = "bytesbytesbytes"B

// some numeric types
let xA = 0xFFy
let xB = 0o7777un
let xC = 0b10010UL
```

```
// print the results
let main() =
    printfn "%A" message
    printfn "%A" dir
    printfn "%A" bytes
    printfn "%A" xA
    printfn "%A" xB
    printfn "%A" xC

// call the main function
main()
```

This example, when executed, returns the following:

```
"Hello
World
        !"
"c:\projects"
[|98uy; 121uy; 116uy; 101uy; 115uy; 98uy; 121uy; 116uy; 101uy; 115uy; 98uy;
  121uy; 116uy; 101uy; 115uy|]
-1y
4095un
18UL
```

Anonymous Functions

In F#, anonymous functions are defined using the keyword fun. The function's arguments are separated by spaces, and the arguments are separated from the function body by a left ASCII arrow (->).

Here is an example of a function that takes two values and adds them together:

```
fun x y -> x + y
```

Notice that this function does not have a name; this is a sort of function literal. Functions defined in this way are referred to as *anonymous functions*, *lambda functions*, or just *lambdas*.

The idea that a function does not need a name may seem a little strange. However, if a function is to be passed as an argument to another function, it may not need a name, especially if the task it's performing is relatively simple.

If you need to give the function a name, you can bind it to an identifier, as described in the next section.

Identifiers and let Bindings

Identifiers are the way you give names to values in F# so you can refer to them later in a program. You define an identifier using the keyword let followed by the name of the identifier, an equal sign, and an expression that specifies the value to which the identifier refers. An expression is any piece of code that represents a computation that will return a value. The following expression shows a value being assigned to an identifier:

```
let x = 42
```

To most people coming from an imperative programming background, this will look like a variable assignment. There are a lot of similarities, but a key difference is that in pure functional programming, once a value is assigned to an identifier, it does not change. This is why I will refer to them throughout this book as *identifiers*, rather than as *variables*.

■ **Note**   Under some circumstances, you can redefine identifiers, which may look a little like an identifier changing value, but is subtly different. Also, in imperative programming in F#, in some circumstances the value of an identifier can change. In this chapter, we focus on functional programming, where identifiers do not change their values.

An identifier can refer to either a value or a function, and since F# functions are really values in their own right, this is hardly surprising. This means F# has no real concept of a function name or parameter name; these are just identifiers. You can bind an anonymous function to an identifier the same way you can bind a string or integer literal to an identifier:

```
let myAdd = fun x y -> x + y
```

However, as it is very common to need to define a function with a name, F# provides a short syntax for this. You write a function definition the same way as a value identifier, except that a function has two or more identifiers between the let keyword and the equal sign, as follows:

```
let raisePowerTwo x = x ** 2.0
```

The first identifier is the name of the function, raisePowerTwo, and the identifier that follows it is the name of the function's parameter, x. If a function has a name, it is strongly recommended that you use this shorter syntax for defining it.

The syntax for declaring *values* and *functions* in F# is indistinguishable because functions *are* values, and F# syntax treats them both similarly. For example, consider the following code:

```
let n = 10

let add a b = a + b
let result = add n 4

printfn "result = %i" result
```

On the first line, the value 10 is assigned to the identifier n; then on the second line, a function named add, which takes two arguments and adds them together, is defined. Notice how similar the syntax is, with the only difference being that a function has parameters that are listed after the function name. Since everything is a value in F#, the literal 10 on the first line is a value, and the result of the expression a + b on the next line is also a value that automatically becomes the result of the add function. Note that there is no need to explicitly return a value from a function as you would in an imperative language.

This example, when executed, returns the following:

```
result = 14
```

Identifier Names

There are some rules governing identifier names. Identifiers must start with an underscore (_) or a letter, and can then contain any alphanumeric character, underscore, or a single quotation mark ('). Keywords cannot be used as identifiers. As F# supports the use of a single quotation mark as part of an identifier name, you can use this to represent "prime" to create identifier names for different but similar values, as in this example:

```
let x = 42
let x' = 43
```

F# supports Unicode, so you can use accented characters and letters from non-Latin alphabets as identifier names, like so:

```
let 标识符 = 42
```

If the rules governing identifier names are too restrictive, you can use double tick marks (``) to quote the identifier name. This allows you to use any sequence of characters—as long as it doesn't include tabs, newlines, or double ticks—as an identifier name. This means you could create an identifier that ends with a question mark (some programmers believe it is useful to have names that represent Boolean values end with a question mark), like so:

```
let ``more? `` = true
```

This can also be useful if you need to use a keyword as an identifier or type name:

```
let ``class`` = "style"
```

For example, you might need to use a member from a library that was not written in F# and has one of F#'s keywords as its name (you'll learn more about using non-F# libraries in Chapter 4). Generally, it's best to avoid overuse of this feature, as it could lead to libraries that are difficult to use from other .NET languages.

Scope

The *scope* of an identifier defines where you can use an identifier (or a type, as discussed in the "Defining Types" section later in this chapter) within a program. It is important to have a good understanding of scope because if you try to use an identifier that's not in scope, you will get a compile error.

All identifiers—whether they relate to functions or values—are scoped from the end of their definitions until the end of the sections in which they appear. So, for identifiers that are at the top level (that is, identifiers that are not local to another function or other value), the scope of the identifier is from the place where it's defined to the end of the source file. Once an identifier at the top level has been assigned a value (or function), this value cannot be changed or redefined. An identifier is available only after its definition has ended, meaning that it is not usually possible to define an identifier in terms of itself.

You will have noticed that in F#, you never need to explicitly return a value; the result of the computation is automatically bound to its associated identifier. So, how do you compute intermediate values within a function? In F#, this is controlled by whitespace. An indentation creates a new scope, and the end of this scope is signaled by the end of the indentation. Indentation means that the let binding is an intermediate value in the computation that is not visible outside this scope. When a scope closes (by the indentation ending), and an identifier is no longer available, it is said to *drop out of scope* or to be *out of scope*.

To demonstrate scope, the next example shows a function that computes the point halfway between two integers. The third and fourth lines show intermediate values being calculated.

```
// function to calculate a midpoint
let halfWay a b =
    let dif = b - a
    let mid = dif / 2
    mid + a

// call the function and print the results
printfn "(halfWay 5 11) = %i" (halfWay 5 11)
printfn "(halfWay 11 5) = %i" (halfWay 11 5)
```

First, the difference between the two numbers is calculated, and this is assigned to the identifier dif using the let keyword. To show that this is an intermediate value within the function, it is indented by four spaces. The choice of the number of spaces is left to the programmer, but the convention is four. After that, the example calculates the midpoint, assigning it to the identifier mid using the same indentation. Finally, the desired result of the function is the midpoint plus a, so the code can simply say mid + a, and this becomes the function's result.

■ **Note**   You cannot use tabs instead of spaces for indenting because these can look different in different text editors, which causes problems when whitespace is significant.

This example, when executed, returns the following:

```
(halfWay 5 11) = 8
(halfWay 11 5) = 8
```

THE F# LIGHTWEIGHT SYNTAX

By default, F# is whitespace-sensitive, with indentation controlling the scope of identifiers. The language F# was based on, Objective Caml (OCaml), is not whitespace-sensitive. In OCaml, scope is controlled though the use of the in keyword. For example, the halfWay function from the previous example would look like the following (note the additional in keyword in the middle two lines):

```
let halfWay a b =
    let dif = b - a in
    let mid = dif / 2 in
    mid + a
```

The F# whitespace-sensitive syntax is said to be a *lightweight* syntax because certain keywords and symbols (such as in, ;, begin, and end) are optional. This means the preceding function definition will be accepted by the F# compiler even with the additional in keywords. If you want to force the use of these keywords, add the declaration #light "off" to the top of each source file.

I believe that significant whitespace is a much more intuitive way of programming, because it helps the programmer decide how the code should be laid out. Therefore, in this book, I cover the F# lightweight syntax.

Identifiers within functions are scoped to the end of the expression in which they appear. Ordinarily, this means they are scoped until the end of the function definition in which they appear. So, if an identifier is defined inside a function, it cannot be used outside it. Consider the following example:

```
let printMessage() =
    let message = "Help me"
    printfn "%s" message

printfn "%s" message
```

This attempts to use the identifier message outside the function printMessage, which is out of scope. If you try to compile this code, you'll get the following error message:

```
Prog.fs(34,17): error: FS0039: The value or constructor 'message' is not defined.
```

Identifiers within functions behave a little differently from identifiers at the top level because within functions they can be redefined using the let keyword. This is useful because it means that you do not need to keep inventing names to hold intermediate values. To demonstrate, the next example shows a function to uppercase a string, where it's possible the input string is null. To handle this, you redefine s as "" if the input string is null; otherwise you use the input value. Then it is safe to call the ToUpperInvariant() method of the string. This is possibly not the most stylish way of handling the situation but it does illustrate the redefining of a value.

```
let SafeUpperCase (s : string) =
    let s = if s = null then "" else s
    s.ToUpperInvariant()
```

Here's what happens when you send the function to F# Interactive and call it with a non-null and with a null string:

```
val SafeUpperCase : s:string -> string
> SafeUpperCase "Hello";;
val it : string = "HELLO"
> SafeUpperCase null;;
val it : string = ""
>
```

Note that this is different from changing the value of an identifier. Because you're redefining the identifier, you're able to change the identifier's type, as shown in the next example, but you still retain type safety.

■ **Note**   *Type safety*, sometimes referred to as *strong typing*, basically means that F# will prevent you from performing an inappropriate operation on a value; for example, you can't treat an integer as if it were a floating-point number. I discuss types and how they lead to type safety in the "Types and Type Inference" section later in this chapter.

```
let changeType () =
    let x = 1                // bind x to an integer
    let x = "change me"      // rebind x to a string
    let x = x + 1            // attempt to rebind to itself plus an integer
    printfn "%s" x
```

This example will not compile because on the third line the value of x changes from an integer to the string "change me", and then on the fourth line it tries to add a string and an integer, which is illegal in F#, so you get the following compile error:

```
prog.fs(55,13): error: FS0001: This expression has type
    int
but is here used with type
    string
stopped due to error
```

If an identifier is redefined, its old value is available while the definition of the identifier is in progress. But after it is defined—that is, at the end of the expression—the old value is hidden. If the identifier is redefined inside a new scope, the identifier will revert to its old value when the new scope is finished.

The following example defines a message and prints it to the console. It then redefines this message inside an inner function called innerFun, which also prints the message. Then it calls the function innerFun, and finally prints the message a third time.

```
let printMessages() =
    // define message and print it
    let message = "Important"
    printfn "%s" message;
    // define an inner function that redefines value of message
    let innerFun () =
        let message = "Very Important"
        printfn "%s" message
    // call the inner function
    innerFun ()
    // finally print the first message again
    printfn "%s" message

printMessages()
```

This example, when executed, returns the following:

```
Important
Very Important
Important
```

A programmer from the imperative world might have expected that message, when printed out for the final time, would be bound to the value Very Important, rather than Important. It holds the value Important because the identifier message is rebound, rather than assigned, to the value Very Important inside the function innerFun, and this binding is valid only inside the scope of the function innerFun. Therefore, once this function has finished, the identifier message reverts to holding its original value.

■ **Note** Using inner functions is a common and excellent way of breaking up a lot of functionality into manageable portions, and you will see their usage throughout the book. They are sometimes referred to as *closures* or *lambdas*, although these two terms actually have more specific meanings. A *closure* means that the function uses values that are defined externally to the function. A *lambda* is an anonymous function.

Capturing Identifiers

You have already seen that in F# you can define functions within other functions. These functions can use any identifier in scope, including definitions that are also local to the function where they are defined. Because these inner functions are values, they could be returned as the result of the function or passed to another function as an argument. This means that although an identifier is defined within a function, so it is not visible to other functions, its actual lifetime may be much longer than the function in which it is defined. Let's look at an example to illustrate this point. Consider the following function, defined as calculatePrefixFunction:

```
// function that returns a function to
let calculatePrefixFunction prefix =
    // calculate prefix
    let prefix' = Printf.sprintf "[%s]: " prefix
    // define function to perform prefixing
    let prefixFunction appendee =
        Printf.sprintf "%s%s" prefix' appendee
    // return function
    prefixFunction

// create the prefix function
let prefixer = calculatePrefixFunction "DEBUG"

// use the prefix function
printfn "%s" (prefixer "My message")
```

This function returns the inner function it defines, prefixFunction. The identifier prefix' is defined as local to the scope of the function calculatePrefixFunction; it cannot be seen by other functions outside calculatePrefixFunction. The inner function prefixFunction uses prefix', so when prefixFunction is returned, the value prefix' must still be available. calculatePrefixFunction creates the function prefixer. When prefixer is called, you see that its result uses a value that was calculated and associated with prefix':

```
[DEBUG]: My message
```

Although you should have an understanding of this process, most of the time you don't need to think about it because it doesn't involve any additional work by the programmer. The compiler will automatically generate a *closure* to handle extending the lifetime of the local value beyond the function in which it is defined. The .NET garbage collection will automatically handle clearing the value from memory. Understanding this process of identifiers being captured in closures is probably more important when programming in the imperative style, where an identifier can represent a value that changes over time. When programming in the functional style, identifiers will always represent values that are constant, making it slightly easier to figure out what has been captured in a closure.

The use Binding

It can be useful to have some action performed on an identifier when it drops out of scope. For example, it's important to close file handles when you've finished reading or writing to the file, so you may want to close the file as soon as the identifier that represents it drops out of scope. More generally, anything that is an operating system resource (such as a network socket) or is precious because it's expensive to create or a limited number is available (such as a database connection) should be closed or freed as quickly as possible.

In .NET, objects that fall into this category should implement the IDisposable interface (for more information about objects and interfaces, see Chapter 5). This interface contains one method, Dispose, which will clean up the resource; for example, in the case of a file, it will close the open file handle. So, in many cases, it's useful to call this method when the identifier drops out of scope. F# provides the use binding to do just that.

A use binding behaves the same as a let binding, except that when the variable drops out of scope, the compiler automatically generates code to ensure that the Dispose method will be called at the end of the scope. The code generated by the compiler will always be called, even if an exception occurs (see the "Exceptions and Exception Handling" section later in this chapter for more information about exceptions). To illustrate this, consider the following example:

```
open System.IO

// function to read first line from a file
let readFirstLine filename =
    // open file using a "use" binding
    use file = File.OpenText filename
    file.ReadLine()

// call function and print the result
printfn "First line was: %s" (readFirstLine "mytext.txt")
```

Here, the function readFirstLine uses the .NET Framework method File.OpenText to open a text file for reading. The StreamReader that is returned is bound to the identifier file using a use binding. The example then reads the first line from the file and returns this as a result. At this point, the identifier file drops out of scope, so its Dispose method will be called and will close the underlying file handle.

Note the following important constraints on the use of use bindings:

- You can use use bindings only with objects that implement the IDisposable interface.

- use bindings cannot be used at the top level. They can be used only within functions because identifiers at the top level never go out of scope.

Recursion

Recursion means defining a function in terms of itself; in other words, the function calls itself within its definition. Recursion is often used in functional programming where you would use a loop in imperative programming. Many believe that algorithms are much easier to understand when expressed in terms of recursion rather than loops.

To use recursion in F#, use the rec keyword after the let keyword to make the identifier available within the function definition. The following example shows recursion in action. Notice how on the fifth line, the function makes two calls to itself as part of its own definition.

```
// a function to generate the Fibonacci numbers
let rec fib x =
    match x with
    | 1 -> 1
    | 2 -> 1
    | x -> fib (x - 1) + fib (x - 2)

// call the function and print the results
printfn "(fib 2) = %i" (fib 2)
printfn "(fib 6) = %i" (fib 6)
printfn "(fib 11) = %i" (fib 11)
```

This example, when executed, returns the following:

```
(fib 2) = 1
(fib 6) = 8
(fib 11) = 89
```

This function calculates the *n*th term in the Fibonacci sequence. The Fibonacci sequence is generated by adding the previous two numbers in the sequence, and it progresses as follows: 1, 1, 2, 3, 5, 8, 13, ... Recursion is most appropriate for calculating the Fibonacci sequence because the definition of any number in the sequence, other than the first two, depends on being able to calculate the previous two numbers, so the Fibonacci sequence is defined in terms of itself.

Although recursion is a powerful tool, you should be careful when using it. It is easy to inadvertently write a recursive function that never terminates. Although intentionally writing a program that does not terminate is sometimes useful, it is rarely the goal when trying to perform calculations. To ensure that recursive functions terminate, it is often useful to think of recursion in terms of a base case and a recursive case:

- The *recursive case* is the value for which the function is defined in terms of itself. For the function fib, this is any value other than 1 and 2.

- The *base case* is the nonrecursive case; that is, there must be some value where the function is not defined in terms of itself. In the fib function, 1 and 2 are the base cases.

Having a base case is not enough in itself to ensure termination. The recursive case must tend toward the base case. In the fib example, if x is greater than or equal to 3, then the recursive case will tend toward the base case, because x will always become smaller and will at some point reach 2. However, if x is less than 1, then x will grow continually more negative, and the function will recurse until the limits of the machine are reached, resulting in a stack overflow error (System.StackOverflowException).

The previous code also uses F# pattern matching, which is discussed in the "Pattern Matching" section later in this chapter.

Operators

In F#, you can think of *operators* as a more aesthetically pleasing way to call functions. F# has two different kinds of operators:

- A *prefix* operator is an operator where the operands come after the operator.

- An *infix* operator comes in between the first and second operands.

F# provides a rich and diverse set of operators that you can use with numeric, Boolean, string, and collection types. The operators defined in F# and its libraries are too numerous to be covered in this section, so rather than looking at individual operators, we'll look at how to use and define operators in F#.

As in C#, F# operators are overloaded, meaning you can use more than one type with an operator; however, unlike in C#, both operands must be the same type, or the compiler will generate an error. F# also allows users to define and redefine operators.

Operators follow a set of rules similar to C#'s for operator overloading resolution; therefore, any class in the .NET Framework Base Class Library (BCL), or any .NET library, that was written to support operator overloading in C# will support it in F#. For example, you can use the + operator to concatenate strings, as well as to add a System.TimeSpan to a System.DateTime, because these types support an overload of the + operator. The following example illustrates this:

```
let rhyme = "Jack " + "and " + "Jill"

open System
let oneYearLater =
    DateTime.Now + new TimeSpan(365, 0, 0, 0, 0)
```

Unlike functions, operators are not values, so they cannot be passed to other functions as parameters. However, if you need to use an operator as a value, you can do this by surrounding it with parentheses. The operator will then behave exactly like a function. Practically, this has two consequences:

- The operator is now a function, and its parameters will appear after the operator:

  ```
  let result = (+) 1 1
  ```

- As it is a value, it could be returned as the result of a function, passed to another function, or bound to an identifier. This provides a very concise way to define the add function:

  ```
  let add = (+)
  ```

You'll see how using an operator as a value can be useful later in this chapter when we look at working with lists.

Users can define their own operators or redefine any of the existing ones if they want (although this is not always advisable because the operators then no longer support overloading). Consider the following perverse example that redefines + to perform subtraction:

```
let (+) a b = a - b
printfn "%i" (1 + 1)
```

User-defined (*custom*) operators must be nonalphanumeric and can be a single character or a group of characters. You can use the following characters in custom operators:

```
!%&*+-./<=>@^|~
```

You can also use a ? character as long as it's not the first in the name.

The syntax for defining an operator is the same as using the let keyword to define a function, except the operator replaces the function name and is surrounded by parentheses so the compiler knows that the symbols are used as a name of an operator, rather than as the operator itself. The following example shows defining a custom operator, +*, which adds its operands and then multiplies them:

```
let (+*) a b = (a + b) * a * b
printfn "(1 +* 2) = %i" (1 +* 2)
```

This example, when executed, returns the following:

```
(1 +* 2) = 6
```

The rules for distinguishing between prefix and infix operators by name are somewhat complex. To quote MSDN,

Only certain operators can be used as prefix operators. Some operators are always prefix operators, others can be infix or prefix, and the rest are always infix operators. Operators that begin with !, except !=, and the operator ~, or repeated sequences of ~, are always prefix operators. The operators +, -, +., -., &, &&, %, and %% can be prefix operators or infix operators. You distinguish the prefix version of these operators from the infix version by adding a ~ at the beginning of a prefix operator when it is defined. The ~ is not used when you use the operator, only when it is defined.

—Microsoft Developer Network

Function Application

Function application simply means calling a function with some arguments. The following example shows the function add being defined and then applied to two arguments. Notice that the arguments are not separated with parentheses or commas; only whitespace is needed to separate them.

```
let add x y = x + y

let result = add 4 5

printfn "(add 4 5) = %i" result
```

This example, when executed, returns the following:

```
(add 4 5) = 9
```

In F#, a function has a fixed number of arguments and is applied to the value that appears next in the source file. You do not necessarily need to use parentheses when calling functions, but F# programmers often use them to define which function should be applied to which arguments. Consider the simple case where you want to add four numbers using the add function. You could bind the result of each function call to a new identifier, but for such a simple calculation, this would be very cumbersome:

```
let add x y = x + y

let result1 = add 4 5
let result2 = add 6 7

let finalResult = add result1 result2
```

Instead, it often better to pass the result of one function directly to the next function. To do this, you use parentheses to show which parameters are associated with which functions:

```
let add x y = x + y

let result =
    add (add 4 5) (add 6 7)
```

Here, the second and third occurrences of the add function are grouped with the parameters 4, 5 and 6, 7, respectively, and the first occurrence of the add function will act on the results of the other two functions.

F# also offers another way to apply functions, using the *pipe-forward* operator (|>). This operator has the following definition:

```
let (|>) x f = f x
```

This simply means it takes a parameter, x, and applies that to the given function, f, so that the parameter is now given before the function. The following example shows a parameter, 0.5, being applied to the function System.Math.Cos using the pipe-forward operator:

```
let result = 0.5 |> System.Math.Cos
```

This reversal can be useful in some circumstances, especially when you want to chain many functions together. Here is the previous add function example rewritten using the pipe-forward operator:

```
let add x y = x + y

let result = add 6 7 |> add 4 |> add 5
```

Some programmers think this style is more readable because it has the effect of making the code read in a more left-to-right manner. The code should now be read as "add 6 to 7, then forward this result to the next function, which will add 4, and then forward this result to a function that will add 5." A more detailed explanation of where it's appropriate to use this style of function application can be found in Chapter 4.

This example also takes advantage of the capability to partially apply functions in F#, as discussed in the next section.

Partial Application of Functions

F# supports the partial application of functions. This means you don't need to pass all the arguments to a function at once. Notice that the final example in the previous section passes a single argument to the add function, which takes two arguments. This is very much related to the idea that functions are values.

Because a function is just a value, if it doesn't receive all its arguments at once, it returns a value that is a new function waiting for the rest of the arguments. So, in the example, passing just the value 4 to the add function results in a new function, which I named addFour because it takes one parameter and adds the value 4 to it. At first glance, this idea can look uninteresting and unhelpful, but it is a powerful part of functional programming that you'll see used throughout the book.

This behavior may not always be appropriate. For example, if the function takes two floating-point parameters that represent a point, it may not be desirable to have these numbers passed to the function separately because they both make up the point they represent. To address this, you may surround a function's parameters with parentheses and separate them with commas, turning them into a *tuple*. You can see this in the following code:

```
let sub (a, b) = a - b

let subFour = sub 4
```

When attempting to compile this example, you will receive the following error message:

```
prog.fs(15,19): error: FS0001: This expression has type
    int
but is here used with type
    'a * 'b
```

This example will not compile because the sub function requires both parameters to be given at once. sub now has only one parameter, the tuple (a, b), instead of two, and although the call to sub in the second line provides only one argument, it's not a tuple. So, the program does not type check, as the code is trying to pass an integer to a function that takes a tuple. Tuples are discussed in more detail in the "Defining Types" section later in this chapter.

In general, functions that can be partially applied–known as *curried functions*–are preferred over functions that use tuples. This is because functions that can be partially applied are more flexible than tuples, giving users of the function more choices about how to use them. This is especially true when creating a library to be used by other programmers. You may not be able to anticipate all the ways your users will want to use your functions, so it is best to give them the flexibility of functions that can be partially applied. Note that when you call your curried F# functions from C#, the curried nature of the arguments is hidden by "compiler magic." You can call the F# function with all its arguments (in brackets, as usual in C#), but since partial application isn't supported by C# you can't call it with just some of its arguments.

Pattern Matching

Pattern matching allows you to look at the value of an identifier and then make different computations depending on its value. It might be compared to the switch statement in C++ and C#, but it is much more powerful and flexible. Programs that are written in the functional style tend to be written as series of transformations applied to the input data. Pattern matching allows you to analyze the input data and decided which transformation should be applied to it, so pattern matching fits in well with programming in the functional style.

The pattern-matching construct in F# allows you to pattern match over a variety of types and values. It also has several different forms and crops up in several places in the language, including its exception-handling syntax, which is discussed in the "Exceptions and Exception Handling" section later in this chapter.

The simplest form of pattern matching is matching over a value. You saw this earlier in this chapter, in the "Recursion" section, where it was used to implement a function that generated numbers in the Fibonacci sequence. To illustrate the syntax, the following code shows an implementation of a function that will produce the Lucas numbers, a sequence of numbers as follows: 1, 3, 4, 7, 11, 18, 29, 47, 76, ... The Lucas sequence has the same definition as the Fibonacci sequence; only the starting points are different.

```
// definition of Lucas numbers using pattern matching
let rec luc x =
    match x with
    | x when x <= 0 -> failwith "value must be greater than 0"
```

```
  | 1 -> 1
  | 2 -> 3
  | x -> luc (x - 1) + luc (x - 2)

// call the function and print the results
printfn "(luc 2) = %i" (luc 2)
printfn "(luc 6) = %i" (luc 6)
printfn "(luc 11) = %i" (luc 11)
printfn "(luc 12) = %i" (luc 12)
```

This example, when executed, returns the following:

```
(luc 2) = 3
(luc 6) = 18
(luc 11) = 199
(luc 12) = 322
```

The syntax for pattern matching uses the keyword match, followed by the identifier that will be matched, then the keyword with, and then all the possible matching rules separated by vertical bars (|). In the simplest case, a rule consists of either a constant or an identifier, followed by an arrow (->), and then by the expression to be used when the value matches the rule. In this definition of the function luc, the second two cases are literals—the values 1 and 2—and these will be replaced with the values 1 and 3, respectively. The fourth case will match any value of x greater than 2, and this will cause two further calls to the luc function.

The rules are matched in the order in which they are defined, and the compiler will issue a warning if pattern matching is incomplete; that is, if there is some possible input value that will not match any rule. This would be the case in the luc function if you had omitted the final rule, because any values of x greater than 2 would not match any rule. The compiler will also issue a warning if there are any rules that will never be matched, typically because there is another rule in front of them that is more general. This would be the case in the luc function if the fourth rule were moved ahead of the first rule. In this case, none of the other rules would ever be matched because the first rule would match any value of x.

You can add a when guard (as in the first rule in the example) to give precise control about when a rule fires. A when guard is composed of the keyword when followed by a Boolean expression. Once the rule is matched, the when clause is evaluated, and the rule will fire only if the expression evaluates to true. If the expression evaluates to false, the remaining rules will be searched for another match. The first rule is designed to be the function's error handler. The first part of the rule is an identifier that will match any integer, but the when guard means the rule will match only those integers that are less than or equal to zero.

If you want, you can omit the first |. This can be useful when the pattern match is small and you want to fit it on one line. You can see this in the following example, which also demonstrates the use of the underscore (_) as a *wildcard*:

```
let booleanToString x =
    match x with false -> "False" | _ -> "True"
```

The _ will match any value and is a way of telling the compiler that you're not interested in using this value. For example, in this booleanToString function, you do not need to use the constant true in the second rule because if the first rule is matched, you know that the value of x will be true. Moreover, you do not need to use x to derive the string "True", so you can ignore the value and just use _ as a wildcard.

CHAPTER 3 ■ FUNCTIONAL PROGRAMMING

Another useful feature of pattern matching is that you can combine two patterns into one rule through the use of the vertical bar (|). The following code, stringToBoolean, demonstrates this:

```
// function for converting a Boolean to a string
let booleanToString x =
    match x with false -> "False" | _ -> "True"

// function for converting a string to a Boolean
let stringToBoolean x =
    match x with
    | "True" | "true" -> true
    | "False" | "false" -> false
    | _ -> failwith "unexpected input"

// call the functions and print the results
printfn "(booleanToString true) = %s"
    (booleanToString true)
printfn "(booleanToString false) = %s"
    (booleanToString false)
printfn "(stringToBoolean \"True\") = %b"
    (stringToBoolean "True")
printfn "(stringToBoolean \"false\") = %b"
    (stringToBoolean "false")
printfn "(stringToBoolean \"Hello\") = %b"
    (stringToBoolean "Hello")
```

The first two rules have two strings that should evaluate to the same value, so rather than having two separate rules, you can just use | between the two patterns. The results of this example, when executed, are as follows:

```
(booleanToString true) = True
(booleanToString false) = False
(stringToBoolean "True") = true
(stringToBoolean "false") = false
Microsoft.FSharp.Core.FailureException: unexpected input
    at FSI_0005.stringToBoolean(String x)
    at <StartupCode$FSI_0005>.$FSI_0005.main@()
```

It is also possible to pattern match over most of the types defined by F#. The next two examples demonstrate pattern matching over tuples, with two functions that implement a Boolean And and Or using pattern matching. Each takes a slightly different approach.

```
let myOr b1 b2 =
    match b1, b2 with
    | true, _ -> true
    | _, true -> true
    | _ -> false
```

```
let myAnd p =
    match p with
    | true, true -> true
    | _ -> false

printfn "(myOr true false) = %b" (myOr true false)
printfn "(myOr false false) = %b" (myOr false false)
printfn "(myAnd (true, false)) = %b" (myAnd (true, false))
printfn "(myAnd (true, true)) = %b" (myAnd (true, true))
```

This example, when executed, returns the following:

```
(myOr true false) = true
(myOr false false) = false
(myAnd (true, false)) = false
(myAnd (true, true)) = true
```

The myOr function has two Boolean parameters, which are placed between the match and with keywords and are separated by commas to form a tuple. The myAnd function has one parameter, which is itself a tuple. Either way, the syntax for creating pattern matches for tuples is the same and is similar to the syntax for creating tuples.

If it's necessary to match values within the tuple, the constants or identifiers are separated by commas, and the position of the identifier or constant defines what it matches within the tuple. This is shown in the first and second rules of the myOr function and in the first rule of the myAnd function. These rules match parts of the tuples with constants, but you could use identifiers if you want to work with the separate parts of the tuple later in the rule definition. Just because you're working with tuples doesn't mean you always need to look at the various parts that make up the tuple.

The third rule of myOr and the second rule of myAnd show the whole tuple matched with a single _ wildcard character. This, too, could be replaced with an identifier if you want to work with the value in the second half of the rule definition.

Because pattern matching is such a common task in F#, the language provides an alternative shorthand syntax. If the sole purpose of a function is to pattern match over something, then it may be worth using this syntax. In this version of the pattern-matching syntax, you use the keyword function, place the pattern where the function's parameters would usually go, and then separate all the alternative rules with |. The following example shows this syntax in action in a simple function that recursively processes a list of strings and concatenates them into a single string:

```
// concatenate a list of strings into single string
let rec concatStringList =
    function head :: tail -> head + concatStringList tail
           | [] -> ""

// test data
let jabber = ["'Twas "; "brillig, "; "and "; "the "; "slithy "; "toves "; "..."]
// call the function
let completJabber = concatStringList jabber
// print the result
printfn "%s" completJabber
```

This example, when executed, returns the following:

```
'Twas brillig, and the slithy toves ...
```

Pattern matching is one of the fundamental building blocks of F#, and we'll return to it several times in this chapter. We'll look at pattern matching over lists, with record types and union types, and with exception handling. The most advanced use of pattern matching is discussed in the "Active Patterns" section toward the end of the chapter. You can find details of how to pattern match over types from non-F# libraries in Chapter 4.

Control Flow

F# has a strong notion of *control flow*. In this way, it differs from many pure functional languages, where the notion of control flow is very loose, because expressions can be evaluated in essentially any order. The strong notion of control flow is apparent in the if ... then ... else ... expression.

In F#, the if ... then ... else ... construct is an expression, meaning it returns a value. One of two different values will be returned, depending on the value of the Boolean expression between the if and then keywords. The next example illustrates this. The if ... then ... else ... expression is evaluated to return either "heads" or "tails", depending on whether the program is run on an even second or an odd second.

```
let result =
    if System.DateTime.Now.Second % 2 = 0 then
        "heads"
    else
        "tails"

printfn "%A" result
```

It's interesting to note that the if ... then ... else ... expression is just a convenient shorthand for pattern matching over a Boolean value. So the previous example could be rewritten as follows:

```
let result =
    match System.DateTime.Now.Second % 2 = 0 with
    | true -> "heads"
    | false ->  "tails"
```

The if ... then ... else ... expression has some implications that you might not expect if you are more familiar with imperative-style programming. F#'s type system requires that the values being returned by the if ... then ... else ... expression must be the same type, or the compiler will generate an error. So, if in the previous example, you replaced the string "tails" with an integer or Boolean value, you would get a compile error. If (very rarely) you really require the values to be of different types, you can create an if ... then ... else ... expression of type obj (F#'s version of System.Object), as shown in the following example, which prints either "heads" or false to the console:

```
let result =
    if System.DateTime.Now.Second % 2 = 0 then
        box "heads"
    else
        box false

printfn "%A" result
```

Imperative programmers may be surprised that an if ... then ... else ... expression must have an else if the expression returns a value. This is pretty logical when you think about it and considering the examples you've just seen. If the else were removed from the code, the identifier result could not be assigned a value when the if evaluated to false, and having uninitialized identifiers is something that F# (and functional programming in general) aims to avoid. There is a way for a program to contain an if ... then expression without the else, but this is very much in the style of imperative programming, so I discuss it in Chapter 4.

Lists

F# *lists* are simple collection types that are built into F#. An F# list can be an *empty list*, represented by square brackets ([ ]), or it can be another list with a value concatenated to it. You concatenate values to the front of an F# list using a built-in operator that consists of two colons (::), pronounced "cons." The following example shows some lists being defined, starting with an empty list on the first line, followed by two lists where strings are placed at the front by concatenation:

```
let emptyList = []
let oneItem = "one " :: []
let twoItem = "one " :: "two " :: []
```

The syntax to add items to a list by concatenation is a little verbose, so if you just want to define a list, you can use shorthand. In this shorthand notation, you place the list items between square brackets and separate them with a semicolon (;), as follows:

```
let shortHand = ["apples "; "pears"]
```

Another F# operator that works on lists is the at symbol (@), which you can use to concatenate two lists together, as follows:

```
let twoLists = ["one, "; "two, "] @ ["buckle "; "my "; "shoe "]
```

All items in an F# list must be of the same type. If you try to place items of different types in a list—for example, you try to concatenate a string to a list of integers—you will get a compile error. If you need a list of mixed types, you can create a list of type obj (the F# equivalent of System.Object), as in the following code:

```
// the empty list
let emptyList = []

// list of one item
let oneItem = "one " :: []

// list of two items
let twoItem = "one " :: "two " :: []

// list of two items
let shortHand = ["apples "; "pairs "]

// concatenation of two lists
let twoLists = ["one, "; "two, "] @ ["buckle "; "my "; "shoe "]
```

```
// list of objects
let objList = [box 1; box 2.0; box "three"]
// print the lists
let main() =
    printfn "%A" emptyList
    printfn "%A" oneItem
    printfn "%A" twoItem
    printfn "%A" shortHand
    printfn "%A" twoLists
    printfn "%A" objList

// call the main function
main()
```

This example, when executed, returns the following:

```
[]
["one "]
["one "; "two "]
["apples "; "pairs "]
["one, "; "two, "; "buckle "; "my "; "shoe "]
[1; 2.0; "three"]
```

I discuss types in F# in more detail in the "Types and Type Inference" section later in this chapter.

F# lists are *immutable*; in other words, once a list is created, it cannot be altered. The functions and operators that act on lists do not alter them, but they create a new, modified version of the list, leaving the old list available for later use if needed. The next example shows this.

```
// create a list of one item
let one = ["one "]
// create a list of two items
let two = "two " :: one
// create a list of three items
let three = "three " :: two

// reverse the list of three items
let rightWayRound = List.rev three

// function to print the results
let main() =
    printfn "%A" one
    printfn "%A" two
    printfn "%A" three
    printfn "%A" rightWayRound
// call the main function
main()
```

An F# list containing a single string is created, and then two more lists are created, each using the previous one as a base. Finally, the List.rev function is applied to the last list to create a new reversed list. When you print these lists, it is easy to see that all the original lists remain unaltered:

```
["one "]
["two "; "one "]
["three "; "two "; "one "]
["one "; "two "; "three "]
```

Pattern Matching Against Lists

The regular way to work with F# lists is to use pattern matching and recursion. The pattern-matching syntax for pulling the head item off a list is the same as the syntax for concatenating an item to a list. The pattern is formed by the identifier representing the head, followed by :: and then the identifier for the rest of the list. You can see this in the first rule of concatList in the next example. You can also pattern match against list constants; you can see this in the second rule of concatList, where there is an empty list.

```
// list to be concatenated
let listOfList = [[2; 3; 5]; [7; 11; 13]; [17; 19; 23; 29]]

// definition of a concatenation function
let rec concatList l =
    match l with
    | head :: tail -> head @ (concatList tail)
    | [] -> []

// call the function
let primes = concatList listOfList

// print the results
printfn "%A" primes
```

This example, when executed, returns the following:

```
[2; 3; 5; 7; 11; 13; 17; 19; 23; 29]
```

Taking the head from a list, processing it, and then recursively processing the tail of the list is the most common way of dealing with lists via pattern matching, but it certainly isn't the only thing you can do with pattern matching and lists. The following example shows a few other uses of this combination of features:

```
// function that attempts to find various sequences
let rec findSequence l =
    match l with
    // match a list containing exactly 3 numbers
    | [x; y; z] ->
        printfn "Last 3 numbers in the list were %i %i %i"
            x y z
```

```
    // match a list of 1, 2, 3 in a row
    | 1 :: 2 :: 3 :: tail ->
        printfn "Found sequence 1, 2, 3 within the list"
        findSequence tail
    // if neither case matches and items remain
    // recursively call the function
    | head :: tail -> findSequence tail
    // if no items remain terminate
    | [] -> ()

// some test data
let testSequence = [1; 2; 3; 4; 5; 6; 7; 8; 9; 8; 7; 6; 5; 4; 3; 2; 1]

// call the function
findSequence testSequence
```

The first rule demonstrates how to match a list of a fixed length—in this case, a list of three items. Here, identifiers are used to grab the values of these items so they can be printed to the console. The second rule looks at the first three items in the list to see whether they are the sequence of integers 1, 2, 3; and if they are, it prints a message to the console. The final two rules are the standard head/tail treatment of a list, designed to work their way through the list, doing nothing if there is no match with the first two rules.

This example, when executed, returns the following:

```
Found sequence 1, 2, 3 within the list
Last 3 numbers in the list were 3 2 1
```

Although pattern matching is a powerful tool for the analysis of data in lists, it's often not necessary to use it directly. The F# libraries provide a number of higher-order functions for working with lists that implement the pattern matching for you, so you don't need repeat the code. To illustrate this, imagine you need to write a function that adds one to every item in a list. You can easily write this using pattern matching.

```
let rec addOneAll list =
    match list with
    | head :: rest ->
        head + 1 :: addOneAll rest
    | [] -> []

printfn "(addOneAll [1; 2; 3]) = %A" (addOneAll [1; 2; 3])
```

This example, when executed, returns the following:

```
(addOneAll [1; 2; 3]) = [2; 3; 4]
```

However, this code is perhaps a little more verbose than you would like for such a simple problem. The clue to solving this comes from noticing that adding one to every item in the list is just an example of a more general problem: the need to apply some transformation to every item in a list. The F# core library contains a function called map, which is defined in the List module. It has the following definition:

```
let rec map func list =
    match list with
    | head :: rest ->
        func head :: map func rest
    | [] -> []
```

You can see that the map function has a very similar structure to the addOneAll function from the previous example. If the list is not empty, you take the head item of the list and apply the function, func, that you are given as a parameter. This is then appended to the results of recursively calling map on the rest of the list. If the list is empty, you simply return the empty list. The map function can then be used to implement adding one to all items in a list in a much more concise manner.

```
let result = List.map ((+) 1) [1; 2; 3]

printfn "List.map ((+) 1) [1; 2; 3] = %A" result
```

This example, when executed, returns the following:

```
(List.map ((+) 1) [1; 2; 3]) = [2; 3; 4]
```

Also note that this example uses the add operator as a function by surrounding it with parentheses, as described earlier in this chapter in the "Operators" section. This function is then partially applied by passing its first parameter but not its second. This creates a function that takes an integer and returns an integer, which is passed to the map function.

The List module contains many other interesting functions for working with lists, such as List.filter and List.fold. These are explained in more detail in Chapter 7, which describes the libraries available with F#.

List Comprehensions

List comprehensions make creating and converting collections easy. You can create F# lists, sequences, and arrays directly using comprehension syntax. I cover arrays in more detail in the next chapter. *Sequences* are collections of type seq, which is F#'s name for the .NET BCL's IEnumerable type. I describe them in the "Lazy Evaluation" section later in this chapter.

The simplest comprehensions specify ranges, where you write the first item you want, either a number or a letter, followed by two periods (..), and then the last item you want, all within square brackets (to create a list) or braces (to create a sequence). The compiler then does the work of calculating all the items in the collection, taking the first number and incrementing it by 1, or similarly with characters, until it reaches the last item specified. The following example demonstrates how to create a list of numbers from 0 through 9 and a sequence of the characters from A through Z:

```
// create some list comprehensions
let numericList = [ 0 .. 9 ]
let alpherSeq = seq { 'A' .. 'Z' }
```

```
// print them
printfn "%A" numericList
printfn "%A" alpherSeq
```

The results of this example are as follows:

```
[0; 1; 2; 3; 4; 5; 6; 7; 8; 9]
seq ['A'; 'B'; 'C'; 'D'; ...]
```

To create more interesting collections, you can also specify a step size for incrementing numbers (note that characters do not support this type of list comprehension). You place the step size between the first and last items, separated by an extra pair of periods (..). The following example shows a list containing multiples of 3, followed by a list that counts backward from 9 to 0:

```
// create some list comprehensions
let multiplesOfThree = [ 0 .. 3 .. 30 ]
let revNumericSeq = [ 9 .. -1 .. 0 ]

// print them
printfn "%A" multiplesOfThree
printfn "%A" revNumericSeq
```

This example, when executed, returns the following:

```
[0; 3; 6; 9; 12; 15; 18; 21; 24; 27; 30]
[9; 8; 7; 6; 5; 4; 3; 2; 1; 0]
```

List comprehensions also allow loops to create a collection from another collection. The idea is that you enumerate the old collection, transform each of its items, and place any generated items in the new collection. To specify such a loop, use the keyword for, followed by an identifier, followed by the keyword in, at the beginning of the list comprehension. The following example creates a sequence of the squares of the first ten positive integers:

```
// a sequence of squares
let squares =
    seq { for x in 1 .. 10 -> x * x }
// print the sequence
printfn "%A" squares
```

The example uses for to enumerate the collection 1 .. 10, assigning each item in turn to the identifier x. It then uses the identifier x to calculate the new item, in this case multiplying x by itself to square it. The results of this example are as follows:

```
seq [1; 4; 9; 16; ...]
```

The use of the F# keyword yield gives you a lot of flexibility when defining list comprehensions. The yield keyword allows you to decide whether or not a particular item should be added to the collection. For example, consider the following example:

```
// a sequence of even numbers
let evens n =
    seq { for x in 1 .. n do
            if x % 2 = 0 then yield x }

// print the sequence
printfn "%A" (evens 10)
```

The goal is to create a collection of even numbers. So you test each number in the collection you are enumerating to see if it is a multiple of two. If it is, you return it using the yield keyword; otherwise, you perform no action. This code results in the following:

```
seq [2; 4; 6; 8; ...]
```

It's also possible to use list comprehensions to iterate in two or more dimensions by using a separate loop for each dimension. The following example defines a function called squarePoints that creates a sequence of points forming a square grid, each point represented by a tuple of two integers:

```
// sequence of tuples representing points
let squarePoints n =
    seq { for x in 1 .. n do
            for y in 1 .. n do
                yield x, y }

// print the sequence
printfn "%A" (squarePoints 3)
```

This example, when executed, returns the following:

```
seq [(1, 1); (1, 2); (1, 3); (2, 1); ...]
```

You'll look at using comprehensions with arrays and collections from the .NET Framework BCL in Chapter 4.

Types and Type Inference

F# is a *strongly typed* language, which means you cannot use a function with a value that is inappropriate. You cannot call a function that has a string as a parameter with an integer argument; you must explicitly convert between the two. The way the language treats the type of its values is referred to as its *type system*. F# has a type system that does not get in the way of routine programming. In F#, all values have a type, and this includes values that are functions.

Ordinarily, you don't need to explicitly declare types; the compiler will work out the type of a value from the types of the literals in the function and the resulting types of other functions it calls. If everything is OK, the compiler will keep the types to itself; only if there is a type mismatch will the compiler inform you by

CHAPTER 3 ■ FUNCTIONAL PROGRAMMING

reporting a compile error. This process is generally referred to as *type inference*. If you want to know more about the types in a program, you can make the compiler display all inferred types with the –i switch. Visual Studio users (and users of other IDEs such as Xamarin Studio and MonoDevelop) get tool tips that show types when they hover the mouse pointer over an identifier.

The way type inference works in F# is fairly easy to understand. The compiler works through the program, assigning types to identifiers as they are defined, starting with the top leftmost identifier and working its way down to the bottom rightmost. It assigns types based on the types it already knows—that is, the types of literals and (more commonly) the types of functions defined in other source files or assemblies.

The following example defines two F# identifiers and then shows their inferred types displayed on the console with the F# compiler's –i switch:

```
let aString = "Spring time in Paris"
let anInt = 42
```

```
val aString : string
val anInt : int
```

The types of these two identifiers are unsurprising—string and int, respectively. The syntax used by the compiler to describe them is fairly straightforward: the keyword val (meaning "value") and then the identifier, a colon, and finally the type.

The definition of the function makeMessage in the next example is a little more interesting:

```
let makeMessage x = (Printf.sprintf "%i" x) + " days to spring time"
let half x = x / 2
```

```
val makeMessage : int -> string
val half : int -> int
```

Note that the makeMessage function's definition is prefixed with the keyword val, just like the two values you saw before; even though it is a function, the F# compiler still considers it to be a value. Also, the type itself uses the notation int -> string, meaning a function that takes an integer and returns a string. The -> between the type names (an *ASCII arrow*, or just *arrow*) represents the transformation of the function being applied. The arrow represents a transformation of the value, but not necessarily the type, because it can represent a function that transforms a value into a value of the same type, as shown in the half function on the second line.

The types of functions that can be partially applied and functions that take tuples differ. The following functions, div1 and div2, illustrate this:

```
let div1 x y = x / y
let div2 (x, y) = x / y

let divRemainder x y = x / y, x % y
```

```
val div1 : int -> int -> int
val div2 : int * int -> int
val divRemainder : int -> int -> int * int
```

The function div1 can be partially applied, and its type is int -> int -> int, representing that the arguments can be passed in separately. Compare this with the function div2, which has the type int * int -> int, meaning a function that takes a pair of integers—a tuple of integers—and turns them into a single integer. You can see this in the function div_remainder, which performs integer division and also returns the remainder at the same time. Its type is int -> int -> int * int, meaning a curried function that returns an integer tuple.

The next function, doNothing, looks inconspicuous enough, but it is quite interesting from a typing point of view.

```
let doNothing x = x
```

```
val doNothing : 'a -> 'a
```

This function has the type 'a -> 'a, meaning it takes a value of one type and returns a value of the same type. Any type that begins with a single quotation mark (') means a *variable* type. F# has a type, obj, that maps to System.Object and represents a value of any type, a concept that you will probably be familiar with from other common language runtime (CLR)-based programming languages (and indeed, many languages that do not target the CLR). However, a variable type is not the same. Notice how the type has an 'a on both sides of the arrow. This means that, even though the compiler does not yet know the type, it knows that the type of the return value will be the same as the type of the argument. This feature of the type system, sometimes referred to as *type parameterization*, allows the compiler to find more type errors at compile time and can help avoid casting.

■ **Note**   The concept of a variable type, or type parameterization, is closely related to the concept of *generics* that was introduced in CLR version 2.0 and later became part of the ECMA specification for CLI version 2.0. When F# targets a CLI that has generics enabled, it takes full advantage of them by using them anywhere it finds an undetermined type. Don Syme, the creator of F#, designed and implemented generics in the .NET CLR before he started working on F#. One might be tempted to infer that he did this so he could create F#!

The function doNothingToAnInt, shown next, is an example of a value being constrained—a *type constraint*. In this case, the function parameter x is constrained to be an int. It is possible to constrain any identifier, not just function parameters, to be of a certain type, although it is more typical to need to constrain parameters. The list stringList here shows how to constrain an identifier that is not a function parameter:

```
let doNothingToAnInt (x: int) = x
let intList = [1; 2; 3]

let (stringList: list<string>) = ["one"; "two"; "three"]
```

```
val doNothingToAnInt _int : int -> int
val intList : int list
val stringList : string list
```

The syntax for constraining a value to be of a certain type is straightforward. Within parentheses, the identifier name is followed by a colon (:), followed by the type name. This is also sometimes called a *type annotation*.

The `intList` value is a list of integers, and the identifier's type is `int list`. This indicates that the compiler has recognized that the list contains only integers, and in this case, the type of its items is not undetermined but is `int`. Any attempt to add anything other than values of type `int` to the list will result in a compile error.

The identifier `stringList` has a type annotation. Although this is unnecessary, since the compiler can resolve the type from the value, it is used to show an alternative syntax for working with undetermined types. You can place the type between angle brackets after the type that it is associated with instead of just writing it before the type name. Note that even though the type of `stringList` is constrained to be `list<string>` (a list of strings), the compiler still reports its type as `string list` when displaying the type, and they mean exactly the same thing. This syntax is supported to make F# types with a type parameter look like generic types from other .NET libraries.

Constraining values is not usually necessary when writing pure F#, though it can occasionally be useful. It's most useful when using .NET libraries written in languages other than F# and for interoperation with unmanaged libraries. In both these cases, the compiler has less type information, so it is often necessary to give it enough information to disambiguate things.

Defining Types

The type system in F# provides a number of features for defining custom types. F#'s type definitions fall broadly into three categories:

- *Tuples* or *records*: A set of types composed to form a composite type (similar to structs in C or classes in C#)

- *Sum* types (sometimes referred to as *union* types)

- *Class* types (which we tackle in Chapter 5)

Tuple and Record Types

Tuples are a way of quickly and conveniently composing values into a group of values. Values are separated by commas and can then be referred to by one identifier, as shown in the first line of the next example. You can then retrieve the values by doing the reverse, as shown in the second line, where identifiers separated by commas appear on the left side of the equal sign, with each identifier receiving a single value from the tuple. If you want to ignore a value in the tuple, you can use _ to tell the compiler you are not interested in the value, as in the third and fourth lines.

```
let pair = true, false
let b1, b2 = pair
let b3, _ = pair
let _, b4 = pair
```

Tuples are different from most user-defined types in F# because you do not need to explicitly declare them using the `type` keyword. To define a type, you use the `type` keyword, followed by the type name, an equal sign, and then the type you are defining. In its simplest form, you can use this to give an alias to any existing type, including tuples. Giving aliases to single types is not often useful, but giving aliases to tuples can be very useful, especially when you want to use a tuple as a type constraint. The following example shows how to give an alias to a single type and a tuple, and also how to use an alias as a type constraint:

```
type Name = string
type Fullname = string * string

let fullNameToSting (x: Fullname) =
    let first, second = x in
    first + " " + second
```

Record types are similar to tuples in that they compose multiple types into a single type. The difference is that in record types, each *field* is named. The following example illustrates the syntax for defining record types:

```
// define an organization with unique fields
type Organization1 = { boss: string; lackeys: string list }
// create an instance of this organization
let rainbow =
    { boss = "Jeffrey";
      lackeys = ["Zippy"; "George"; "Bungle"] }

// define two organizations with overlapping fields
type Organization2 = { chief: string; underlings: string list }
type Organization3 = { chief: string; indians: string list }

// create an instance of Organization2
let (thePlayers: Organization2) =
    { chief = "Peter Quince";
      underlings = ["Francis Flute"; "Robin Starveling";
                    "Tom Snout"; "Snug"; "Nick Bottom"] }
// create an instance of Organization3
let (wayneManor: Organization3) =
    { chief = "Batman";
      indians = ["Robin"; "Alfred"] }
```

You place field definitions between braces and separate them with semicolons. A field definition is composed of the field name followed by a colon and the field's type. The type definition Organization1 is a record type where the field names are unique. This means you can use a simple syntax to create an instance of this type where there is no need to mention the type name when it is created. To create a record, you place the field names followed by equal signs and the field values between braces ({}), as shown in the Rainbow identifier.

F# does not force field names to be unique across multiple record types, so sometimes the compiler cannot infer which record type you intended to reference. If this happens, you can use a type annotation, as described in the previous section. Using a type annotation is illustrated by the types Organization2 and Organization3, and their instances, thePlayers and wayneManor. You can see the type of the identifier given explicitly just after its name.

Accessing the fields in a record is fairly straightforward. You simply use the syntax record identifier name, followed by a dot, followed by field name. The following example illustrates this, showing how to access the chief field of the Organization record:

```
// define an organization type
type Organization = { chief: string; indians: string list }

// create an instance of this type
let wayneManor =
    { chief = "Batman";
      indians = ["Robin"; "Alfred"] }

// access a field from this type
printfn "wayneManor.chief = %s" wayneManor.chief
```

Records are immutable by default. To an imperative programmer, this may sound like records are not very useful, since there will inevitably be situations where you need to change a value in a field. For this purpose, F# provides a simple syntax for creating a copy of a record with updated fields. To create a copy of a record, place the name of that record between braces, followed by the keyword with, followed by a list of fields to be changed, with their updated values. The advantage of this is that you don't need to retype the list of fields that have not changed. The following example demonstrates this approach. It creates an initial version of wayneManor and then creates wayneManor', in which "Robin" has been removed:

```
// define an organization type
type Organization = { chief: string; indians: string list }

// create an instance of this type
let wayneManor =
    { chief = "Batman";
      indians = ["Robin"; "Alfred"] }
// create a modified instance of this type
let wayneManor' =
    { wayneManor with indians = [ "Alfred" ] }

// print out the two organizations
printfn "wayneManor = %A" wayneManor
printfn "wayneManor' = %A" wayneManor'
```

```
wayneManor = {chief = "Batman";
 indians = ["Robin"; "Alfred"];}
wayneManor' = {chief = "Batman";
 indians = ["Alfred"];}
```

Another way to access the fields in a record is using pattern matching; that is, you can use pattern matching to match fields within the record type. As you would expect, the syntax for examining a record using pattern matching is similar to the syntax used to construct it. You can compare a field to a constant with field = constant. You can assign the values of fields with identifiers with field = identifier. You can ignore a field with field = _. The findDavid function in the next example illustrates using pattern matching to access the fields in a record.

```
// type representing a couple
type Couple = { him : string ; her : string }

// list of couples
let couples =
    [ { him = "Brad" ; her = "Angelina" };
      { him = "Becks" ; her = "Posh" };
      { him = "Chris" ; her = "Gwyneth" };
      { him = "Michael" ; her = "Catherine" } ]

// function to find "David" from a list of couples
let rec findDavid l =
    match l with
    | { him = x ; her = "Posh" } :: tail -> x
    | _ :: tail -> findDavid tail
    | [] -> failwith "Couldn't find David"

// print the results
printfn "%A" (findDavid couples)
```

The first rule in the findDavid function is the one that does the real work: checking the her field of the record to see whether it is "Posh", David's wife. The him field is associated with the identifier x so it can be used in the second half of the rule.

This example, when executed, returns the following:

Becks

It's important to note that you can use only literal values when you pattern match over records like this. So, if you want to generalize the function to allow you to change the person you are searching for, you need to use a when guard in your pattern matching, like so:

```
let rec findPartner soughtHer l =
    match l with
    | { him = x ; her = her } :: tail when her = soughtHer -> x
    | _ :: tail -> findPartner soughtHer tail
    | [] -> failwith "Couldn't find him"
```

Field values can also be functions. Since this technique is mainly used in conjunction with a mutable state to form values similar to objects, I will cover this usage in Chapter 5.

Union or Sum Types (Discriminated Unions)

Union types, sometimes called *sum types* or *discriminated unions*, are a way of bringing together data that may have a different meaning or structure. You define a union type using the type keyword, followed by the type name, followed by an equal sign, just as with all type definitions. Then comes the definition of the different *constructors*, separated by vertical bars. The first vertical bar is optional.

A constructor is composed of a name that must start with a capital letter, which is intended to avoid the common bug of getting constructor names mixed up with identifier names. The name can optionally be followed by the keyword of and then the types that make up that constructor. Multiple types that make up a constructor are separated by asterisks. The names of constructors within a type must be unique. If several union types are defined, then the names of their constructors can overlap; however, you should be careful when doing this because it can be that further type annotations are required when constructing and consuming union types.

The next example defines a type Volume whose values can have three different meanings: liter, US pint, or imperial pint. Although the structure of the data is the same and is represented by a float, the meanings are quite different. Mixing up the meaning of data in an algorithm is a common cause of bugs in programs, and the Volume type is, in part, an attempt to avoid this.

```
type Volume =
    | Liter of float
    | UsPint of float
    | ImperialPint of float

let vol1 = Liter 2.5
let vol2 = UsPint 2.5
let vol3 = ImperialPint (2.5)
```

The syntax for constructing a new instance of a union type is the constructor name followed by the values for the types, with multiple values separated by commas. Optionally, you can place the values in parentheses. You use the three different Volume constructors to construct three different identifiers: vol1, vol2, and vol3.

You can optionally provide names for the fields that make up a union type. Consider a union type that describes several kinds of shapes, like so:

```
// union type using field labels
type Shape =
| Square of side:float
| Rectangle of width:float * height:float
| Circle of radius:float
```

Note how each field is assigned a label. You can use these labels when constructing an instance, but you don't have to.

```
// create an instance of a union type without using the field label
let sq = Square 1.2
// create an instance of a union type using the field label
let sq2 = Square(side=1.2)
// create an instance of a union type using multiple field labels
// and assigning the field out-of-order
let rect3 = Rectangle(height=3.4, width=1.2)
```

To deconstruct the values of union types into their basic parts, you always use pattern matching. When pattern matching over a union type, the constructors make up the first half of the pattern-matching rules. You don't need a complete list of rules, but if the list is incomplete, there must be a default rule, using either an identifier or a wildcard to match all remaining rules. The first part of a rule for a constructor consists of the constructor name followed by identifiers or wildcards to match the various values within it. The following convertVolumeToLiter, convertVolumeUsPint, and convertVolumeImperialPint functions demonstrate this syntax:

```
// type representing volumes
type Volume =
    | Liter of float
    | UsPint of float
    | ImperialPint of float

// various kinds of volumes
let vol1 = Liter 2.5
let vol2 = UsPint 2.5
let vol3 = ImperialPint 2.5

// some functions to convert between volumes
let convertVolumeToLiter x =
    match x with
    | Liter x -> x
    | UsPint x -> x * 0.473
    | ImperialPint x -> x * 0.568
let convertVolumeUsPint x =
    match x with
    | Liter x -> x * 2.113
    | UsPint x -> x
    | ImperialPint x -> x * 1.201
let convertVolumeImperialPint x =
    match x with
    | Liter x -> x * 1.760
    | UsPint x -> x * 0.833
    | ImperialPint x -> x

// a function to print a volume
let printVolumes x =
    printfn "Volume in liters = %f,
in us pints = %f,
in imperial pints = %f"
        (convertVolumeToLiter x)
        (convertVolumeUsPint x)
        (convertVolumeImperialPint x)

// print the results
printVolumes vol1
printVolumes vol2
printVolumes vol3
```

This example, when executed, returns the following:

```
Volume in liters = 2.500000,
in us pints = 5.282500,
in imperial pints = 4.400000
Volume in liters = 1.182500,
in us pints = 2.500000,
in imperial pints = 2.082500
Volume in liters = 1.420000,
in us pints = 3.002500,
in imperial pints = 2.500000
```

An alternative solution to this problem is to use F#'s units of measure. This is discussed in the "Units of Measure" section later in the chapter.

Type Definitions with Type Parameters

Both union and record types can be parameterized. Parameterizing a type means leaving one or more of the types within the type being defined to be determined later by the consumer of the types. This is a similar concept to the variable types discussed earlier in this chapter. When defining types, you must be a little more explicit about which types are variable.

F# supports two syntaxes for type parameterization. In the first, you place the type being parameterized between the keyword type and the name of the type, as follows:

```
type 'a BinaryTree =
| BinaryNode of 'a BinaryTree * 'a BinaryTree
| BinaryValue of 'a

let tree1 =
    BinaryNode(
        BinaryNode ( BinaryValue 1, BinaryValue 2),
        BinaryNode ( BinaryValue 3, BinaryValue 4) )
```

In the second syntax, you place the types being parameterized in angle brackets after the type name, as follows:

```
type Tree<'a> =
| Node of Tree<'a> list
| Value of 'a

let tree2 =
    Node( [ Node( [Value "one"; Value "two"] ) ;
        Node( [Value "three"; Value "four"] ) ]  )
```

Like variable types, the names of type parameters always start with a single quote (') followed by an alphanumeric name for the type. Typically, just a single letter is used. If multiple parameterized types are required, you separate them with commas. You can then use the type parameters throughout the type definition. The previous examples defined two parameterized types using the two different syntaxes that F# offers. The BinaryTree type used OCaml-style syntax, where the type parameters are placed before the name of the type. The tree type used .NET-style syntax, with the type parameters in angle brackets after the type name.

The syntax for creating and consuming an instance of a parameterized type does not change from that of creating and consuming a nonparameterized type. This is because the compiler will automatically infer the type parameters of the parameterized type. You can see this in the following construction of tree1 and tree2, and their consumption by the functions printBinaryTreeValues and printTreeValues:

```
// definition of a binary tree
type 'a BinaryTree =
    | BinaryNode of 'a BinaryTree * 'a BinaryTree
    | BinaryValue of 'a

// create an instance of a binary tree
let tree1 =
    BinaryNode(
        BinaryNode ( BinaryValue 1, BinaryValue 2),
        BinaryNode ( BinaryValue 3, BinaryValue 4) )

// definition of a tree
type Tree<'a> =
    | Node of Tree<'a> list
    | Value of 'a

// create an instance of a tree
let tree2 =
    Node( [ Node( [Value "one"; Value "two"] ) ;
        Node( [Value "three"; Value "four"] ) ] )

// function to print the binary tree
let rec printBinaryTreeValues x =
    match x with
    | BinaryNode (node1, node2) ->
        printBinaryTreeValues node1
        printBinaryTreeValues node2
    | BinaryValue x ->
        printf "%A, " x

// function to print the tree
let rec printTreeValues x =
    match x with
    | Node l -> List.iter printTreeValues l
    | Value x ->
        printf "%A, " x

// print the results
printBinaryTreeValues tree1
printfn ""
printTreeValues tree2
```

This example, when executed, returns the following:

```
1, 2, 3, 4,
"one", "two", "three", "four",
```

You may have noticed that although I've discussed defining types, creating instances of them, and examining these instances, I haven't discussed updating them. It is not possible to update these kinds of types because the idea of a value that changes over time goes against the idea of functional programming. However, F# does have some types that are updatable, and I discuss them in Chapter 4.

Recursive Type Definitions

If a type needs to reference a type declared later in the compilation order, it cannot typically do so, even if the referenced type is declared later in the same file. Sometimes, however, it is useful for two types in the same file to reference each other. The only reason you'll need to do this is if types are *mutually recursive*.

F# provides a special syntax for defining types that are mutually recursive. The types must be declared together, in the same block. Types declared in the same block must be declared next to each other; that is, without any value definitions in between, and the keyword type is replaced by the keyword and for every type definition after the first one.

Types declared in this way are not any different from types declared the regular way. They can reference any other type in the block, and they can even be mutually referential.

The next example shows how you might represent an XML tree in F#, using union types and record types. Two types in this example are mutually recursive, XmlElement and XmlTree, and they are declared in the same block. If they were declared separately, XmlElement would not be able to reference XmlTree because XmlElement is declared before XmlTree; because their declarations are joined with the keyword and, XmlElement can have a field of type XmlTree.

```
// represents an XML attribute
type XmlAttribute =
    { AttribName: string;
      AttribValue: string; }

// represents an XML element
type XmlElement =
    { ElementName: string;
      Attributes: list<XmlAttribute>;
      InnerXml: XmlTree }

// represents an XML tree
and XmlTree =
  | Element of XmlElement
  | ElementList of list<XmlTree>
  | Text of string
  | Comment of string
  | Empty
```

Active Patterns

Active patterns provide a flexible way to use F#'s pattern-matching constructs. They allow you to execute a function to see whether a match has occurred or not, which is why they are called *active*. Their design goal is to permit you to make better reuse of pattern-matching logic in your application.

All active patterns take an input and then perform some computation with that input to determine whether a match has occurred. There are two sorts of active patterns:

- *Complete active patterns* allow you to break a match down into a finite number of cases.

- *Partial active patterns* can either match or fail.

First, we'll look at complete active patterns.

Complete Active Patterns

The syntax for defining an active pattern is similar to the syntax for defining a function. The key difference is that the identifier that represents an active pattern is surrounded by *banana brackets* (sometimes also known as *banana clips*), which are formed of parentheses and vertical bars ((| |)). The names of the different cases of the active pattern go between the banana brackets, separated by vertical bars. The body of the active pattern is just an F# function that must return each case of the active pattern given in the banana brackets. Each case may also return additional data, just like a union type. This can be seen in the first part of the following example, which shows an active pattern for parsing input string data:

```
open System
```

```
// definition of the active pattern
let (|Bool|Int|Float|String|) input =
    // attempt to parse a bool
    let success, res = Boolean.TryParse input
    if success then Bool(res)
    else
        // attempt to parse an int
        let success, res = Int32.TryParse input
        if success then Int(res)
        else
            // attempt to parse a float (Double)
            let success, res = Double.TryParse input
            if success then Float(res)
            else String(input)
```

```
// function to print the results by pattern
// matching over the active pattern
let printInputWithType input =
    match input with
    | Bool b -> printfn "Boolean: %b" b
    | Int i -> printfn "Integer: %i" i
    | Float f -> printfn "Floating point: %f" f
    | String s -> printfn "String: %s" s
```

```
// print the results
printInputWithType "true"
printInputWithType "12"
printInputWithType "-12.1"
```

The pattern is designed to decide if the input string is a Boolean, integer, floating-point, or string value. The case names are Bool, Int, Float, and String. The example uses the TryParse method provided by the base class library to decide, in turn, if the input value is a Boolean, integer, or floating-point value; if it is not one of these, then it is classified as a string. If parsing is successful, this is indicated by returning the case name along with the value parsed.

In the second half of the example, you see how the active pattern is used. The active pattern allows you to treat a string value as if it were a union type. You can match against each of the four cases and recover the data returned by the active pattern in a strongly typed manner.

This example, when executed, returns the following:

```
Boolean: true
String: 12
Floating point: -12.100000
```

Partial Active Patterns

To define a partial active pattern, you use a syntax similar to that for a complete active pattern. A partial active pattern has only one case name, which is placed between banana brackets, as with the complete active pattern. The difference is that a partial active pattern must be followed by a vertical bar and an underscore to show it is partial (as opposed to a complete active pattern with just one case).

Remember that the key difference between complete and partial active patterns is that complete active patterns are guaranteed to return one of their cases, whereas active patterns either match or fail to match. So, a partial active pattern is the option type. The option type is a simple union type that is already built into the F# base libraries. It has just two cases: Some and None. It has the following definition:

```
type option<'a> =
    | Some of 'a
    | None
```

This type, as it name suggests, is used to represent either the presence or absence of a value. So, a partial active pattern returns either Some, along with any data to be returned, to represent a match, or None to represent failure.

All active patterns can have additional parameters, as well as the input they act on. Additional parameters are listed before the active pattern's input.

The next example reimplements the problem from the previous example using a partial active pattern that represents the success or failure of a .NET regular expression. The regular expression pattern is given as a parameter to the active pattern.

```
open System.Text.RegularExpressions

// the definition of the active pattern
let (|Regex|_|) regexPattern input =
    // create and attempt to match a regular expression
    let regex = new Regex(regexPattern)
    let regexMatch = regex.Match(input)
```

```
    // return either Some or None
    if regexMatch.Success then
        Some regexMatch.Value
    else
        None

// function to print the results by pattern
// matching over different instances of the
// active pattern
let printInputWithType input =
    match input with
    | Regex "$true|false^" s -> printfn "Boolean: %s" s
    | Regex @"$-?\d+^" s -> printfn "Integer: %s" s
    | Regex "$-?\d+\.\d*^" s -> printfn "Floating point: %s" s
    | _ -> printfn "String: %s" input

// print the results
printInputWithType "true"
printInputWithType "12"
printInputWithType "-12.1"
```

While complete active patterns behave in exactly the same way as a union type—meaning the compiler will raise a warning only if there are missing cases—a partial active pattern will always require a final catch-all case to avoid the compiler raising a warning. However, partial active patterns do have the advantage that you can chain multiple active patterns together, and the first case that matches will be the one that is used. This can be seen in the preceding example, which chains three of the regular expression active patterns together. Each active pattern is parameterized with a different regular expression pattern: one to match Boolean input, another to match integer input, and the third to match floating-point input.

This example, when executed, returns the following:

```
Boolean: true
String: 12
Floating point: -12.1
```

Units of Measure

Units of measure are an interesting addition to the F# type system. They allow you to classify numeric values into different units. The idea of this is to prevent you from accidentally using a numeric value incorrectly—for example, adding together a value that represents inches with a value that represents centimeters without first performing the proper conversion.

To define a unit of measure, you declare a type name and prefix it with the attribute Measure. Here is an example of creating a unit of type meters (abbreviated to m):

```
[<Measure>]type m
```

To create a value with a unit, you simply postfix the value with the name of the unit in angled brackets. So, to create a value of the meter type, use the following syntax:

```
let meters = 1.0<m>
```

Now we are going to revisit the example from the "Defining Types" section, which used union types to prevent various units of volume from being mixed up. This example implements something similar using units of measure. It starts by defining a unit of measure for liters and another for pints. Then it defines two identifiers that represent different volumes: one with a pint unit and one with a liter. Finally, it tries to add these two values, an operation that should result in an error, since you can't add pints and liters without first converting them.

```
[<Measure>]type liter
[<Measure>]type pint

let vol1 = 2.5<liter>
let vol2 = 2.5<pint>

let newVol = vol1 + vol2
```

This program will not compile, resulting in the following error:

```
Program.fs(7,21): error FS0001: The unit of measure 'pint' does not match the unit of
measure 'liter'
```

The addition or subtraction of different units of measure is not allowed, but the multiplication or division of different units of measure is allowed and will create a new unit of measure. For example, you know that to convert a pint to a liter, you need to multiply it by the ratio of liters to pints. One liter is made up of approximately 1.76 pints, so you can now calculate the correct conversion ratio in the program.

```
let ratio =  1.0<liter> / 1.76056338<pint>
```

The identifier `ratio` will have the type float<liter/pint>, which makes it clear that it is the ratio of liters to pints. Furthermore, when a value of type float<pint> is multiplied by a value of type float<liter/pint>, the resulting type will automatically be of type float<liter>, as you would expect. This means you can now write the following program, which ensures that pints are safely converted to liters before adding them:

```
// define some units of measure
[<Measure>]type liter
[<Measure>]type pint

// define some volumes
let vol1 = 2.5<liter>
let vol2 = 2.5<pint>

// define the ratio of pints to liters
let ratio =  1.0<liter> / 1.76056338<pint>
```

```
// a function to convert pints to liters
let convertPintToLiter pints =
    pints * ratio

// perform the conversion and add the values
let newVol = vol1 + (convertPintToLiter vol2)
```

Note that in versions of F# up to and including 3.1, you have to strip off the unit of measure by casting, before printing or formatting the value using sprintf, printf, or printtfn. For example,

```
// stripping off unit of measure (<= F# 3.1)
printfn "The volume is %f" (float vol1)
```

From F# 4.0 onwards, this requirement has been removed. You can apply format placeholders like %f and %i directly to values having units of measure.

```
// using a format placeholder with a unit-of-measure value (>= F# 4.0)
printfn "The volume is %f" vol1
```

Exceptions and Exception Handling

Defining exceptions in F# is similar to defining a constructor of a union type, and the syntax for handling exceptions is similar to pattern matching.

You define exceptions using the exception keyword, followed by the name of the exception, and then optionally the keyword of and the types of any values the exception should contain, with multiple types separated by asterisks. The following example shows the definition of an exception, WrongSecond, which contains one integer value:

```
exception WrongSecond of int
```

You can raise exceptions with the raise keyword, as shown in the else clause in the following testSecond function. F# also has an alternative to the raise keyword, the failwith function, as shown in the following if clause. If, as is commonly the case, you just want to raise an exception with a text description of what went wrong, you can use failwith to raise a generic exception that contains the text passed to the function, like so:

```
// define an exception type
exception WrongSecond of int

// list of prime numbers
let primes =
    [ 2; 3; 5; 7; 11; 13; 17; 19; 23; 29; 31; 37; 41; 43; 47; 53; 59 ]

// function to test if current second is prime
let testSecond() =
    try
        let currentSecond = System.DateTime.Now.Second in
        // test if current second is in the list of primes
        if List.exists (fun x -> x = currentSecond) primes then
            // use the failwith function to raise an exception
            failwith "A prime second"
```

```
        else
            // raise the WrongSecond exception
            raise (WrongSecond currentSecond)
    with
    // catch the wrong second exception
    WrongSecond x ->
        printf "The current was %i, which is not prime" x

// call the function
testSecond()
```

As shown in testSecond, the try and with keywords handle exceptions. The expressions that are subject to error handling go between the try and with keywords, and one or more pattern-matching rules must follow the with keyword. When trying to match an F# exception, the syntax follows that of trying to match an F# constructor from a union type. The first half of the rule consists of the exception name, followed by identifiers or wildcards to match values that the exception contains. The second half of the rule is an expression that states how the exception should be handled. One major difference between this and the regular pattern-matching constructs is that no warning or error is issued if pattern matching is incomplete. This is because any exceptions that are unhandled will propagate until they reach the top level and stop execution. The example handles exception wrongSecond, while leaving the exception raised by failwith to propagate.

F# also supports a finally keyword, which is used with the try keyword. You can't use the finally keyword in conjunction with the with keyword. The finally expression will be executed whether or not an exception is thrown. The following example shows a finally block being used to ensure a file is closed and disposed of after it is written to:

```
// function to write to a file
let writeToFile() =
    // open a file
    let file = System.IO.File.CreateText("test.txt")
    try
        // write to it
        file.WriteLine("Hello F# users")
    finally
        // close the file, this will happen even if
        // an exception occurs writing to the file
        file.Dispose()

// call the function
writeToFile()
```

■ **Caution**   Programmers coming from an OCaml background should be careful when using exceptions in F#. Because of the architecture of the CLR, throwing an exception is pretty expensive—quite a bit more expensive than in OCaml. If you throw a lot of exceptions, profile your code carefully to decide whether the performance costs are worth it. If the costs are too high, revise the code appropriately. As a more general stylistic point: avoid using exceptions for "expected" flow of control.

Lazy Evaluation

Lazy evaluation goes hand in hand with functional programming. The theory is that if there are no side effects in the language, the compiler or runtime is free to choose the evaluation order of expressions.

As you know, F# allows functions to have side effects, so it's not possible for the compiler or runtime to have a free hand in function evaluation; therefore, F# is said to have a strict evaluation order, or to be a *strict language*. You can still take advantage of lazy evaluation, but you must be explicit about which computations can be delayed—that is, evaluated in a lazy manner.

You use the keyword `lazy` to delay a computation (invoke lazy evaluation). The computation within the lazy expression remains unevaluated until evaluation is explicitly forced with the `force` function from the Lazy module. When the `force` function is applied to a particular lazy expression, the value is computed, and the result is cached. Subsequent calls to the `force` function return the cached value–whatever it is—even if this means raising an exception.

The following code shows a simple use of lazy evaluation:

```
let lazyValue = lazy ( 2 + 2 )
let actualValue = Lazy.force lazyValue

printfn "%i" actualValue
```

The first line delays a simple expression for evaluation later. The next line forces evaluation. Finally, the value is printed.

The value has been cached, so any side effects that take place when the value is computed will occur only the first time the lazy value is forced. This is fairly easy to demonstrate, as shown by this example:

```
let lazySideEffect =
    lazy
        ( let temp = 2 + 2
          printfn "%i" temp
          temp )

printfn "Force value the first time: "
let actualValue1 = Lazy.force lazySideEffect
printfn "Force value the second time: "
let actualValue2 = Lazy.force lazySideEffect
```

In this example, a lazy value has a side effect when it is calculated: it writes to the console. To show that this side effect takes place only once, it forces the value twice. As you can see from the result, writing to the console takes place only once:

```
Force value the first time:
4
Force value the second time:
```

Laziness can also be useful when working with collections. The idea of a lazy collection is that elements in the collection are calculated on demand. Some collection types also cache the results of these calculations, so there is no need to recalculate elements. The collection most commonly used for lazy programming in F# is the seq type, a shorthand for the BCL's IEnumerable type. seq values are created and manipulated using functions in the Seq module. Many other values are also compatible with the type seq; for example, all F# lists and arrays are compatible with this type, as are most other collection types in the F# libraries and the BCL.

Possibly the most important function for creating lazy collections, and probably the most difficult to understand, is unfold. This function allows you to create a lazy list. What makes it complicated is that you must provide a function that will be repeatedly evaluated to provide the elements of the list. The function passed to Seq.unfold can take any type of parameter and must return an option type. An option type, recall, is a union type that can be either None or Some(x), where x is a value of any type. In the context of Seq.unfold, None is used to represent the end of a list. The Some constructor must contain a tuple. The first item in the tuple represents the value that will become the first value in the list. The second value in the tuple is the value that will be passed into the function the next time it is called. You can think of this value as an accumulator.

The next example shows how this works. The identifier lazyList contains three values. If the value passed into the function is less than 13, it appends the list using this value to form the list element, and then adds 1 to the value passed to the list. This will be the value passed to the function the next time it is called. If the value is greater than or equal to 13, the example terminates the list by returning None.

```
// the lazy list definition
let lazyList =
    Seq.unfold
        (fun x ->
            if x < 13 then
                // if smaller than the limit return
                // the current and next value
                Some(x, x + 1)
            else
                // if great than the limit
                // terminate the sequence
                None)
        10

// print the results
printfn "%A" lazyList
```

This example, when executed, returns the following:

```
10
11
12
```

Sequences are useful to represent lists that don't terminate. A nonterminating list can't be represented by a classic list, which is constrained by the amount of memory available. The next example demonstrates this by creating fibs, an infinite list of all the Fibonacci numbers. To display the results conveniently, the example uses the function Seq.take to turn the first 20 items into an F# list, but carries on calculating many more Fibonacci numbers, as it uses F# bigint integers, so it is not limited by the size of a 32-bit integer.

```
// create an infinite list of Fibonacci numbers
let fibs =
    Seq.unfold
        (fun (n0, n1) ->
            Some(n0, (n1, n0 + n1)))
        (1I,1I)
```

```
// take the first twenty items from the list
let first20 = Seq.take 20 fibs

// print the finite list
printfn "%A" first20
```

This example, when executed, returns the following:

```
[1I; 1I; 2I; 3I; 5I; 8I; 13I; 21I; 34I; 55I; 89I; 144I; 233I; 377I; 610I; 987I;
1597I; 2584I; 4181I; 6765I]
```

Note that both of these sequences could also be created using the list comprehension discussed earlier in this chapter. If list comprehensions are based on sequences, they are automatically lazy.

Summary

In this chapter, you looked at the major functional programming constructs in F#. This is the core of the language, and I hope you've developed a good feel for how to approach writing algorithms and handling data in F#. The next chapter covers imperative programming, and you'll see how to mix functional and imperative programming techniques to handle tasks such as input and output.

CHAPTER 4

■ ■ ■

Imperative Programming

As you saw in Chapter 3, you can use F# for pure functional programming. However, some issues, most notably I/O, are almost impossible to address without some kind of state change. F# does not require that you program in a stateless fashion. It allows you to use *mutable* identifiers whose values can change over time. F# also has other constructs that support imperative programming. You saw some in Chapter 3. Any example that wrote to the console included a few lines of imperative code alongside functional code. In this chapter, you'll explore these constructs—and many others—in much more detail.

First, you'll look at F#'s unit type, a special type that means "no value," which enables some aspects of imperative programming. Second, you'll look at some of the ways F# can handle *mutable state*, or types whose values can change over time. These include mutable identifiers, the ref type, mutable record types, and arrays. Finally, you'll look at using .NET libraries. The topics will include calling static methods, creating objects and working with their members, using special members such as indexers and events, and using the F# |> operator.

The Unit Type

Any function that does not accept or return values is of type unit, which is similar to the type void in C# and System.Void in the CLR. To a functional programmer, a function that doesn't accept or return a value might not seem interesting because a function that doesn't accept or return a value doesn't do anything. In the imperative paradigm, you know that side effects exist, so even if a function accepts or returns nothing, you know it can still have its uses. The unit type is represented as a *literal value* in the form of a pair of parentheses (()). This means that whenever you want a function that doesn't take or return a value, you put () in the code, like so:

```
let aFunction() =
    ()
```

In this example, aFunction is a function because you placed parentheses after the identifier, where its parameters would go. If you hadn't done this, it would have meant aFunction was not a function, but a value. You probably know that all functions are values, but here the difference between a function and a nonfunction value is important. If aFunction were a nonfunction value, the expressions within it would be evaluated only once. Because it is a function, the expressions will be evaluated each time it is called.

Similarly, placing () after the equals sign tells the compiler you will return nothing. Ordinarily, you need to put something between the equals sign and the empty parentheses, or the function is pointless. For the sake of keeping things simple, I'll leave this function pointless. Now you'll see the type of aFunction.

© Robert Pickering and Kit Eason 2016
R. Pickering and K. Eason, *Beginning F# 4.0*, DOI 10.1007/978-1-4842-1374-2_4

The easiest way to see a function's type is by using the tool tips that are available in Visual Studio and other IDEs, or by compiling it using F# Interactive. Alternatively, you can use the compiler's `fsc -i` switch. In all cases, the result is as follows:

```
val aFunction: unit -> unit
```

As you can see, the type of aFunction is a function that accepts unit and transforms it into a value of type unit. Because the compiler now knows that the function doesn't return anything, you can now use it with some special imperative constructs. To call the function, you can use the let keyword followed by a pair of parentheses and the equals sign. This is a special use of the let keyword, which here means "call a function that does not return a value." Alternatively, you can use the keyword do, or you can simply call the function without any extra keywords at all, by placing the function at the top level.

```
let aFunction() =
  ()

let () = aFunction ()
// -- or --
do aFunction ()
// -- or --
aFunction ()
```

Similarly, you can chain functions that return unit together within a function; just make sure they all share the same indentation. The next example shows several printfn functions chained together to print text to the console:

```
let poem() =
  printfn "I wandered lonely as a cloud"
  printfn "That floats on high o'er vales and hills,"
  printfn "When all at once I saw a crowd,"
  printfn "A host, of golden daffodils"

poem()
```

It's not quite true that the only functions that return a unit type can be used in this manner; however, using them with a type other than unit will generate a warning, which is something most programmers want to avoid. To avoid this, it's sometimes useful to turn a function that does return a value into a function of type unit, typically because the function has a side effect, as well as returning a value. The need to do this is fairly rare when you're using only F# libraries written in F# (although situations where it is useful do exist), but it is more common when using .NET libraries that were not written in F#.

The next example shows how to throw away the value of the result of a function, so that the resulting function returns unit:

```
let getShorty() = "shorty"
let _ = getShorty()
// -- or --
ignore(getShorty())
// -- or --
getShorty() |> ignore
```

You begin by defining a function called getShorty that returns a string. Now imagine that you want to call this function and ignore its result. The next two lines demonstrate different ways to do this. First, you can use a let expression with an underscore (_) character in place of the identifier. The underscore tells the compiler this is a value in which you aren't interested. Second, this is such a common thing to do that it has been wrapped into a function named ignore, which is available in the F# base libraries and is demonstrated on the third line. The final line shows an alternative way of calling ignore that uses the pipe-forward operator to pass the result of getShorty() to the ignore function. (See the "The |> Operator" section for more information about the pipe-forward operator.)

The Mutable Keyword

In Chapter 3, I talked about how you could bind identifiers to values using the keyword let and noted how, under some circumstances, you could redefine and rebind, but not modify, these identifiers. If you want to define an identifier whose value can change over time, you can do this using the mutable keyword. A special operator, the *left ASCII arrow* (or just *left arrow*), is composed of a less-than sign and a dash (<-). You use it to update these identifiers. An update operation using the left arrow has type unit, so you can chain these operations together as discussed in the previous section. The following example demonstrates how to define a mutable identifier of type string and then change the value that it holds:

```
// a mutable idendifier
let mutable phrase = "How can I be sure, "

// print the phrase
printfn "%s" phrase
// update the phrase
phrase <- "In a world that's constantly changing"
// reprint the phrase
printfn "%s" phrase
```

The results are as follows:

```
How can I be sure,
In a world that's constantly changing
```

At first glance, this doesn't look too different from redefining an identifier, but it has a couple of key differences. When you use the left arrow to update a mutable identifier, you can change its value but not its type; when you redefine an identifier, you can do both. A compile error is produced if you try to change the type, as this example demonstrates:

```
let mutable number = "one"
phrase <- 1
```

If you attempt to compile this code, you get the following error message:

```
Prog.fs(9,10): error: FS0001: This expression has type
    int
but is here used with type
    string
```

The other major difference is where these changes are visible. When you redefine an identifier, the change is visible only within the scope of the new identifier. When it passes out of scope, it reverts to its old value. This is not the case with mutable identifiers. Any changes are permanent, whatever the scope, as this example demonstrates:

```
// demonstration of redefining X
let redefineX() =
    let x = "One"
    printfn "Redefining:\r\nx = %s" x
    if true then
        let x = "Two"
        printfn "x = %s" x
    printfn "x = %s" x

// demonstration of mutating X
let mutableX() =
    let mutable x = "One"
    printfn "Mutating:\r\nx = %s" x
    if true then
        x <- "Two"
        printfn "x = %s" x
    printfn "x = %s" x

// run the demos
redefineX()
mutableX()
```

Executing the preceding code produces the following results:

```
Redefining:
x = One
x = Two
x = One
Mutating:
x = One
x = Two
x = Two
```

In versions of F# before 4.0, identifiers defined as mutable are somewhat limited because you can't mutate them within a subfunction, as this example illustrates:

```
let mutableY() =
    let mutable y = "One"
    printfn "Mutating:\r\nx = %s" y
    let f() =
        // this causes an error as
        // mutables can't be captured
        y <- "Two"
        printfn "x = %s" y
  f()
  printfn "x = %s" y
```

If you attempt to compile this program using a version of F# before 4.0, you get the following error message:

```
Prog.fs(35,16): error FS0191: The mutable variable 'y' is used in an invalid way. Mutable
  variables may not be captured by closures. Consider eliminating this use of mutation or
  using a heap-allocated mutable reference cell via 'ref' and '!'.
```

Fortunately, from F# 4.0 onwards this restriction has largely been eliminated, and you can normally use a mutable value in this kind of context.

If you are using earlier versions of F#, or in rare situations where a mutable still cannot be used, you can use a ref type. Use of this type is covered in a following section.

Defining Mutable Records

In Chapter 3, when you first met record types, I discussed how to update their fields using the *with* syntax. This is because record types are immutable by default. Alternatively, you can use the mutable keyword to allow you to update the fields in record types. (Other types of values can be declared as mutable; I discuss this in the next chapter.) You make record fields mutable by using the keyword mutable before the field in a record type. I should emphasize that this operation changes the contents of the record's field, rather than changing the record itself.

```
// a record with a mutable field
type Couple = { Her: string; mutable Him: string }

// a create an instance of the record
let theCouple = { Her = "Elizabeth Taylor "; Him = "Nicky Hilton" }

// function to change the contents of
// the record over time
let changeCouple() =
    printfn "%A" theCouple
    theCouple.Him <- "Michael Wilding"
    printfn "%A" theCouple
    theCouple.Him <- "Michael Todd"
    printfn "%A" theCouple
    theCouple.Him <- "Eddie Fisher"
    printfn "%A" theCouple
    theCouple.Him <- "Richard Burton"
    printfn "%A" theCouple
    theCouple.Him <- "Richard Burton"
    printfn "%A" theCouple
    theCouple.Him <- "John Warner"
    printfn "%A" theCouple
    theCouple.Him <- "Larry Fortensky"
    printfn "%A" theCouple

// call the fucntion
changeCouple()
```

Executing the preceding code produces the following results:

```
{Her = "Elizabeth Taylor ";
 Him = "Nicky Hilton";}
{Her = "Elizabeth Taylor ";
 Him = "Michael Wilding";}
{Her = "Elizabeth Taylor ";
 Him = "Michael Todd";}
{Her = "Elizabeth Taylor ";
 Him = "Eddie Fisher";}
{Her = "Elizabeth Taylor ";
 Him = "Richard Burton";}
{Her = "Elizabeth Taylor ";
 Him = "Richard Burton";}
{Her = "Elizabeth Taylor ";
 Him = "John Warner";}
{Her = "Elizabeth Taylor ";
 Him = "Larry Fortensky";}
```

This example shows a mutable record in action. A type, couple, is defined where the field him is mutable, but the field her is not. Next, an instance of couple is initialized, after which you change the value of him many times, each time displaying the results. Note that the mutable keyword applies per field, so any attempt to update a field that is not mutable will result in a compile error. For example, the next example will fail on the second line:

```
theCouple.Her <- "Sybil Williams"
printfn "%A" theCouple
```

If you attempt to compile this program, you get the following error message:

```
prog.fs(2,4): error: FS0005: This field is not mutable
```

The Reference Type

The ref type is a simple way for a program to use mutable state, or values that change over time, in those few situations where simply using the mutable keyword isn't permitted. From F# 4.0 onwards, these situations are rare, but in previous versions you weren't allowed to mutate a mutable value within a "closure," such as an inner function or a sequence generator. The ref type is a record type with a single mutable field that is defined in the F# libraries. Some operators are defined to make accessing and updating the field as straightforward as possible. F#'s definition of the ref type uses *type parameterization*, a concept introduced in the previous chapter. Thus, although the value of the ref type can be of any type, you cannot change the type of the value once you create an instance of the value.

Creating a new instance of the `ref` type is easy; you use the keyword `ref`, followed by whatever item represents the initial value of the `ref`. The next example shows the compiler's output (using the `-i` option, which shows that the type of `phrase` is `string ref`, or a reference type that can only contain strings):

```
let phrase = ref "Inconsistency"
```

```
val phrase : string ref
```

This syntax is similar to defining a union type's constructors, also shown in the previous chapter. The `ref` type has two built-in operators to access it: the exclamation point (`!`) provides access to the value of the reference type, and an operator composed of a colon followed by an equals sign (`:=`) enables you to update it. The `!` operator always returns a value of the type that matches the `ref` type's contents, known to the compiler thanks to type parameterization. The `:=` operator has the type `unit` because it doesn't return anything.

The next example shows how to use a `ref` type to total the contents of an array. (Of course, in practice the easiest way to do this is to use `Array.sum` in the Array module.) On the third line of `totalArray`, you see the creation of the `ref` type. In this case, it is initialized to hold the value 0. On the seventh line, the let binding after the array definition, you see the `ref` type being both accessed and updated. First, `!` is used to access the value with the `ref` type; second, after it has been added to the current value held in the array, the value of the `ref` type is updated through the use of the `:=` operator. Now the code will correctly print 6 to the console.

```
let totalArray () =
    // define an array literal
    let array = [| 1; 2; 3 |]
    // define a counter
    let total = ref 0
    // loop over the array
    for x in array do
        // keep a running total
        total := !total + x
    // print the total
    printfn "total: %i" !total

totalArray()
```

Executing the preceding code produces the following result:

```
total: 6
```

■ **Caution**   If you are used to programming in one of the C family of programming languages, you should be careful here. When reading F# code, it is quite easy to misinterpret the `ref` type's `!` operator as a Boolean "not" operator. F# uses a function called `not` for Boolean "not" operations.

The ref type is a useful way to share mutable values between several functions. An identifier can be bound to a ref type defined in scope that is common to all functions that want to use the value; then the functions can use the value of the identifier as they like, changing it or merely reading it. Because you can pass around functions in F# as if they were values, the value follows the function everywhere it goes. This process is known as *capturing a local* or *creating a closure*.

The next example demonstrates this by defining three functions: inc, dec, and show, which all share a common ref type holding an integer. The functions inc, dec, and show are all defined in their own private scopes and then returned to the top level as a *tuple*, so they are visible everywhere. Note how n is not returned; it remains private, but inc, dec, and show are all still able to access n. This is a useful technique for controlling what operations can take place on mutable data.

```
// capture the inc, dec, and show funtions
  let inc, dec, show =
      // define the shared state
      let n = ref 0
      // a function to increment
      let inc () =
          n := !n + 1
      // a function to decrement
      let dec () =
          n := !n - 1
      // a function to show the current state
      let show () =
          printfn "%i" !n

    // return the functions to the top level
    inc, dec, show

// test the functions
inc()
inc()
dec()
show()
```

Executing the preceding code produces the following result:

1

From F# 4.0 onwards, the preceding code can be rewritten using a mutable value, like so:

```
// this will work from F# 4.0
let inc, dec, show =
    // define the shared state
    let mutable n = 0
    // a function to increment
    let inc () =
        n <- n + 1
    // a function to decrement
    let dec () =
        n <- n - 1
```

```
    // a function to show the current state
    let show () =
        printfn "%i" n

    // return the functions to the top level
    inc, dec, show

// test the functions
inc()
inc()
dec()
show()
```

Arrays

Arrays are a concept that most programmers are familiar with, as almost all programming languages have some sort of array type. The F# array type is based on the BCL System.Array type, so anyone who has used arrays in C# or Visual Basic will find the underlying concepts the same.

Arrays are a mutable collection type in F#; it's useful to compare them to the immutable list type explained in Chapter 3. Arrays and lists are both collections, but the values within arrays are updatable, whereas the values in lists are not. One-dimensional arrays are sometimes referred to as *vectors*, and multidimensional arrays are sometimes called *matrices*. Array literals are defined by a sequence of items separated by semicolons (;) and delimited by an opening square bracket and a vertical bar ([|) and a closing bar and square bracket (|]). The syntax for referencing an array element is the name of the identifier of the array followed by a period (.) and then the index of the element in square brackets ([ ]). The syntax for retrieving the value of an element stops there. The syntax for setting the value of an element is the left arrow (<-) followed by the value to be assigned to the element.

The next example shows you how to read from and write to an array. First, you define an array, rhymeArray, and then you read all the members from it. Next, you insert new values into the array, and finally, you print out all the values you have.

```
// define an array literal
let rhymeArray =
    [| "Went to market";
       "Stayed home";
       "Had roast beef";
       "Had none" |]

// unpack the array into identifiers
let firstPiggy = rhymeArray.[0]
let secondPiggy = rhymeArray.[1]
let thirdPiggy = rhymeArray.[2]
let fourthPiggy = rhymeArray.[3]

// update elements of the array
rhymeArray.[0] <- "Wee,"
rhymeArray.[1] <- "wee,"
rhymeArray.[2] <- "wee,"
rhymeArray.[3] <- "all the way home"
```

```
// give a short name to the new line characters
let nl = System.Environment.NewLine

// print out the identifiers & array
printfn "%s%s%s%s%s%s%s"
    firstPiggy nl
    secondPiggy nl
    thirdPiggy nl
    fourthPiggy
printfn "%A" rhymeArray
```

When you execute this code, you see the following results:

```
Went to market
Stayed home
Had roast beef
Had none
[|"Wee,"; "wee,"; "wee,"; "all the way home"|]
```

Arrays, like lists, use type parameterization, so the type of the array's contents makes up part of the array's type. This is written as content type, followed by the array's type. Thus, rhymeArray has the type `string array`, which you might also write like `string[]` or `array<string>`.

Multidimensional arrays in F# come in two, slightly different flavors: jagged and rectangular. As the name suggests, jagged arrays are arrays where the second dimension is not a regular shape; rather they are arrays whose contents happen to be other arrays, and the length of the inner arrays is not forced to be the same. In *rectangular* arrays, all inner arrays are of the same length; in fact, there is no concept of an inner array because the whole array is the same object. The method of getting and setting items in the two different types of arrays differs slightly.

For jagged arrays, you use the period followed by the index in parentheses, but you have to use this twice (one time for each dimension) because the first time you get back the inner array, and the second time you get the element within it.

The next example demonstrates a simple jagged array called `jagged`. You can access the array members in two different ways. The first inner array (at index 0) is assigned to the identifier `singleDim`, and then its first element is assigned to `itemOne`. On the fourth line, the first element of the second inner array is assigned to `itemTwo`, using one line of code.

```
// define a jagged array literal
let jagged = [| [| "one" |] ; [| "two" ; "three" |] |]

// unpack elements from the arrays
let singleDim = jagged.[0]
let itemOne = singleDim.[0]
let itemTwo = jagged.[1].[0]

// print some of the unpacked elements
printfn "%s %s" itemOne itemTwo
```

When you compile and execute the results of this example, you get the following result:

```
one two
```

To reference elements in rectangular arrays, use a period (.) followed by all the indexes in square brackets, separated by commas. Unlike jagged arrays, which are multidimensional but use the same ([| |]) syntax as single-dimensional arrays, you must create rectangular arrays with the create function of the Array2D and Array3D modules, which support two- and three-dimensional arrays, respectively. This doesn't mean rectangular arrays are limited to three dimensions because it's possible to use the System.Array class to create rectangular arrays with more than three dimensions; however, you should consider such an approach carefully because adding extra dimensions can quickly lead to extremely large objects.

In the following example, you create a rectangular array, square, and then populate its elements with the integers 1, 2, 3, and 4:

```
// create a square array,
// initally populated with zeros
let square = Array2D.create 2 2 0

// populate the array
square.[0,0] <- 1
square.[0,1] <- 2
square.[1,0] <- 3
square.[1,1] <- 4

// print the array
printfn "%A" square
```

Now let's look at the differences between jagged and rectangular arrays. First, you create a jagged array to represent Pascal's Triangle. Next, you create a rectangular array that contains various number sequences that are hidden within pascalsTriangle.

```
// define Pascal's Triangle as an
// array literal
let pascalsTriangle =
    [| [|1|];
       [|1; 1|];
       [|1; 2; 1|];
       [|1; 3; 3; 1|];
       [|1; 4; 6; 4; 1|];
       [|1; 5; 10; 10; 5; 1|];
       [|1; 6; 15; 20; 15; 6; 1|];
       [|1; 7; 21; 35; 35; 21; 7; 1|];
       [|1; 8; 28; 56; 70; 56; 28; 8; 1|]; |]

// collect elements from the jagged array
// assigning them to a square array
let numbers =
    let length = (Array.length pascalsTriangle) in
    let temp = Array2D.create 3 length 0 in
```

```
    for index = 0 to length - 1 do
        let naturelIndex = index - 1 in
        if naturelIndex >= 0 then
            temp.[0, index] <- pascalsTriangle.[index].[naturelIndex]
    let triangularIndex = index - 2 in
    if triangularIndex >= 0 then
        temp.[1, index] <- pascalsTriangle.[index].[triangularIndex]
    let tetrahedralIndex = index - 3 in
    if tetrahedralIndex >= 0 then
        temp.[2, index] <- pascalsTriangle.[index].[tetrahedralIndex]
    done
    temp

// print the array
printfn "%A" numbers
```

When you compile and execute this code, you get the following results:

```
[|[|0; 1; 2; 3; 4; 5; 6; 7; 8|]; [|0; 0; 1; 3; 6; 10; 15; 21; 28|];
  [|0; 0; 0; 1; 4; 10; 20; 35; 56|]|]
```

The following results show the types displayed when you use the compiler's -i switch:

```
val pascalsTriangle: int array array
val numbers: int [,]
```

As you might expect, jagged and rectangular arrays have different types. The type of a jagged array is the same as a single-dimensional array, except that it has an array per dimension, so the type of pascalsTriangle is int array array. Rectangular arrays use a notation more similar to C#. It begins with the name of the type of the array's elements, and then includes square brackets ([]) with one comma for every dimension greater than 1, so the type of your two-dimensional numbers array is int[,].

Array Comprehensions

I introduced comprehension syntax for lists and sequences in Chapter 3. You can use a corresponding syntax to create arrays. The only difference between this and the list and sequence syntax is the characters that delimit the array. You use vertical bars surrounded by square brackets for arrays.

```
// an array of characters
let chars = [| '1' .. '9' |]

// an array of tuples of number, square
let squares =
    [| for x in 1 .. 9 -> x, x*x |]

// print out both arrays
printfn "%A" chars
printfn "%A" squares
```

Executing the preceding code produces the following results:

```
[|'1'; '2'; '3'; '4'; '5'; '6'; '7'; '8'; '9'|]
[|(1, 1); (2, 4); (3, 9); (4, 16); (5, 25); (6, 36); (7, 49); (8, 64); (9, 81)|]
```

Array Slicing

It's often useful to pull out some range of the values in an array. This can be done using *array slicing*. A simple slice of an array can be taken like this:

```
let arr = [|1; 3; 5; 7; 11; 13|]
let middle = arr.[1..4] // [|3; 5; 7; 11|]
```

Omit the starting or ending index to start from the beginning or end of the input array, like so:

```
let start = arr.[..3] // [|1; 3; 5; 7|]
let tail = arr.[1..] // [|3; 5; 7; 11; 13|]
```

Slicing also works for multi-dimensional arrays, as in this simple implementation of part of a "Battleships" game:

```
let ocean = Array2D.create 100 100 0
// Create a ship:
for i in 3..6 do
    ocean.[i, 5] <- 1
// Pull out an area hit by a 'shell':
let hitArea = ocean.[2..5, 2..5]
```

If you want to include all of the elements in one of the dimensions, use a *:

```
// We can see a rectangular area by 'radar':
let radarArea = ocean.[3..4, *]
```

Note that from F# 4.0 onwards, the same slicing syntax can also be applied to F# lists.

Control Flow

Unlike the pseudo-control-flow syntax described in Chapter 3, F# does have some imperative control-flow constructs. In addition to the imperative use of if, there are also while and for loops.

The major difference from using the if expression in the imperative style—that is, using it with a function that returns the type unit—is that you aren't forced to use an else, as the following example demonstrates:

```
if System.DateTime.Now.DayOfWeek = System.DayOfWeek.Sunday then
    printfn "Sunday Playlist: Lazy On A Sunday Afternoon - Queen"
```

Although it isn't necessary to have an else expression if the if expression has the type unit, you can add one if necessary. This too must have the type unit, or the compiler will issue an error.

```
if System.DateTime.Now.DayOfWeek = System.DayOfWeek.Monday then
    printfn "Monday Playlist: Blue Monday - New Order"
else
    printfn "Alt Playlist: Fell In Love With A Girl - White Stripes"
```

You can use whitespace to detect where an if expression ends. You indent the code that belongs to the if expression, and the if expression ends when it goes back to its original indentation. In the following example, the string "Tuesday Playlist: Ruby Tuesday - Rolling Stones" will be printed on a Tuesday, while "Everyday Playlist: Eight Days A Week - Beatles" will be printed every day of the week:

```
if System.DateTime.Now.DayOfWeek = System.DayOfWeek.Tuesday then
    printfn "Tuesday Playlist: Ruby Tuesday - Rolling Stones"
printfn "Everyday Playlist: Eight Days A Week - Beatles"
```

If you want multiple statements to be part of the if statement, you can give them the same indention, as shown in the following example, where both strings will be printed only on a Friday:

```
if System.DateTime.Now.DayOfWeek = System.DayOfWeek.Friday then
    printfn "Friday Playlist: Friday I'm In Love - The Cure"
    printfn "Friday Playlist: View From The Afternoon - Arctic Monkeys"
```

Most programmers are familiar with for loops because they are commonly found in imperative programming languages. In F#, for loops are overloaded, so a for loop can either enumerate a collection, behaving in a similar way to the foreach loop available in many programming languages, or it can specify an identifier that will be incremented by one for each iteration of the loop.

First, let's look at using for to enumerate collections. In this case, the for loop performs an imperative action, one that returns the unit on each element in the collection. This is probably the most common imperative usage of for loops in F#. The syntax begins with the for keyword, followed by the identifier that will be bound to each item in the collection. Next comes the keyword in, followed by the collection, and then the keyword do. The code for processing each item in the collection comes next; you indent this to show that it belongs to the for loop. The following example demonstrates this syntax, enumerating an array of strings and printing each one:

```
// an array for words
let words = [| "Red"; "Lorry"; "Yellow"; "Lorry" |]

// use a for loop to print each element
for word in words do
    printfn "%s" word
```

Executing the preceding code produces the following results:

```
Red
Lorry
Yellow
Lorry
```

As you'll see later in this chapter and in many examples throughout the book, this can be a convenient way to work with typed or untyped collections returned by .NET BCL methods.

The other usage of a for loop is to declare an identifier, whose scope is the for loop, that increases or decreases its value by 1 (or some other specified amount) after each iteration of the loop. The identifier is given a starting value and an end value, and the end value provides the condition for loop termination. F# follows this syntax. It starts with the keyword for, followed by the identifier that will hold the counter value; next comes an equals sign, followed by an expression for the initial counter value, the keyword to, and then an expression for the terminal value, and finally the keyword do. The body of the loop follows, normally in an indented scope. The for loop has the type unit, so the code that forms the body of the loop should have the type unit; otherwise, the compiler will issue a warning.

The next example demonstrates a common usage of a for loop: to enumerate all the values in an array. The identifier index will take on values starting at 0 and ending at 1 less than the length·of the array. You can use this identifier as the index for the array.

```
// a Ryunosuke Akutagawa haiku array
let ryunosukeAkutagawa = [| "Green "; "frog,";
    "Is"; "your"; "body"; "also";
    "freshly"; "painted?" |]

// for loop over the array printing each element
for index = 0 to Array.length ryunosukeAkutagawa - 1 do
    printf "%s " ryunosukeAkutagawa.[index]
```

When you compile and execute this code, you get the following results:

```
Green frog, Is your body also freshly painted?
```

In a regular for loop, the initial value of the counter must always be *less* than the final value, and the value of the counter will increase as the loop continues. There is a variation on this, where you replace to with downto. In this case, the initial counter value must always be *greater* than the final value, and the counter will decrease as the loop continues. You can see how to use downto in this example:

```
// a Shuson Kato hiaku array (backwards)
let shusonKato = [| "watching."; "been"; "have";
    "children"; "three"; "my"; "realize"; "and";
    "ant"; "an"; "kill"; "I";
    |]

// loop over the array backwards printing each word
for index = Array.length shusonKato - 1 downto 0 do
    printf "%s " shusonKato.[index]
```

When you compile and execute this code, you get the following results:

```
I kill an ant and realize my three children have been watching.
```

An alternative (and commonly used) syntax for for loops uses range notation for the index value. You can have both upward- and downward-counting loops, and even loops that increment or decrement the index value by more than 1.

```
// Count upwards:
for i in 0..10 do
    printfn "%i green bottles" i
// Count downwards:
for i in 10..-1..0 do
    printfn "%i green bottles" i
// Count upwards in tens
for i in 0..10..100 do
    printfn "%i green bottles" i
```

The while loop is another familiar imperative language construct. It is an expression that creates a loop over a section of code until a Boolean expression evaluates to false. To create a while loop in F#, you use the keyword while followed by a Boolean expression that determines whether the loop should continue. As with for loops, you place the body of the loop after the keyword do, and the body should have the type unit; otherwise, the compiler will issue a warning. This code illustrates how to create a while loop:

```
// a Matsuo Basho hiaku in a mutable list
let mutable matsuoBasho = [ "An"; "old"; "pond!";
    "A"; "frog"; "jumps"; "in-";
    "The"; "sound"; "of"; "water" ]

while (List.length matsuoBasho > 0) do
    printf "%s " (List.head matsuoBasho)
    matsuoBasho <- List.tail matsuoBasho
```

This program enumerates the list, and the Boolean expression to terminate the loop is based on whether the list is empty. Within the body of the loop, you print the head of the list and then remove it, shortening the list on each iteration.

When you compile and execute this code, you get the following results:

```
An old pond! A frog jumps in- The sound of water
```

Calling Static Methods and Properties from .NET Libraries

One extremely useful feature of imperative programming in F# is the ability to use just about any library written in a .NET programming language, including the many methods and classes available as part of the BCL itself. I consider this to be imperative programming because libraries written in other languages make no guarantees about how state works inside them, so you can't know whether a method you call has side effects.

A distinction should be made between calling libraries written in F# and libraries written in any other language. This is because libraries written in F# have metadata that describes extra details about the library, such as whether a method takes a tuple or whether its parameters can be curried. This metadata is specific to F#, and it is stored in a binary format as a resource to the generated assembly. This is largely why the Microsoft.FSharp.Reflection API is provided: to bridge the gap between F# and .NET metadata.

You use the same basic syntax when calling static or instance properties or methods. Method calls to a non-F# library must have their arguments separated by commas and surrounded by parentheses. (Remember, F# function calls usually use whitespace to separate arguments, and you need to use parentheses only to impose precedence.) Method calls to a non-F# library cannot be curried; in fact, methods from non-F# libraries behave as though they take a tuple of arguments. Despite this difference, calling a method from a non-F# library is straightforward. You start off by using static properties and methods, like so:

```
open System.IO
// test whether a file "test.txt" exist
if File.Exists("test.txt") then
    printfn "Text file \"test.txt\" is present"
else
    printfn "Text file \"test.txt\" does not exist"
```

This example calls a static method from the .NET Framework BCL. Calling a static method is almost identical to calling an F# function. You begin with the class name followed by a period (.) and then the name of the method; the only real difference is in the syntax for passing the arguments, which are surrounded by parentheses and separated by commas. You make a call to the System.IO.File class's Exists method to test whether a file exists and print an appropriate message, depending on the result.

You can treat static methods from other .NET libraries as values in the same way that you can treat F# functions as values and pass them to other function as parameters. The following example shows how to pass the File.Exist method to the F# library function List.map:

```
open System.IO

// list of files to test
let files1 = [ "test1.txt"; "test2.txt"; "test3.txt" ]

// test if each file exists
let results1 = List.map File.Exists files1

// print the results
printfn "%A" results1
```

Because .NET methods behave as if they take tuples as arguments, you can also treat a method that has more than one argument as a value. Here you see how to apply the File.WriteAllBytes to a list of tuples; the tuples contain the file path (a string) and the desired file contents (an array of bytes):

```
open System.IO

// list of files names and desired contents
let files2 = [ "test1.bin", [| 0uy |];
               "test2.bin", [| 1uy |];
               "test3.bin", [| 1uy; 2uy |]]

// iterate over the list of files creating each one
List.iter File.WriteAllBytes files2
```

Often, you want to use the functionality of an existing .NET method, but you also want the ability to curry it. A common pattern in F# to achieve this is to *import* the .NET method function by writing a thin F# wrapper, as in the following example:

```
open System.IO

// import the File.Create function
let create size name =
    File.Create(name, size, FileOptions.Encrypted)

// list of files to be created
let names = [ "test1.bin"; "test2.bin"; "test3.bin" ]

// open the files create a list of streams
let streams = List.map (create 1024) names
```

Here you see how to import the `File.Create`; in this case, you use the overload that takes three parameters, but you expose only two of them as parameters: the buffer size (`size`) and the file name (`name`). Notice how you specify that the size parameter comes first. You do it this way because it's more likely that you'll want to create several files with the same buffer size than with the same name. In the final line of the listing, you apply the `create` function to a list of file names to create a list of file streams. You want each stream to be created with a buffer size of 1024 bytes, so you pass the literal 1024 to the `create` function, like so: (`create 1024`). This returns a new function, which is then used with the `List.map` function.

When using .NET methods with lots of arguments, it can sometimes be helpful to know the names of the arguments to help you keep track of what each argument is doing. F# lets you use named arguments, where you give the name of the argument, an equals sign, and then the value of the argument. The following example demonstrates this with an overload of `File.Open()` that takes four arguments:

```
open System.IO

// open a file using named arguments
let file = File.Open(path = "test.txt",
                     mode = FileMode.Append,
                     access = FileAccess.Write,
                     share = FileShare.None)

// close it!
file.Close()
```

Using Objects and Instance Members from .NET Libraries

Using classes from non-F# libraries is also straightforward. The syntax for instantiating an object consists of the keyword new, the name of the class you want to instantiate, and then constructor arguments separated by commas within parentheses. You can use the let keyword to bind an instance of a class to an identifier. Once associated with an identifier, the object behaves a lot like a record type; the object referred to cannot be changed, but its contents can. Also, if the identifier is not at the top level, then it can be redefined or hidden by an identifier of the same name in another scope. C# and Visual Basic programmers should find accessing fields, properties, events, and methods to be intuitive because the syntax is similar. To access any member, you use the identifier of the object followed by a period (.) and then the name of the member. Arguments to instance methods follow the same convention as for static methods, and they must be within parentheses and separated by commas. To retrieve the value of a property or field, you need only the name of member, and you set it using the left arrow (<-).

The following example demonstrates how to create a System.IO.FileInfo object and then use various members of the class to manipulate it in different ways. On the first line, you make the System.IO namespace available to F#. On the second, you create the FileInfo object, passing it the name of the file in which you're interested. Next, you check whether the file exists using the Exists instance property. If it doesn't exist, you create a new file using the CreateText() instance method and then set it to read-only using the Attributes instance property. Here, you use the use binding to clean up resources, by calling their Dispose method when they drop out of scope.

```
open System.IO
// create a FileInfo object
let file = new FileInfo("test.txt")

// test if the file exists,
// if not create a file
if not file.Exists then
    use stream = file.CreateText()
    stream.WriteLine("hello world")
    file.Attributes <- FileAttributes.ReadOnly

// print the full file name
printfn "%s" file.FullName
```

I explained this fully in Chapter 3. F# also allows you to set properties when constructing an object. It's quite common to set object properties as part of the process of initially configuring the object. To set a property at construction time, you place the property name inside the constructor call, followed by an equals sign and then by the value for the property. Separate multiple properties with commas. The following is a variation on the previous example; it sets the ReadOnly attribute when the object is the constructor:

```
open System.IO
// file name to test
let filename = "test.txt"

// bind file to an option type, depending on whether
// the file exist or not
let file =
    if File.Exists(filename) then
        Some(new FileInfo(filename, Attributes = FileAttributes.ReadOnly))
    else
        None
```

Note that you need to test for the file's existence to avoid a runtime exception when trying to set the Attributes property. F# allows you to set type parameters when calling a constructor because it is not always possible to infer the type parameter when making a constructor call. The type parameters are surrounded by angle brackets (<>) and separated by commas. The next example demonstrates how to set a type parameter when calling a constructor. You can create an instance of System.Collections.Generic.List, which you can

use with integers only by setting its type parameter when you create it. In F#, System.Collections.Generic.
List is called ResizeArray to avoid confusion with F# lists.

```
open System

// an integer list
let intList =
    let temp = new ResizeArray<int>()
    temp.AddRange([| 1; 2; 3 |]);
    temp

// print each int using the ForEach member method
intList.ForEach( fun i -> Console.WriteLine(i) )
```

Executing the preceding code produces the following results:

```
1
2
3
```

The previous example also demonstrates another nice feature of F# when interoperating with non-F#
libraries. .NET APIs often use a .NET construct called *delegates*, which are conceptually a kind of function
value. F# functions will automatically be converted to .NET delegate objects if their signatures match. You can
see this on the last line, where an F# function is passed directly to a method that takes a .NET delegate type.

To keep methods as flexible as possible, you might prefer not to specify a type parameter when you
import methods that take generic delegates or when you create a wrapper F# function around constructors
for a non-F# library. You achieve this by using the underscore (_) in place of the type parameter, as in the
first line of the next example (which also uses the forward operator, |>, which I explain in the
"The |> Operator" section):

```
open System
// how to wrap a method that take a delegate with an F# function
let findIndex f arr = Array.FindIndex(arr, new Predicate<_>(f))

// define an array literal
let rhyme = [| "The"; "cat"; "sat"; "on"; "the"; "mat" |]

// print index of the first word ending in 'at'
printfn "First word ending in 'at' in the array: %i"
    (rhyme |> findIndex (fun w -> w.EndsWith("at")))
```

When you compile and execute this example, you get the following result:

```
First word ending in 'at' in the array: 1
```

Here you import the FindIndex method from the System.Array class, so you can use it in a curried
style. If you had not explicitly created a delegate, the identifier f would have represented a predicate
delegate rather than a function. This means all calls to findIndex would need to create a delegate object
explicitly, which is not ideal. However, if you had specified a type when creating the Predicate delegate in

the definition of findIndex, then you would have limited the use of the findIndex function to arrays of a specific type. Occasionally, this might be what you want to do, but that's not usually the case. By using the underscore, you avoid having to specify a type for the findIndex function, while keeping it nice and flexible.

Using Indexers from .NET Libraries

Indexers are a .NET concept that is designed to make a collection class look more like an array. Under the hood, an indexer is a special property that is always called Item and has one or more parameters. It is important that you have easy access to an indexer property because many classes within the BCL have indexers.

F# offers two different syntaxes for accessing properties. You can explicitly use the Item property, or you can use an array-like syntax, with brackets instead of parentheses around the index, like so:

```
open System.Collections.Generic

// create a ResizeArray
let stringList =
    let temp = new ResizeArray<string>()
    temp.AddRange([| "one"; "two"; "three" |]);
    temp

// unpack items from the resize array
let itemOne = stringList.Item(0)
let itemTwo = stringList.[1]

// print the unpacked items
printfn "%s %s" itemOne itemTwo
```

This example associates the strings "one" and "two" with the identifiers itemOne and itemTwo, respectively. The association of "one" with itemOne demonstrates how to use the Item property explicitly. The association of "two" with itemTwo uses the bracket syntax.

■ **Note**   This example also demonstrates a common pattern in F#. Note how you want to create the identifier stringList as an object from a non-F# library, yet at the same time initialize it to a certain state. To do this, you assign the object to a temporary identifier and then call an instance member on the object to manipulate its state. Finally, you return the temporary identifier, so it becomes the value of stringList. In this way, you keep the object creation and initialization logic close together.

Working with Events from .NET Libraries

Events are special properties of objects that allow you to attach functions to them. The functions you attach to events are sometimes referred to as *handlers*. When the event occurs, it executes all the functions that have been attached to it. For example, you might create a Button object that exposes a Click event, which occurs when a user clicks the button. This would mean that any functions that have been attached to the button's Click event would execute when the button is clicked. This is extremely useful because it's common to need notifications of what the user has done when creating user interfaces.

Adding a handler to an event is fairly straightforward. Each event exposes a method called Add, and the handling function is passed to this method. Events come from non-F# libraries, so the Add method follows the convention that its arguments must be surrounded by parentheses. In F#, it is common to place the handler function inside the Add method itself, using F#'s anonymous function feature. The type of the handler function must match the type of the Add method's parameter, and this parameter has the type 'a -> unit. This means that for events exposed by objects in the BCL, the parameter of the Add method will have a type similar to EventArgs -> Unit.

The next example shows the creation of a Timer object and a function being added to the timer's Elapsed event. A Timer object is an object that fires its Elapsed event at regular intervals. In this case, the handler prints a message to the user. Notice how you do not care about the argument that will be passed to the handler function, so you ignore it using the underscore.

```fsharp
#if INTERACTIVE
#else
module HandlersDemo
#endif

open System.Timers

let timedMessages() =
    // define the timer
    let timer = new Timer(Interval = 3000.0,
                          Enabled = true)

    // a counter to hold the current message
    let mutable messageNo = 0

    // the messages to be shown
    let messages = [ "bet"; "this"; "gets";
                     "really"; "annoying";
                     "very"; "quickly" ]

    // add an event to the timer
    timer.Elapsed.Add(fun _ ->
        // print a message
        printfn "%s" messages.[messageNo]
        messageNo <- messageNo + 1
        if messageNo = messages.Length then
            timer.Enabled <- false)

timedMessages()
```

To run this example, select all lines and send them to F# Interactive. You should see a series of words appear in the interactive console, one every three seconds. The words will stop when the last one in the array has been printed, because at that point the code sets the Enabled property of the timer to false.

```
> bet
this
gets
really
annoying
very
quickly
>
```

It is also possible to remove handlers from events. To do this, you must keep the function you will add to the event in scope, so you can later pass it to the event's RemoveHandler method. The RemoveHandler method accepts a delegate, which is an object that wraps a regular .NET method to allow it to be passed around like a value. This means the handler function must be given to the event already wrapped in a delegate and you must therefore use the event's AddHandler (or RemoveHandler) method instead of its Add (or Remove) method. Creating a delegate in F# is straightforward. You simply call the delegate's constructor, the same way you call any constructor for an object from any non-F# library, passing it the function that delegate should wrap:

```
#if INTERACTIVE
#else
module HandlersDemo
#endif

open System.Timers

let timedMessagesViaDelegate() =
    // define the timer
    let timer = new Timer(Interval = 3000.0,
                          Enabled = true)

    // a counter to hold the current message number
    let mutable messageNo = 0

    // the messages to be shown
    let messages = [ "bet"; "this"; "gets";
                     "really"; "annoying";
                     "very"; "quickly" ]

    // function to print a message
    let printMessage = fun _ _ ->
        // print a message
        printfn "%s" messages.[messageNo]
        messageNo <- (messageNo + 1) % messages.Length

    // wrap the function in a delegate
    let del = new ElapsedEventHandler(printMessage)

    // add the delegate to the timer
    timer.Elapsed.AddHandler(del) |> ignore

    // return the time and the delegate so we can
    // remove one from the other later
    (timer, del)

// Run this first:
let timer, del = timedMessagesViaDelegate()

// Run this later:
timer.Elapsed.RemoveHandler(del)
```

To run this example, select all lines other than the last and send to F# Interactive. You should see a series of words appear in the interactive console, one every three seconds.

```
> bet
this
gets
really
annoying
very
```

To stop the flow of words, send the last line of the example to F# Interactive.

The way this example works is very similar to the previous one. The difference is that you wrap the function to be called when the timer fires in a delegate, by passing it to the constructor of ElapsedEventHandler. Then you add the delegate to the timer via AddHandler (instead of Add) and return both the timer and the delegate (as a tuple) to the caller. This means that the timer and the delegate are available later so that the handler can be removed from the timer via RemoveHandler, as in the last line of the example.

Pattern Matching over .NET Types

As you saw in Chapter 3, pattern matching is a powerful feature of F#. Pattern matching allows a programmer to specify that different computations are executed depending on the value being matched against. F# has a construct that allows pattern matching over .NET types. The rule to match a .NET type is formed with a colon and question mark operator (:?) followed by the name of the .NET type you want to match. Because it is impossible to have an exhaustive list of .NET types, you must always provide a default rule when pattern matching over .NET types.

```
// a list of objects
let simpleList = [ box 1; box 2.0; box "three" ]

// a function that pattern matches over the
// type of the object it is passed
let recognizeType (item : obj) =
    match item with
    | :? System.Int32 -> printfn "An integer"
    | :? System.Double -> printfn "A double"
    | :? System.String -> printfn "A string"
    | _ -> printfn "Unknown type"

// iterate over the list of objects
List.iter recognizeType simpleList
```

Executing the preceding code produces the following results:

```
An integer
A double
A string
```

This example shows a function named recognizeType that is designed to recognize three of the .NET basic types via pattern matching. This function is then applied to a list. This function has a couple of noteworthy details. First, the function takes an argument of the type obj, and you need to use a type annotation to make sure it does. If you didn't use the type annotation, the compiler would infer that the function can take any type and would use type 'a. This would be a problem because you cannot use pattern matching of this kind over F#'s types, only over .NET types. Second, the function's default case uses the underscore to ignore the value.

Once you recognize that a value is of a certain type, it's common to want to do something with that value. To use the value on the right side of a rule, you can use the as keyword followed by an identifier. You can see this in the next example, where you rewrite recognizeType to include the value in the message that is printed when a type is recognized:

```
// list of objects
let anotherList = [ box "one"; box 2; box 3.0 ]

// pattern match and print value
let recognizeAndPrintType (item : obj) =
    match item with
    | :? System.Int32 as x -> printfn "An integer: %i" x
    | :? System.Double as x -> printfn "A double: %f" x
    | :? System.String as x -> printfn "A string: %s" x
    | x -> printfn "An object: %A" x

// interate over the list pattern matching each item
List.iter recognizeAndPrintType anotherList
```

When you compile and execute this example, you get the following results:

```
A string: one
An integer: 2
A double: 3.000000
```

Notice how you use an identifier for a final default rule. You don't need to match it to a type because you already know it will be of the type obj, as the value being matched over is already of the type obj.

Pattern matching over .NET types is also useful for handling exceptions thrown by .NET methods. You form the pattern match rules in the same way, except you use them with the try … with construct instead of the match construct. The next example shows how to match and catch two .NET exceptions. You match over the exceptions thrown and then print a different message to the console depending on the type of exception thrown.

```
try
    // look at current time and raise an exception
    // based on whether the second is a multiple of 3
    if System.DateTime.Now.Second % 3 = 0 then
        raise (new System.Exception())
    else
        raise (new System.ApplicationException())
with
| :? System.ApplicationException ->
    // this will handle "ApplicationException" case
    printfn "A second that was not a multiple of 3"
| _ ->
    // this will handle all other exceptions
    printfn "A second that was a multiple of 3"
```

The | > Operator

You met the pipe-forward operator (|>) in the Function Application section in Chapter 3. This operator allows you to pass a value to a function, reversing the order that the function and parameter would normally appear in the source file. As a quick reminder, the following example shows the operator's definition and usage:

```
// the definition of the pipe-forward operator
let (|>) x f = f x

// pipe the parameter 0.5 to the sin function
let result = 0.5 |> System.Math.Sin
```

This technique proves especially useful when working with .NET libraries because it helps the compiler infer the correct types for a function's parameters, without the need for explicit type annotations.

To understand why this operator is useful, it is helpful to probe a little deeper into how left-to-right type inference works. Consider the following simple example, where you define a list of integers, called intList, of the type int list, and then pass this list as the second argument to the library function List.iter. The first argument to List.iter is a function of the type int -> unit.

```
let intList = [ 1; 2; 3 ]
    // val printInt: int list

let printInt = printf "%i"
    // val printInt: int -> unit

List.iter printInt intList
```

Now you need to understand how these expressions in the program were assigned their types. The compiler started at the top of the input file, found the identifier intList, and inferred its type from the literal that is bound to it. Then it found the identifier printInt and inferred its type to be int -> unit because this is the type of the function returned from the call to the printfn function. Next, it found the function List.iter and knew that its type is ('a -> unit) -> 'a list -> unit. Because it has a generic or undetermined type 'a within it, the compiler examines the next identifier to the right, in this case the function printInt. This function has the type int -> unit, so the compiler infers that the type of the generic parameter 'a is int, which means the list passed to the function must be of the type int list.

So it is the type of the function that determines what the type of the list must be. However, it is often useful to have the type of the function inferred from the type of the list that it will be applied to. This is especially true when working with .NET types, as it allows you to access their members without a type annotation. The pipe forward operator lets you do this by allowing you to place the list before the function that operates on it. Consider the following example:

```
open System

// a date list
let importantDates = [ new DateTime(1066,10,14);
                       new DateTime(1999,01,01);
                       new DateTime(2999,12,31) ]

// printing function
let printInt = printf "%i "
```

```
// case 1: type annotation required
List.iter (fun (d: DateTime) -> printInt d.Year) importantDates

// case 2: no type annotation required
importantDates |> List.iter (fun d -> printInt d.Year)
```

Here you have two ways of printing the year from a list of dates. In the first case, you need to add a type annotation to access the methods and properties on the DateTime structure. The type annotation is required because the compiler has not yet encountered the importantDates, so it has no information it can use to infer the type of the parameter d of the anonymous function. In the second case, the compiler infers automatically that d is of the type DateTime because it has encountered the importantDates list already, which means it has enough information to infer the type of d.

The pipe-forward operator also proves useful when trying to chain functions together–that is, when one function operates on the result of another. Consider the next example, where you obtain a list of all the .NET assemblies in memory and then process this list until you end up with a list of all the .NET methods in memory. As each function operates on the result of the previous function, the forward operator is used to show the results being piped or passed forward to the next function. You don't need to declare intermediate variables to hold the results of a function.

```
// grab a list of all methods in memory
let methods = System.AppDomain.CurrentDomain.GetAssemblies()
                |> List.ofArray
                |> List.map ( fun assm -> assm.GetTypes() )
                |> Array.concat
                |> List.ofArray
                |> List.map ( fun t -> t.GetMethods() )
                |> Array.concat

// print the list
printfn "%A" methods
```

■ **Note**   This example will take a few moments to run, especially on Linux.

You'll find this a useful technique, and it will crop up now and again throughout the rest of the book.

Summary

In this chapter, you learned about the imperative features of F#. Combining this information with the functional features covered in Chapter 3 gives you a full range of techniques to attack any computing problem. F# allows you to choose techniques from the appropriate paradigm and combine them whenever necessary. In the next chapter, you'll see how F# supports the third major programming paradigm, *object-oriented programming*.

CHAPTER 5

■ ■ ■

Object-Oriented Programming

Object-oriented programming is the third major programming paradigm. There has been a tendency to paint the functional paradigm and the object-oriented paradigm as competing, but I believe them to be complementary techniques that work well together, which I will try to demonstrate in this chapter. At its heart, object-oriented programming has a few simple ideas, sometimes referred to as the tenets of object-oriented programming: encapsulation, polymorphism, and inheritance.

Possibly the most important tenet is *encapsulation*, the idea that the implementations and state should be *encapsulated*, or hidden behind well-defined boundaries. This makes the structure of a program easier to manage. In F#, you hide things by using signatures for modules and type definitions, as well as by simply defining them locally to an expression or class construction (you'll see examples of both in this chapter).

The second tenet, *polymorphism*, is the idea that you can implement abstract entities in multiple ways. You've met a number of simple abstract entities already, such as function types. A function type is abstract because you can implement a function with a specific type in many different ways; for example, you can implement the function type int -> int as a function that increments the given parameter, a function that decrements the parameter, or any one of millions of mathematical sequences. You can also build other abstract entities out of existing abstract components, such as the interface types defined in the .NET BCL. You can also model more sophisticated abstract entities using user-defined interface types. Interface types have the advantage that you can arrange them hierarchically; this is called *interface inheritance*. For example, the .NET BCL includes a hierarchical classification of collection types, available in the System. Collections and System.Collections.Generic namespaces.

In OOP, you can sometimes arrange implementation fragments hierarchically. This is called *implementation inheritance*, and it tends to be less important in F# programming because of the flexibility that functional programming provides for defining and sharing implementation fragments. However, it is significant for domains such as graphical user interface (GUI) programming.

While the tenets of object-oriented programming are important, object-oriented programming has also become synonymous with organizing your code around the values of the system (*nouns*) and then providing operations (*verbs*) on those values as members, functions, or methods that operate on these values. This is often as simple as taking a function written in the style where the function is applied to a value (such as String.length s) and rewriting it using the dot notation (such as s.Length). This simple act can often make your code a good deal clearer. In this chapter, you'll see how F# allows you to attach members to any of its types, not just its classes, enabling you to organize all your code in an object-oriented style if you wish.

F# provides a rich object-oriented programming model that allows you to create classes, interfaces, and objects that behave similarly to those created by C# and VB.NET. Perhaps more importantly, the classes you create in F# are indistinguishable from those that are created in other languages when packaged in a library and viewed by a user of that library–provided that you don't expose any F#-specific data types. However, object-oriented programming is more than simply defining objects, as you'll see when you start looking at how you can program in an object-oriented style using F# native types.

© Robert Pickering and Kit Eason 2016

R. Pickering and K. Eason, *Beginning F# 4.0*, DOI 10.1007/978-1-4842-1374-2_5

Records As Objects

It is possible to use the record types you met in Chapter 3 to simulate object-like behavior. This is because records can have fields that are functions, which you can use to simulate an object's methods. While this technique does have some limitations compared to using F# classes, it also has some advantages. Only the function's type (or as some prefer, its *signature*) is given in the record definition, so you can easily swap the implementation without having to define a derived class, as you would in object-oriented programming. I discuss defining new implementations of objects in greater detail in the "Object Expressions" and "Inheritance" sections later in this chapter.

Let's take a look at a simple example of using records as objects. The next example defines a type, Shape, that has two members. The first member, Reposition, is a function type that moves the shape; and the second member, Draw, draws the shape. You use the function makeShape to create a new instance of the shape type. The makeShape function implements the reposition functionality for you; it does this by accepting the initPos parameter, which is then stored in a mutable ref cell and updated when the reposition function is called. This means the position of the shape is encapsulated, accessible only through the reposition member. Hiding values in this way is a common technique in F# programming.

■ **Note** To get this example to work, create a new F# Library project and add a reference to System.Drawing. Then paste the example code into the project's Library1.fs file, replacing its existing contents. You can run the example by selecting all of the code and sending it to F# Interactive.

```
#if INTERACTIVE
#r "System.Drawing.dll"
#else
module Shapes
#endif
open System.Drawing

// a Shape record that will act as our object
type Shape =
    { Reposition: Point -> unit;
      Draw: unit -> unit }

// create a new instance of Shape
let makeShape initPos draw =
    // currPos is the internal state of the object
    let currPos = ref initPos
    { Reposition =
        // the Reposition member updates the internal state
        (fun newPos -> currPos := newPos);
      Draw =
        // draw the shape passing the current position
        // to given draw function
        (fun () -> draw !currPos); }
```

```
// "draws" a shape, prints out the shapes name and position
let draw shape (pos: Point) =
    printfn "%s, with x = %i and y = %i"
        shape pos.X pos.Y

// creates a new circle shape
let circle initPos =
    makeShape initPos (draw "Circle")

// creates a new square shape
let square initPos =
    makeShape initPos (draw "Square")

// list of shapes in their inital positions
let shapes =
    [ circle (new Point (10,10));
      square (new Point (30,30)) ]

// draw all the shapes
let drawShapes() =
    shapes |> List.iter (fun s -> s.Draw())

let main() =
    drawShapes() // draw the shapes
    // move all the shapes
    shapes |> List.iter (fun s -> s.Reposition (new Point (40,40)))
    drawShapes() // draw the shapes

// start the program
do main()
```

When the program is run, it doesn't yet actually draw the shapes, but it simulates doing so by printing messages to the console. The first two lines of output represent the shapes as originally created when the Shapes array is constructed. The second two lines of output represent the same shapes after their Reposition method has been called.

```
Circle, with x = 10 and y = 10
Square, with x = 30 and y = 30
Circle, with x = 40 and y = 40
Square, with x = 40 and y = 40
```

This example might seem trivial, but you can go quite a long way with this technique. The next example takes things to their natural conclusion, drawing the shapes on a form.

■ **Note** To get this example to work, create a new F# Library project and add references to System.Drawing and System.Windows.Forms. Then paste the example code into the project's Library1.fs file, replacing its existing contents. You can run the example by selecting all of the code and sending it to F# Interactive.

```
#if INTERACTIVE
#r "System.Drawing.dll"
#r "System.Windows.Forms.dll"
#else
module ShapesWithDrawing
#endif

open System
open System.Drawing
open System.Windows.Forms

// a Shape record that will act as our object
type Shape =
    { Reposition: Point -> unit;
      Draw : Graphics -> unit }

// create a new instance of Shape
let movingShape initPos draw =
    // currPos is the internal state of the object
    let currPos = ref initPos in
    { Reposition =
        // the Reposition member updates the internal state
        (fun newPos -> currPos := newPos);
      Draw =
        // draw the shape passing the current position
        // and graphics object to given draw function
        (fun g -> draw !currPos g); }

// create a new circle Shape
let movingCircle initPos diam =
    movingShape initPos (fun pos g ->
        g.DrawEllipse(Pens.Blue,pos.X,pos.Y,diam,diam))

// create a new square Shape
let movingSquare initPos size =
    movingShape initPos (fun pos g ->
        g.DrawRectangle(Pens.Blue,pos.X,pos.Y,size,size) )

// list of shapes in their inital positions
let shapes =
    [ movingCircle (new Point (10,10)) 20;
      movingSquare (new Point (30,30)) 20;
      movingCircle (new Point (20,20)) 20;
      movingCircle (new Point (40,40)) 20; ]

// create the form to show the items
let mainForm =
    let form = new Form()
    let rand = new Random()
```

```
  // add an event handler to draw the shapes
  form.Paint.Add(fun e ->
    shapes |> List.iter (fun s ->
    s.Draw e.Graphics))
  // add an event handler to move the shapes
  // when the user clicks the form
  form.Click.Add(fun e ->
    shapes |> List.iter (fun s ->
    s.Reposition(new Point(rand.Next(form.Width),
                 rand.Next(form.Height)))
    form.Invalidate()))
  form

// Show the form
#if INTERACTIVE
do mainForm.ShowDialog() |> ignore
#else
[<STAThread>]
do Application.Run(mainForm)
#endif
```

This application produces a GUI, as shown in Figure 5-1.

Figure 5-1. *Drawing shapes using records to simulate objects*

Again, you define a Shape record type that has the members Reposition and Draw. Next, you define the functions makeCircle and makeSquare to create different kinds of shapes, using them to define a list of Shape records. Finally, you define the form that will hold your records. Here you must do a bit more work than perhaps you would like. Because you don't use inheritance, the BCL's System.Winows.Forms.Form doesn't know anything about your shape *objects*, and you must iterate though the list, explicitly drawing each shape. This is quite simple to do, and it takes only three lines of code for you add an event handler to mainForm's Paint event:

```
temp.Paint.Add(
    fun e ->
      List.iter (fun s -> s.draw e.Graphics) shapes);
```

This example shows how you can quickly create multifunctional records without having to worry about any unwanted features you might also be inheriting. In the next section, you'll look at how to represent operations on these objects in a more natural way: by adding members to F# types.

F# Types with Members

It is possible to add functions to both F#'s record and union types. You can call a function added to a record or union type using dot notation, just as you can a member of a class from a library not written in F#. This also proves useful when you want to expose types you define in F# to other .NET languages. (I discuss this in more detail in Chapter 12.) Many programmers prefer to see function calls made on an instance value, and this technique provides a nice way of doing this for all F# types.

The syntax for defining an F# record or union type with members is the same as the syntax you learned in Chapter 3, except here it includes member definitions that always come at the end, after the with keyword. The definition of the members themselves start with the keyword member, followed by an identifier that represents the parameter of the type the member is being attached to, followed by a dot, the function name, and then any other parameters the function takes. After this comes an equals sign followed by the function definition, which can be any F# expression.

The following example defines a record type, Point. It has two fields, Left and Top, plus a member function, Swap. The function Swap is a simple function that creates a new point with the values of Left and Top swapped over. Note how you use the x parameter, given before the function name Swap, within the function definition to access the record's other members.

```
#if INTERACTIVE
#else
module Points
#endif

// A point type
type Point =
    { Top: int;
      Left: int }
    with
        // the swap member creates a new point
        // with the left/top coords reveresed
        member x.Swap() =
          { Top = x.Left;
            Left = x.Top }

// create a new point
let myPoint =
    { Top = 3;
      Left = 7 }
```

```
// print the inital point
printfn "%A" myPoint
// create a new point with the coords swapped
let nextPoint = myPoint.Swap()
// print the new point
printfn "%A" nextPoint
```

When you execute this example, you get the following results:

```
{Top = 3;
 Left = 7;}
{Top = 7;
 Left = 3;}
```

You might have noticed the x parameter in the definition of the function Swap:

```
member x.Swap() =
  { Top = x.Left;
    Left = x.Top }
```

This is the parameter that represents the object on which the function is being called. Now look at the case where you call a function on a value:

```
let nextPoint = myPoint.Swap()
```

The value you call the function on is passed to the function as an argument. This is logical when you think about it because the function needs to be able to access the fields and methods of the value on which you call it. Some OO languages use a specific keyword for this, such as this or Me, but F# lets you choose the name of this parameter by specifying a name for it after the keyword member—x, in this case.

Union types can have member functions, too. You define them in the same way that you define record types. The following example shows a union type, DrinkAmount, that has a function added to it:

```
// a type representing the amount of a specific drink
type DrinkAmount =
    | Coffee of int
    | Tea of int
    | Water of int
    with
       // get a string representation of the value
       override x.ToString() =
          match x with
          | Coffee x -> Printf.sprintf "Coffee: %i" x
          | Tea x -> Printf.sprintf "Tea: %i" x
          | Water x -> Printf.sprintf "Water: %i" x

// create a new instance of DrinkAmount
let t = Tea 2

// print out the string
printfn "%s" (t.ToString())
```

When you execute this code, you get the following result:

```
Tea: 2
```

Note how this code uses the keyword override in place of the keyword member. This has the effect of replacing, or *overriding*, an existing function of the base type. This is not that common a practice with function members associated with union types and record types because only four methods are available to be overridden: ToString, Equals, GetHashCode, and Finalize. Every .NET type inherits these from System.Object. Because of the way some of these methods interact with the CLR, the only one I recommend routinely overriding is ToString. Only four methods are available for overriding because record and union types can't act as base or derived classes, so you cannot inherit methods to override (except from System.Object).

Object Expressions

Object expressions are at the heart of succinct object-oriented programming in F#. They provide a concise syntax to create an object that inherits from an existing type. This is useful if you want to provide a short implementation of an abstract class or interface, or if you want to tweak an existing class definition. An object expression allows you to provide an implementation of a class or interface while at the same time creating a new instance of it.

You surround the definition of an object expression with braces. You put the name of the class or interfaces at the beginning. You must follow the name of a class with a pair of parentheses that can have any values passed to the constructor between them. Interface names need nothing after them, though both class names and interface names can have a type parameter following them; you need to surround this type parameter with angled brackets. Next, you include the keyword with and the definition of the methods of the class or interfaces you want to implement. You declare these methods just as you declare members on records and union types (see the previous section for more information on this). You declare each new method using the keywords member or override, followed by the instance parameter, a dot, and the method name. The name of the method must be the same as the name of a virtual or abstract method in the class or interface definition, and its parameters must be surrounded by parentheses and separated by commas, just as .NET methods must be (unless the method has one parameter, in which case you can get away with excluding the parentheses). Ordinarily you don't need to give type annotations; however, if the base class contains several overloads for a method, then you might have to give type annotations. You include an equals sign after the name of a method and its parameters, followed by the implementation of the method's body, which is an F# expression that must match the return value of the method.

```
open System
open System.Collections.Generic

// a comparer that will compare strings in their reversed order
let comparer =
    { new IComparer<string>
      with
        member x.Compare(s1, s2) =
          // function to reverse a string
          let rev (s: String) =
             new String(Array.rev (s.ToCharArray()))
          // reverse 1st string
          let reversed = rev s1
```

```
        // compare reversed string to 2nd strings reversed
        reversed.CompareTo(rev s2) }

// Eurovision winners in a random order
let winners =
    [| "Sandie Shaw"; "Bucks Fizz"; "Dana International" ;
        "Abba"; "Lordi" |]

// print the winners
printfn "%A" winners
// sort the winners
Array.Sort(winners, comparer)
// print the winners again
printfn "%A" winners
```

When you execute this example, you get the following results:

```
[|"Sandie Shaw"; "Bucks Fizz"; "Dana International"; "Abba"; "Lordi"|]
[|"Abba"; "Lordi"; "Dana International"; "Sandie Shaw"; "Bucks Fizz"|]
```

This short snippet shows how to implement the IComparer interface. This is an interface with one method, Compare, that takes two parameters and returns an integer that represents the result of the parameter comparison. It accepts one type parameter; in this case, you pass it a string. You can see this on the second line of the definition of the identifier comparer. Next, you include the definition of the method body, which in this case compares reversed versions of the string parameters. Finally, you use the comparer by defining an array and then sorting, displaying the before and after results in the console.

It is possible to implement multiple interfaces on a class and several other interfaces within one object expression. It's also possible to attach an interface to a preexisting class without altering any of the class methods. However, it is not possible to implement more than one class within an object expression, basically because neither F# nor the CLR allow multiple inheritances of classes. When you implement a class and an interface, the class must always come first in the expression. Regardless, the implementation of any other interfaces after the first interface or class must come after the definitions of all the methods of the first interface or class. You prefix the name of the interface with the keyword interface and follow that with the keyword with. The definition of the methods is the same as for the first interface or class. If you don't change any methods on the class, then you don't use the keyword with.

■ **Note**   To get this example to work, create a new F# Library project and add references to System.Drawing and System.Windows.Forms. Then paste the example code into the project's Library1.fs file, replacing its existing contents. You can run the example by selecting all of the code and sending it to F# Interactive.

```
#if INTERACTIVE
#r "System.Drawing.dll"
#r "System.Windows.Forms.dll"
#else
module ObjectExpressions
#endif
```

```fsharp
open System
open System.Drawing
open System.Windows.Forms

// create a new instance of a number control
let makeNumberControl (n: int) =
    { new TextBox(Tag = n, Width = 32, Height = 16, Text = n.ToString())
        // implement the IComparable interface so the controls
        // can be compared
        interface IComparable with
          member x.CompareTo(other) =
            let otherControl = other :?> Control in
            let n1 = otherControl.Tag :?> int in
            n.CompareTo(n1) }

// a sorted array of the numbered controls
let numbers =
    // initalize the collection
    let temp = new ResizeArray<Control>()
    // initalize the random number generator
    let rand = new Random()
    // add the controls collection
    for index = 1 to 10 do
      temp.Add(makeNumberControl (rand.Next(100)))
    // sort the collection
    temp.Sort()
    // layout the controls correctly
    let height = ref 0
    temp |> Seq.iter
      (fun c ->
          c.Top <- !height
          height := c.Height + !height)
    // return collection as an array
    temp.ToArray()

// create a form to show the number controls
let numbersForm =
    let temp = new Form() in
    temp.Controls.AddRange(numbers);
    temp

// Show the form
#if INTERACTIVE
do numbersForm.ShowDialog() |> ignore
#else
[<STAThread>]
do Application.Run(numbersForm)
#endif
```

The previous example shows the definition of the object expression that implements the interface IComparable for the TextBox class. IComparable allows objects that implement this interface to be compared, primarily so they can be sorted. In this case, the implementation of IComparable's CompareTo method sorts the controls according to which number is displayed as the text of the TextBox. After you implement the makeNumberControl function, you create an array of controls called numbers. The definition of numbers is a little complicated. Begin by initializing it so it's full of controls in a random order, and then you sort the array. Finally, ensure that each control is displayed at the appropriate height. You can see the resulting user interface in Figure 5-2.

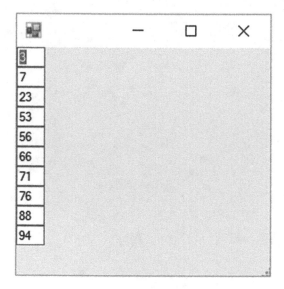

Figure 5-2. *Sorted text box controls*

You might also want to override methods from the object in the object expression. To do so in this case, you would use the same syntax, except you would follow the object name with the keyword with. Imagine that, instead of displaying the numbers in a text box, you want to custom draw them by overriding an object's OnPaint method. Use the following code to replace the makeNumberControl function in the previous example:

```
// create a new instance of a number control
let makeNumberControl (n: int) =
    { new Control(Tag = n, Width = 32, Height = 16) with
        // override the controls paint method to draw the number
        override x.OnPaint(e) =
            let font = new Font(FontFamily.Families.[0], 10.0F)
            e.Graphics.DrawString(n.ToString(),
                                  font,
                                  Brushes.Black,
                                  new PointF(0.0F, 0.0F))
```

```
// implement the IComparable interface so the controls
// can be compared
interface IComparable with
    member x.CompareTo(other) =
        let otherControl = other :?> Control in
        let n1 = otherControl.Tag :?> int in
        n.CompareTo(n1) }
```

You can see the resulting user interface in Figure 5-3.

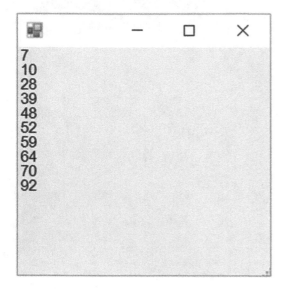

Figure 5-3. *Sorted, custom-drawn controls*

Object expressions are a powerful mechanism to quickly and concisely introduce object-oriented functionality from objects in non-F# libraries into your F# code. However, they do not allow you to add extra properties or methods to these objects. For example, in the previous example, notice how it was necessary to place the number associated with the control in the control's Tag property. This is more of a workaround than a proper solution. However, sometimes you don't need extra properties or methods on a type, and this syntax can be useful for those cases.

Defining Classes

You have already seen quite a few examples of using classes defined in the BCL library; next, you'll learn how to define your own classes. In object-oriented programming, a class should model some concept used within the program or library you are creating. For example, the String class models a collection of characters, and the Process class models an operating system process.

A class is a type, so a class definition starts with the type keyword, followed by the name of the class and the parameters of the class's constructor between parentheses. Next comes an equals sign, followed by a class's member definitions. The most basic member of a class is called a *method*, which is a function that has access to the parameters of the class.

The following example shows a class that represents a user. The user class's constructor takes two parameters: the user's name and a hash of the user's password. Your class provides two member methods: Authenticate, which checks whether the user's password is valid, and LogonMessage, which gets a user-specific logon message.

```
#if INTERACTIVE
#else
module Classes
#endif

// a very crude hasher - don't
// use this method in real code!
let hash (s : string) =
    s.GetHashCode()

// a class that represents a user
// its constructor takes two parameters, the user's
// name and a hash of their password
type User(name, passwordHash) =
    // hashes the users password and checks it against
    // the known hash
    member x.Authenticate(password) =
        let hashResult = hash password
        passwordHash = hashResult

    // gets the users logon message
    member x.LogonMessage() =
        sprintf "Hello, %s" name

// Create a user using the primary constructor
let user1 = User("kiteason", 1234)
// Access a method of the User instance
printfn "*** %s" (user1.LogonMessage())
```

The last part of the example demonstrates how to use the class. It behaves exactly like other classes you've seen from the BCL. You can create a new instance of User by calling its constructor (optionally using the new keyword) and then calling its member methods.

It's often useful to define values that are internal to your classes. Perhaps you need to precalculate a value that you share between several member methods, or maybe you need to retrieve some data for the object from an external data source. To enable this, objects can have let bindings that are internal to the object, but shared between all members of the object. You place the let bindings at the beginning of the class definition, after the equals sign, but before the first member definition. These let bindings execute when the object is constructed; if the let bindings have any side effects, then these too will occur when the object is constructed. If you need to call a function that has the unit type, such as when logging the object's construction, you must prefix the function call with the do keyword.

The next example demonstrates private let bindings by taking your User class and modifying it slightly. Now the class constructor takes a firstName and lastName, which you use in the let binding to calculate the user's fullName. To see what happens when you call a function with a side effect, you can print the user's fullName to the console:

```fsharp
// a class that represents a user
// its constructor takes three parameters, the user's
// first name, last name and a hash of their password
type User(firstName, lastName, passwordHash) =
    // calculate the user's full name and store of later use
    let fullName = Printf.sprintf "%s %s" firstName lastName
    // print users fullname as object is being constructed
    do printfn "User: %s" fullName

    // hashes the users password and checks it against
    // the known hash
    member x.Authenticate(password) =
        let hashResult = hash password
        passwordHash = hashResult

    // retrieves the users full name
    member x.GetFullname() = fullName
```

Notice how the members also have access to the class's let bindings; the member GetFullName returns the pre-calculated fullName value.

It's common to need to be able to change values within classes. For example, you might need to provide a ChangePassword method to reset the user's password in the User class. F# gives you two approaches to accomplish this. You can make the object immutable; in this case, you copy the object's parameters, changing the appropriate value as you go. This method is generally considered to fit better with functional-style programming, but it can be a little inconvenient if the object has a lot of parameters or is expensive to create. For example, doing this might be computationally expensive, or it might require a lot of I/O to construct it. The next example illustrates this approach. Notice how in the ChangePassword method you call the hash function on the password parameter, passing this to the User object's constructor along with the user's name.

```fsharp
// a class that represents a user
// its constructor takes two parameters, the user's
// name and a hash of their password
type User(name, passwordHash) =
    // hashes the users password and checks it against
    // the known hash
    member x.Authenticate(password) =
        let hashResult = hash password
        passwordHash = hashResult

    // gets the user's logon message
    member x.LogonMessage() =
        Printf.sprintf "Hello, %s" name

    // creates a copy of the user with the password changed
    member x.ChangePassword(password) =
        new User(name, hash password)
```

The alternative to an immutable object is to make the value you want to change mutable. You do this by binding it to a mutable let binding. You can see this in the following example, where you bind the class's parameter passwordHash to a mutable let binding of the same name:

```
// a class that represents a user
// its constructor takes two parameters, the user's
// name and a hash of their password
type User(name, passwordHash) =
    // store the password hash in a mutable let
    // binding, so it can be changed later
    let mutable passwordHash = passwordHash

    // hashes the users password and checks it against
    // the known hash
    member x.Authenticate(password) =
        let hashResult = hash password
        passwordHash = hashResult

    // gets the users logon message
    member x.LogonMessage() =
        Printf.sprintf "Hello, %s" name

    // changes the users password
    member x.ChangePassword(password) =
        passwordHash <- hash password
```

This means you are free to update the passwordHash using a mutable assignment, as you do in the ChangePassword method.

Optional Parameters

Member methods of classes (as well as member methods of other types) and class constructors can have optional parameters. These are useful because they allow you to set default input values. This means users of your class don't have to specify all its arguments, which can help make client code look cleaner and less cluttered.

You mark a parameter as optional by prefixing it with a question mark. You can have more than one optional parameter, but optional parameters must always appear at the end of the parameter list. Also, you must use *tuple* style in cases where you have a member method that contains more than one argument with one or more optional arguments. You do this by surrounding optional arguments with parentheses, separated by commas. An optional parameter might (or might not) have a type annotation. This type annotation appears after the parameter name, separated by a colon. Optional parameters are always of the option<'a> type, so you must not include "option" in the type annotation.

The following example shows some optional parameters in action. Here you define a class, AClass, that has an optional integer as a parameter of its constructor. This class has one member method, PrintState, and two parameters (the second parameter is optional). As you might expect, you use pattern matching over the option<'a> type to test whether the optional parameters were passed as an argument.

```
type AClass(?someState:int) =
    let state =
        match someState with
        | Some x -> string x
        | None -> "<no input>"
      member x.PrintState (prefix, ?postfix) =
        match postfix with
        | Some x -> printfn "%s %s %s" prefix state x
        | None -> printfn "%s %s" prefix state

let aClass = new AClass()
let aClass' = new AClass(109)

aClass.PrintState("There was ")
aClass'.PrintState("Input was:", ", which is nice.")
```

The last part of the example shows some of the class's client code. You create two instances of the class: you create the first class without any arguments being passed to the constructor; and you create the second with a value of 109 being passed to the constructor. Next, you call the PrintState member of the class, calling it initially without the optional argument, and then calling it again with the optional argument. Executing this code produces the following results:

```
There was <no input>
Input was: 109, which is nice.
```

Functions defined by let bindings can't have optional parameters.

Additional Constructors

Sometimes it is useful to define a type with more than one constructor. To do this, specify each additional constructor using the keyword new followed by the constructor arguments in brackets, and then the body of the constructor. The additional constructor must end by calling the main constructor. Additional constructor definitions must come after any let bindings in the main constructor.

Here is an example that extends your User type to allow an instance to be created, specifying not the password hash, but the actual raw password:

```
// a class that represents a user
// its constructor takes two parameters, the user's
// name and a hash of their password
type User(name, passwordHash) =
    // store the password hash in a mutable let
    // binding, so it can be changed later
    let mutable passwordHash = passwordHash

    // additional constructor to create a user given the
    // raw password
    new(name : string, password : string) =
        User(name, (hash password))
```

```
// hashes the users password and checks it against
// the known hash
member x.Authenticate(password) =
    let hashResult = hash password
    passwordHash = hashResult

// gets the users logon message
member x.LogonMessage() =
    Printf.sprintf "Hello, %s" name

// changes the users password
member x.ChangePassword(password) =
    passwordHash <- hash password
```

Additional constructors can often defeat F#'s type inference. You may find that, as in this example, you need to give the compiler a little help by specifying the argument types of the additional constructors.

Defining Interfaces

Interfaces can contain only abstract methods and properties–in other words, members that you declare using the keyword abstract. Interfaces define a *contract* for all classes that implement them, exposing those components that clients can use while insulating clients from their actual implementation. A class can inherit from only one base class, but it can implement any number of interfaces. Because any class implementing an interface can be treated as being of the interface type, interfaces provide similar benefits to multiple-class inheritance, while avoiding the complexity of that approach.

You define interfaces by defining a type that has no constructor and where all the members are abstract. The following example defines an interface that declares two methods: Authenticate and LogonMessage. Notice how the interface name starts with a capital I; this is a naming convention that is strictly followed thought the BCL, and you should follow it in your code too because it will help other programs distinguish between classes and interfaces when reading your code.

```
// an interface "IUser"
type IUser =
    // hashes the user's password and checks it against
    // the known hash
    abstract Authenticate: evidence: string -> bool
    // gets the users logon message
    abstract LogonMessage: unit -> string

let logon (user: IUser) (password : string) =
    // authenticate user and print appropriate message
    if user.Authenticate(password) then
        printfn "%s" (user.LogonMessage())
    else
        printfn "Logon failed"
```

The second half of the example illustrates the advantages of interfaces. You can define a function that uses the interface without knowing the implementation details. You define a logon function that takes an IUser parameter and uses it to perform a logon. This function will then work with any implementations of IUser. This is extremely useful in many situations; for example, it enables you to write one set of client code that you can reuse with several different implementations of the interface.

Implementing Interfaces

To implement an interface, use the keyword `interface`, followed by the interface name, the keyword `with`, and then the code to implement the interface members. You can implement interfaces by either classes or structs. You will learn how to create classes in some detail in the following sections, and you will learn more about structs in the "Structs" section later in this chapter.

The next example defines, implements, and uses an interface. The interface is the same IUser interface you implemented in the previous section; here you implement it in a class called User.

```
#if INTERACTIVE
#else
module Classes
#endif

// a very crude hasher - don't
// use this method in real code!
let hash (s : string) =
    s.GetHashCode()

// an interface "IUser"
type IUser =
    // hashes the user's password and checks it against
    // the known hash
    abstract Authenticate: evidence: string -> bool
    // gets the users logon message
    abstract LogonMessage: unit -> string

type User(name, passwordHash) =
    interface IUser with

        // Authenticate implementation
        member x.Authenticate(password) =
          let hashResult = hash (password)
          passwordHash = hashResult

        // LogonMessage implementation
        member x.LogonMessage() =
            Printf.sprintf "Hello, %s" name

// create a new instance of the user
// 281887125 is the hash of "mypassword"
let user = User("Robert", 281887125)

// get the logon message by casting to IUser then calling LogonMessage
let logonMessage = (user :> IUser).LogonMessage()

let logon (user: IUser) (password : string) =
    // authenticate user and print appropriate message
    if user.Authenticate(password) then
        printfn "%s" (user.LogonMessage())
```

```
    else
        printfn "Logon failed"

do logon (user:>IUser) "mypassword"

do logon (user:>IUser) "guess"
```

Notice how in the middle of example you see *casting* for the first time; you can find a more detailed explanation of casting at the end of the chapter in the "Casting" section. But for now here's a quick summary of what happens: the identifier user is cast to the interface IUser via the upcast operator, :>.

```
// create a new instance of the user
// 281887125 is the hash of "mypassword"
let user = User("Robert", 281887125)

// get the logon message by casting to IUser then calling LogonMessage
let logonMessage = (user :> IUser).LogonMessage()
```

This is necessary because interfaces are explicitly implemented in F#. Before you can use the method LogonMessage, you must have an identifier that is of the type IUser and not just of a class that implements IUser. The situation is different when a downcast needs to happen. For instance, the function logon takes a parameter of the IUser type:

```
let logon (user: IUser) (password : string) =
```

When you call logon with a class that implements IUser, the class is implicitly downcast to this type.

You can add the interface members to the definition of the class if you want the methods of the interface to be available directly on the class that implements it, instead of forcing the users of your class to cast the object to the interface. To revise the example, you simply add the methods Authenticate and LogonMessage as members of the class User. Now it is no longer necessary for the caller to cast the identifier user. You'll learn about adding members to methods in the "Classes and Methods" section later in the chapter.

```
// a class that represents a user
// its constructor takes two parameters, the user's
// name and a hash of their password
type User(name, passwordHash) =
    interface IUser with

        // Authenticate implementation
        member x.Authenticate(password) =
            let hashResult = hash (password)
            passwordHash = hashResult

        // LogonMessage implementation
        member x.LogonMessage() =
            Printf.sprintf "Hello, %s" name
    // Expose Authenticate implementation
    member x.Authenticate(password) = x.Authenticate(password)
    // Expose LogonMessage implementation
    member x.LogonMessage() = x.LogonMessage()
```

Classes and Inheritance

I covered inheritance in a limited way in the "Object Expressions" and "Implementing Interfaces" sections. Inheritance allows you to extend a class that is already defined; it also allows you to add new functionality or possibly to modify or replace the original functionality. Like most modern, object-oriented languages, F# allows single inheritance (from one base class), as well as the implementation of multiple interfaces (see the previous sections, "Defining Interfaces" and "Implementing Interfaces"). This section will cover the basics of inheriting from a base class and adding new functionality. The next section, "Methods and Inheritance," will show you how to implement methods to make full use of inheritance.

You specify inheritance with the inherit keyword, which must come directly after the equals sign, which follows a class's constructor. After the keyword inherit, you provide the name of the class you want to inherit from, followed by the arguments you intend to pass to its constructor. Let's kick things off by looking at a simple example of inheritance between two F# types. The following example shows an F# class, Sub, that derives from a base class, Base. The class Base has one method, GetState; and the class Sub also has one method, called GetOtherState. This example shows that how the Sub-derived class can use both methods because GetState is inherited from the base class.

```
type Base() =
    member x.GetState() = 0

type Sub() =
    inherit Base()
    member x.GetOtherState() = 0

let myObject = new Sub()

printfn
    "myObject.state = %i, myObject.otherState = %i"
    (myObject.GetState())
    (myObject.GetOtherState())
```

When you execute this example, you get the following results:

```
myObject.state = 0, myObject.otherState = 0
```

Methods and Inheritance

The preceding sections gave you the basics of inheritance between classes. Now you'll take a look at getting the most out of object-oriented programming by learning how to override methods and give them new behaviors. A derived class can define new methods, as well as override methods inherited from its base class.

You define methods using one of four keywords: member, override, abstract, or default. You've already seen the keywords member and abstract, which you use to define methods. The member keyword defines a simple method that cannot be overridden with an implementation, while the abstract keyword defines a method with no implementation that must be overridden in a derived class. The override keyword defines a method that overrides an inherited method that has an implementation in a base class. Finally, the keyword default has a similar meaning to the override keyword, except it is used only to override an abstract method.

The following example illustrates how to use all four kinds of methods:

```
// a base class
type Base() =
    // some internal state for the class
    let mutable state = 0
    // an ordinary member method
    member x.JiggleState y = state <- y
    // an abstract method
    abstract WiggleState: int -> unit
    // a default implementation for the abstract method
    default x.WiggleState y = state <- y + state
    member x.GetState() = state

// a sub class
type Sub() =
    inherit Base()
    // override the abstract method
    default x.WiggleState y = x.JiggleState (x.GetState() &&& y)

// create instances of both methods
let myBase = new Base()
let mySub = new Sub()

// a small test for our classes
let testBehavior (c : #Base) =
    c.JiggleState 1
    printfn "%i" (c.GetState())
    c.WiggleState 3
    printfn "%i" (c.GetState())

// run the tests
let main() =
    printfn "base class: "
    testBehavior myBase
    printfn "sub class: "
    testBehavior mySub

do main()
```

When you execute this example, you get the following results:

```
base class:
1
4
sub class:
1
1
```

You first implement a method, JiggleState, in class Base. The method cannot be overridden, so all derived classes will inherit this implementation. You then define an abstract method, WiggleState, that can be overridden (and, in fact, must be) by derived classes. To define a new method that can be overridden, you always need to use a combination of the abstract and default keywords. This could mean that you use abstract on the base class, while you use default on the derived class; however, you will often use them together in the same class, as shown in the previous example. This requires you to give types explicitly to a method you provide to be overridden. Although the F# philosophy doesn't generally require the programmer to give explicit types, leaving it to the compiler to work them out, the compiler has no way to infer these types, so you must give them explicitly.

As shown in the preceding results, the behavior remains the same in both the base class and the derived class when JiggleState is called; this is in contrast to the behavior of WiggleState, which changes because it is overridden.

Accessing the Base Class

When accessing a virtual method within a class, the version of the method in the most-derived class is called. This means that if you try to call a method on the base class that has been overridden by the derived class, it will automatically call the version on the derived class.

To get access to methods on the base class, you use the base keyword. The following example shows an implementation of a class that derives from System.Windows.Form. The identifier base is assigned to base class Form, as shown at the top of the definition of the MySquareForm class. The example uses implicit class construction, indicated by the fact that the type MySquareForm takes a single parameter, color.

■ **Note**   To get this example to work, create a new F# Library project and add references to System.Drawing and System.Windows.Forms. Then paste the example code into the project's Library1.fs file, replacing its existing contents. You can run the example by selecting all of the code and sending it to F# Interactive.

```
#if INTERACTIVE
#r "System.Drawing.dll"
#r "System.Windows.Forms.dll"
#else
module ShapesWithDrawing
#endif

open System
open System.Drawing
open System.Windows.Forms

// define a class that inherits from 'Form'
type MySquareForm(color) =
    inherit Form()
    // override the OnPaint method to draw on the form
    override x.OnPaint(e) =
        e.Graphics.DrawRectangle(color,
                                 10, 10,
                                 x.Width - 30,
                                 x.Height - 50)
        base.OnPaint(e)
```

```
    // override the OnResize method to respond to resizing
    override x.OnResize(e) =
        x.Invalidate()
        base.OnResize(e)

// create a new instance of the form
let form = new MySquareForm(Pens.Blue)

// Show the form
#if INTERACTIVE
do form.ShowDialog() |> ignore
#else
[<STAThread>]
do Application.Run(form)
#end
```

In this form, you override two methods, OnPaint and OnResize, and in these methods, you use the keyword base, which grants access to the base class that you use to call the base class's implementation of this method.

Properties and Indexers

A property is a special type of method that looks like a value to the code that calls it. Indexers fulfill a similar purpose; they make a method look a bit like a collection to the calling code. Both properties and indexers have accessors, which include a get accessor for reading and a set accessor for writing.

A property definition starts the same way as a method definition, with the keyword member followed by the parameter that represents the object. Next, you include a dot and then the member name. Instead of using the method parameters after this, you use the keyword with, followed by either get or set. The parameters come next; a get method must take unit, and a set method must take a single parameter. An equals sign follows next, and then an expression that forms the method body. If a second method is required, you use the keyword and to join them together.

The following example shows the definition of a class that has a single property, MyProp, which returns a random number. Setting the property resets the seed of the random-number generator.

```
// a class with properties
type Properties() =
    let mutable rand = new System.Random()
    // a property definition
    member x.MyProp
        with get () = rand.Next()
        and set y = rand <- new System.Random(y)

// create a new instance of our class
let prop = new Properties()

// run some tests for the class
prop.MyProp <- 12
printfn "%d" prop.MyProp
printfn "%d" prop.MyProp
printfn "%d" prop.MyProp
```

When you execute this example, you get the following results:

```
2137491492
726598452
334746691
```

You can also declare abstract properties. The syntax is similar, but you replace the keyword member with abstract, and you omit the parameter that represents the object, just as you do for a method. After the member name, you include the name of the type, separated from the member name by a colon. The keyword with comes next, followed by either get or set, which represents whether the inheritor must implement a get or set method, or both, separated by a comma. Properties look exactly like a field to the calling code.

The next example revises the previous one so now it uses an interface, IAbstractProperties. Note how the derived class ConcreteProperties must implement the get and set methods using the keywords with and and.

```
// an interface with an abstract property
type IAbstractProperties =
    abstract MyProp: int
        with get, set

// a class that implements our interface
type ConcreteProperties() =
    let mutable rand = new System.Random()
    interface IAbstractProperties with
        member x.MyProp
            with get() = rand.Next()
            and set(y) = rand <- new System.Random(y)
```

Indexers are properties that take two or more parameters, one to represent the element being placed in the pseudo-collection and others to represent the index in it. In C#, all indexers are called Item in the underlying implementation, but the programmer never uses this name because it is always implicit. In F#, the programmer can choose the name of the indexer property. If the programmer chooses the name Item, then F# provides special syntax for accessing the property.

The syntax for creating an indexer is the same as for a property, except that a get method has one or more parameters, and a set method has two or more parameters. The next step is to access an element in an indexer. If its name is Item, you can use a special syntax that looks like array access:

```
// a class with indexers
type Indexers(vals:string[]) =
    // a normal indexer
    member x.Item
        with get y = vals.[y]
        and set y z = vals.[y] <- z
    // an indexer with an unusual name
    member x.MyString
        with get y = vals.[y]
        and set y z = vals.[y] <- z
```

```
// create a new instance of the indexer class
let index = new Indexers [|"One"; "Two"; "Three"; "Four"|]

// test the set indexers
index.[0] <- "Five";
index.Item(2) <- "Six";
index.MyString(3) <- "Seven";

// test the get indexers
printfn "%s" index.[0]
printfn "%s" (index.Item(1))
printfn "%s" (index.MyString(2))
printfn "%s" (index.MyString(3))
```

When you execute this example, you get the following results:

```
Five
Two
Six
Seven
```

■ **Note**   When working with indexers with a name other than Item, you should keep in mind that it will be difficult for other .NET languages to use your classes.

Autoproperties

In the previous section, I introduced properties in a way that will seem familiar to C# developers: I used a mutable value as a backing store, and get and set functions to read and write the property. This is such a common pattern (when working in mutable style) that F# provides a shortcut, known as *autoproperties* or *auto-implemented properties*. Consider a simple Circle type that just has one settable property, its radius:

```
type Circle() =
    let mutable radius = 0.0
    member x.Radius
        with get() = radius
        and set(r) = radius <- r
```

This can instead be expressed using member val:

```
type Circle() =
    member val Radius = 0.0 with get, set
```

117

The radius of the circle can be set and retrieved in exactly the same way as for a mutable backing field accessed via get and set:

```
let c = Circle()
c.Radius <- 99.9
printf "Radius: %f" c.Radius // 99.9
```

To make the property read-only, simply omit the set keyword.

Overriding Methods from Non-F# Libraries

When overriding methods from non-F# libraries, you must implement the method definition in the tuple style; that is, you must surround the parameters with parentheses and separate them by commas.

The following example shows a class that implements the interface named System.Net.ICredentials. Its single method, GetCredential, has two parameters. Just after the place where you implement the interface, you can see how to use the interface as a value in the method GetCredentialList.

```
type CredentialsFactory() =
    interface System.Net.ICredentials with
        member x.GetCredential(uri, authType) =
            new System.Net.NetworkCredential("rob", "whatever", "F# credentials")
    member x.GetCredentialList uri authTypes =
        let y = (x :> System.Net.ICredentials)
        let getCredential s = y.GetCredential(uri, s)
        List.map getCredential authTypes
```

You will learn more about the relationship between F# signatures and C# signatures in Chapter 12.

Abstract Classes

The generally accepted way of defining a contract in F# is to use an interface, which works well for the most part. However, interfaces have one significant drawback: any change to an interface's definition is a breaking change to client code. This isn't a problem if you're creating the application, and you have complete control over the code base. Indeed, it can even be useful because the compiler will automatically notify you of all the code than needs changing. However, if you're shipping the interface as part of a library, then you are likely to run into problems if you change your interface's definition. This is where abstract classes prove useful. For example, assume you have an interface that an abstract class defines as a *contract*; the important difference here is that abstract base classes can have concrete methods and properties. This makes versioning an abstract base class easier than versioning an interface because you can add a concrete member without making breaking changes. Unlike interfaces, an abstract class can have concrete members, which means a class can only inherit from one abstract class.

The abstract class syntax is exactly the same as the syntax for a class, except an abstract class can have abstract members. To ensure that you haven't made a mistake in adding an abstract member that you didn't provide an implementation for, you need to mark the abstract class with the [<AbstractClass>] attribute. The following example shows what your User example might look like if you were to choose to use an abstract class:

```
// a abstract class that represents a user
// its constructor takes one parameter,
// the user's name
```

```
[<AbstractClass>]
type User(name) =
    // the implmentation of this method should hashes the
    // user's password and checks it against the known hash
    abstract Authenticate: evidence: string -> bool

    // gets the users logon message
    member x.LogonMessage() =
       Printf.sprintf "Hello, %s" name
```

Classes and Static Methods

Static methods are like instance methods, except they are not specific to any instance of a class, so they have no access to a class's fields. To create a static method, you use the keyword `static`, followed by the keyword `member`. Next, you include the method name, its parameters, an equals sign, and then the method definition. This is basically the same as declaring an instance method, but with the addition of the keyword `static` and the removal of the parameter that represents the object. Removing the parameter that represents the object is quite logical because the method has no access to the object's properties.

Static methods are useful for providing alternative ways of creating a new instance of an object. F# provides no way of overloading class constructors, so you provide a static method that calls the class's constructor. In the next example, you return to the `User` class example, this time adding a static method that allows you to create a user from its unique identifier in the database:

```
#if INTERACTIVE
#else
module Classes
#endif

// a very crude hasher - don't
// use this method in real code!
let hash (s : string) =
  s.GetHashCode()

// pretend to get a user from a database
let getUserFromDB id =
  ((sprintf "someusername%i" id), 1234)

// a class that represents a user
// its constructor takes two parameters, the user's
// name and a hash of their password
type User(name, passwordHash) =
  // hashes the users password and checks it against
  // the known hash
  member x.Authenticate(password) =
    let hashResult = hash password
    passwordHash = hashResult

  // gets the users logon message
  member x.LogonMessage() =
    Printf.sprintf "Hello, %s" name
```

```
// a static member that provides an alterative way
// of creating the object
static member FromDB id =
  let name, ph = getUserFromDB id
  new User(name, ph)

// Create a user using the primary constructor
let user1 = User("kiteason", 1234)
// Create a user using a static method
let user2 = User.FromDB 999
```

Notice that the static methods called use the name of the type they are associated with, rather than a value of the type the method is associated with.

Static methods can also be useful for providing operators for your classes to use. The basic syntax for declaring an operator is the same as for declaring any other static method, except that you replace the name of the method with the operator in brackets. You must provide the parameters of the operator as a tuple; typically, you need to use type annotations to indicate their types.

The following example assumes that you want to reimplement the int type in a class called MyInt. The MyInt class has a plus operator defined on it.

```
type MyInt(state:int) =
    member x.State = state
    static member ( + ) (x:MyInt, y:MyInt) : MyInt = new MyInt(x.State + y.State)
    override x.ToString() = string state

let x = new MyInt(1)
let y = new MyInt(1)

printfn "(x + y) = %A" (x + y)
```

When you execute the preceding example, you get the following result:

```
(x + y) = 2
```

Casting

You already encountered casting, which was discussed briefly in the "Implementing Interfaces" section of this chapter. Casting is a way of explicitly altering the static type of a value by either throwing information away, which is known as *upcasting*, or rediscovering it, which is known as *downcasting*. In F#, upcasts and downcasts have their own operators. The type hierarchy starts with obj (or System.Object) at the top, with all its descendants below it. An upcast moves a type up the hierarchy, while a downcast moves a type down the hierarchy.

Upcasts change a value's static type to one of its ancestor types. This is a safe operation. The compiler can always tell whether this will work because the compiler always knows all the ancestors of a type, so it's able to use static analysis to determine whether an upcast will be successful. An upcast is represented by a colon, followed by the greater-than sign (:>). The following code shows you how to use an upcast to convert a string to an obj:

```
let myObject = ("This is a string" :> obj)
```

Generally, you must use upcasts when defining collections that contain disparate types. If you don't use an upcast, the compiler will infer that the collection has the type of the first element and give a compile error if elements of other types are placed in the collection. The next example demonstrates how to create an array of controls, a common task when working with WinForms. Notice that you upcast all of the individual controls to their common base class, Control.

```
open System.Windows.Forms

let myControls =
    [| (new Button() :> Control);
       (new TextBox() :> Control);
       (new Label() :> Control) |]
```

An upcast also has the effect of automatically boxing any value type. Value types are held in memory on the program stack, rather than on the managed heap. Boxing means that the value is pushed onto the managed heap, so it can be passed around by reference. The following example demonstrates how to box a value:

```
let boxedInt = (1 :> obj)
```

A downcast changes a value's static type to one of its descendant types; thus, it recovers information hidden by an upcast. Downcasting is dangerous because the compiler doesn't have any way to determine statically whether an instance of a type is compatible with one of its derived types. This means you can get it wrong, and this will cause an invalid cast exception (System.InvalidCastException) to be issued at runtime. Due to the inherent danger of downcasting, many developers prefer to replace it with pattern matching over .NET types, as demonstrated in Chapter 3. Nevertheless, a downcast can be useful in some places, so a downcast operator, which consists of a colon, question mark, and a greater-than sign (:?>), is available. The following example shows you how to use downcasting:

```
open System.Windows.Forms

let moreControls =
    [| (new Button() :> Control);
       (new TextBox() :> Control) |]

let control =
    let temp = moreControls.[0]
    temp.Text <- "Click Me!"
    temp

let button =
    let temp = (control :?> Button)
    temp.DoubleClick.Add(fun e -> MessageBox.Show("Hello") |> ignore)
    temp
```

This example creates an array of two Windows control objects, upcasting them to their base class, Control. Next, it binds the first control to the control identifier; downcasts this to its specific type, Button; and adds a handler to its DoubleClick event, an event not available on the Control class.

Type Tests

Closely related to casting is the idea of type tests. You can bind an identifier to an object of a derived type, as you did earlier when you bound a string to an identifier of type obj:

```
let myObject = ("This is a string" :> obj)
```

You can bind an identifier to an object of a derived type, so it is often useful to be able to test what this type is. To do this, F# provides a type-test operator, which consists of a colon followed by a question mark (:?). To compile, the operator and its operands must be surrounded by parentheses. If the identifier in the type test is of the specified type or a type derived from it, the operator returns true; otherwise, it returns false. The next example shows two type tests, one that returns true and another that returns false:

```
let anotherObject = ("This is a string" :> obj)

if (anotherObject :? string) then
    printfn "This object is a string"
else
    printfn "This object is not a string"

if (anotherObject :? string[]) then
    printfn "This object is a string array"
else
    printfn "This object is not a string array"
```

First, you create an identifier, anotherObject, of type obj, binding it to a string. Then you test whether the anotherObject is a string, which returns true. Next, you test whether it is a string array, which, of course, returns false.

Defining Delegates

A delegate is the mechanism that both C# and Visual Basic use to treat their methods as values. A delegate basically acts as a .NET object that wraps the method and provides an invoke method so the method can be called. You rarely need to define delegates in F# because it can treat a function as a value, without the need for any wrapper. However, sometimes delegates prove useful, such as when you need to define delegates to expose F# functionality to other .NET languages in a friendlier manner, or you need to define callbacks for directly calling C# code from F#.

To define a delegate, you use the keyword delegate, followed directly by the keyword of, and the type of the delegate's signature, which follows the standard F# type annotation.

The following example shows the definition of a delegate, MyDelegate, which takes an int and returns unit. You then create a new instance of this delegate and apply it to a list of integers. As you saw in Chapter 3, you implement this functionality in F# in a much shorter way:

```
type MyDelegate = delegate of int -> unit

let inst = new MyDelegate (fun i -> printf "%i" i)
let ints = [1 ; 2 ; 3 ]

ints
|> List.iter (fun i -> inst.Invoke(i))
```

When you execute this example, you get the following result:

123

Structs

You define structs in a similar manner to classes. The main difference between a class and struct is the area of memory where the object will be allocated. When used as a local variable or parameter, a struct is allocated on the stack, while a class is allocated on the managed heap. Since structs are allocated on the stack, they are not garbage collected, but automatically deallocated when a function exits. Generally, it's slightly faster to access a struct's fields than a class's; however, it's slightly slower to pass them to methods. That said, these differences tend to be quite small. Because they are allocated on the stack, it is generally best to create structs with a small number of fields to avoid stack overflow. You can't use inheritance when implementing structs, which means structs can't define virtual methods or abstract methods.

The next example defines a struct that represents an IP address:

```
type IpAddress = struct
    val first : byte
    val second : byte
    val third : byte
    val fourth : byte
    new(first, second, third, fourth) =
        { first = first;
          second = second;
          third = third;
          fourth = fourth }
    override x.ToString() =
        Printf.sprintf "%O.%O.%O.%O" x.first x.second x.third x.fourth
    member x.GetBytes() = x.first, x.second, x.third, x.fourth
end
```

So when should you use a class, and when should you use a struct? A good rule of thumb is to avoid structs, using them only when absolutely necessary, such as when interoperating with unmanaged C/C++ code (see Chapter 12 for more details on this).

Enums

Enums allow you to define a type made up of a finite set of identifiers, with each identifier mapping to an integer. This defines a type that can then take the value associated with any one of the defined identifiers.

You define an enum by giving the names of the identifiers followed by the equals sign and the values of the constants associated with the identifiers. You separate the identifiers that are members of the enum with vertical bars. The following example shows you how to define an enum named Scale:

```
type Scale =
| C = 1
| D = 2
| E = 3
```

```
| F = 4
| G = 5
| A = 6
| B = 7
```

It's quite common to define enums that you intend to combine logically. To do this, choose constants so that each number is represented by a single bit, or the numbers 0, 1, 2, 4, 8, and so on. F#'s binary literals are a great help here because it's easy to see how you might combine the constants:

```
[<System.Flags>]
type ChordScale =
| C = 0b0000000000000001
| D = 0b0000000000000010
| E = 0b0000000000000100
| F = 0b0000000000001000
| G = 0b0000000000010000
| A = 0b0000000000100000
| B = 0b0000000001000000
```

The module Enum provides functionality for dealing with enums in F#. (You will learn more about this module in Chapter 7.)

Summary

You've now seen how to use the three major programming paradigms in F# and how flexible F# is for coding in any mix of styles. In the next chapter, you'll look at how code is organized in F#, as well as how to annotate and "quote" it.

CHAPTER 6

■ ■ ■

Organizing, Annotating, and Quoting Code

An important part of any programming language is the ability to organize code into logical units. F# provides *modules* and *namespaces* for this; you can learn more about them in this chapter's "Modules," "Namespaces," and "Opening Namespaces and Modules" sections. To attain a good understanding of F#'s module system, it's also important that you understand the scope of a module, as well as how it will be initialized and executed. You can learn more about these two concepts in the in "Module Scope" and "Module Execution" sections.

For a module to be effective, it's important to able to make parts of the module private, so it cannot be seen by the outside world. F# provides two different ways to achieve this; you'll learn how to do this in the "Signature Files" and "Private and Internal let Bindings and Members" sections.

It's also important to be able to annotate code with notes about what it does for future users, maintainers, and even yourself; you will learn how to do this in the "Comments" section.

To support cross-compiling with OCaml and other advanced scenarios, it's often useful to have optional compilation. F# provides two forms of this, one of which is specifically designed for cross-compiling with OCaml and is covered in the "Comments for Cross-Compilation" section. The other, more general form is described in the "Optional Compilation" section.

It has also become common to use attributes and data structures to annotate assemblies and the types and values within them. Other libraries or the CLR can then interpret these attributes. You will learn about this technique of marking functions and values with attributes in this chapter's "Attributes" Section. The technique of compiling code into data structures is known as *quoting*, which you will learn about in the "Quoted Code" section toward the end of the chapter.

Modules

F# code is organized into modules, which are basically a way of grouping values and types under a common name. This organization has an effect on the scope of identifiers. Inside a module, identifiers can reference each other freely, although forward-references aren't allowed even to other items later in the module. To reference identifiers in a module from code outside the module, you must qualify the identifier with the module name unless the module is explicitly opened with the open directive (see the "Opening Namespaces and Modules" section later in this chapter).

You name a module using the keyword module. The keyword has two modes of operation: the first gives the same name to the whole of the source file, while the second gives a name to a section of a source file. This enables you to make several modules appear in a source file.

© Robert Pickering and Kit Eason 2016

R. Pickering and K. Eason, *Beginning F# 4.0*, DOI 10.1007/978-1-4842-1374-2_6

To include the entire contents of a source file in the same, explicitly named module, you must place the module keyword at the top of the source file. A module name in this case can contain dots, and these separate the name into parts, as you can see in this snippet:

```
module Strangelights.Beginning.ModuleDemo
```

You can define nested modules within the same source file. A module name in this case cannot contain dots. After the nested module's name, you include an equals sign followed by the indented module definition. You can also use the keywords begin and end. To wrap the module definition, you can nest submodules. The following code defines three submodules: FirstModule, SecondModule, and ThirdModule. ThirdModule is nested within SecondModule.

```
// create a top level module
module ModuleDemo

// create a first module
module FirstModule =
    let n = 1

// create a second module
module SecondModule =
    let n = 2
    // create a third module
    // nested inside the second
    module ThirdModule =
        let n = 3
```

■ **Note**   You cannot use the module keyword without an equals sign in F# Interactive. When you use the module keyword without an equals sign, it affects the whole of the source file, and F# Interactive does not have the concept of a source file; instead all code entered is treated as if it were in the same source file. This means that when you use the version of the module keyword without an equals sign in F# Interactive, you get an error. You can still use module with an equals sign to create submodules in F# Interactive.

Note that different submodules can contain the same identifiers without any problems. Modules affect the scope of an identifier. To access an identifier outside of its module, you need to qualify it with the module name, so there is no ambiguity between identifiers in different modules. In the previous example, you define the identifier n in all three modules. The following example shows how to access the identifier n specific to each of the modules:

```
// unpack the values defined in each module
let x = ModuleDemo.FirstModule.n
let y = ModuleDemo.SecondModule.n
let z = ModuleDemo.SecondModule.ThirdModule.n
```

This code compiles into a .NET class, with the values becoming methods and fields within that class. You can find more details about what an F# module looks like compared to other .NET programming languages in Chapter 12.

Namespaces

Namespaces help you organize your code hierarchically. To help keep module names unique across assemblies, you qualify the module name with a namespace name, which is just a character string with parts separated by dots. For example, F# provides a module named List, and the .NET BCL provides a class named List. There is no name conflict because the F# module is in the namespace Microsoft.FSharp. Collections, and the BCL class is in the namespace System.Collections.Generic. Namespaces keep the module names of compiled code separate, so they are not allowed in F# Interactive because they serve no purpose.

It's important that namespace names be unique. The most popular convention is to start namespace names with the name of a company or organization, followed by a specific name that indicates a piece of functionality. You aren't obligated to do this, but the convention is so widely followed that if you intend to distribute your code, especially in the form of a class library, then you should adopt this practice, too.

■ **Note**   There is no real concept of namespaces at the IL level of F#. The name of a class or module is nothing more than a long identifier that might or might not contain dots. You implement namespaces at the compiler level. When you use an open directive, you tell the compiler to do some extra work; to qualify all your identifiers with the given name, if it needs to; and to see whether this results in a match with a value or type.

In the simplest case, you can place a module in a namespace by using a module name with dots in it. The module and namespace names will be the same. You can also explicitly define a namespace for a module with the namespace directive. For example, look at this code:

```
module Strangelights.Beginning.ModuleDemo
```

You could replace the preceding code with this to get the same result:

```
namespace Strangelights.Beginning
module ModuleDemo =
```

This might not be too useful for modules, but as noted in the previous section, submodule names cannot contain dots, so you use the namespace directive to place submodules within a namespace, as in this example:

```
// put the file in a name space
namespace Strangelights.Beginning

// create a first module
module FirstModule =
    let n = 1
// create a second module
module SecondModule =
    let n = 2
    // create a third module
    // nested inside the second
    module ThirdModule =
        let n = 3
```

After you compile this code to the outside world, the first instance of n will be accessible using the identifier Strangelights.Beginning.FirstModule.n rather than just FirstModule.n. It's also possible to place several namespace declarations in the same source file, but you must declare them at the top level. In the previous example, this means you could have declared FirstModule and SecondModule in separate namespaces. You can't declare SecondModule and ThirdModule in separate namespaces; because ThirdModule is nested inside SecondModule, you can't declare a separate namespace for ThirdModule.

It's possible to define a namespace without also using a module directive, but then the namespace can contain only type definitions, as in this example:

```
// a namespace definition
namespace Strangelights.Beginning

// a record defintion
type MyRecord = { Field: string }
```

The following example will not compile because you can't place a value definition directly into a namespace without explicitly defining a module or submodule within the namespace:

```
// a namespace definition
namespace Strangelights.Beginning

// a value defintion, which is illegal
// directly inside a namespace
let value = "val"
```

In fact, the namespace directive has some interesting and subtle effects on what your code looks like to other languages; you can learn more about this in Chapter 12.

Opening Namespaces and Modules

As you saw in the previous two sections, you must use its qualified name to specify a value or type that is not defined in the current module. This can quickly become tedious because some qualified names can be quite long. Fortunately, F# provides the open directive, so you can use simple names for types and values.

You follow the open keyword by the name of the namespace or module you want to open. For example, consider this code:

```
System.Console.WriteLine("Hello world")
```

You could replace the preceding code with this:

```
open System

Console.WriteLine("Hello world")
```

Note that you don't need to specify the whole namespace name. You can specify the front part of it and use the remaining parts to qualify simple names. For example, you can specify System.Collections rather than the namespace, System.Collections.Generic, and then use Generic.List to create an instance of the generic List class, as follows:

```
open System.Collections
// create an instance of a dictionary
let wordCountDict =
    new Generic.Dictionary<string, int>()
```

■ **Caution** The technique of using partially qualified names, such as Generic.Dictionary, can make programs difficult to maintain. You should use either the name and the full namespace or the name only.

You can open F# modules, but you cannot open classes from non-F# libraries. If you open a module, you can reference values and types within it by using their simple names. Some argue that this ability to open modules directly should be used sparingly because it can make it difficult to figure out where identifiers originated. Note that many modules from the F# libraries cannot be opened directly. In fact, you can typically divide modules into two categories: those that are designed to be accessed using qualified names, and those that are designed to be opened directly. Most modules are designed to be accessed with qualified names; a few are designed to be directly opened. The typical reason to open a module directly is so that you can use operators within it directly. The following example defines a custom module that contains a *triple equals* operator and then opens this module to use the operator:

```
// module of operators
module MyOps =
    // check equality via hash code
    let (===) x y =
        x.GetHashCode() =
          y.GetHashCode()

// open the MyOps module
open MyOps

// use the triple equal operator
let equal = 1 === 1
let nEqual = 1 === 2
```

If you open two namespaces that contain modules or classes of the same name, it won't cause a compile error. You can even use values from the modules or classes with the same name, as long as the names of the values are not the same. You can see the open namespace System in Figure 6-1. You can see that it contains the class Array; you can also see a module named Array that's available in F#'s libraries. In the figure, you can see both static methods from BCL's Array class, which all start with a capital letter, and values from F#'s Array module, which start with a small letter.

Figure 6-1. *Visual Studio's IntelliSense*

Giving Modules Aliases

You might occasionally find it useful to give an alias to a module to avoid naming clashes. This is useful when two modules share the same name and a value with a common name, and it can also be a convenient way of switching some of your code to use two different implementations of similar modules. You can only give module aliases to modules that have been created in F#.

The syntax for this is the module keyword, followed by an identifier, an equals sign, and then the name of the namespace or module you want to alias. The following example defines ArrayThreeD as the alias for the namespace Microsoft.FSharp.Collections.Array3:

```
// give an alias to the Array3 module
module ArrayThreeD = Microsoft.FSharp.Collections.Array3D

// create an matrix using the module alias
let matrix =
    ArrayThreeD.create 3 3 3 1
```

Signature Files

Signature files give you a way of making function and value definitions private to a module. You've already seen the syntax for the definition of a signature file in Chapter 2. A signature file can be generated using the compiler's –i switch. Any definitions that appear in a signature file are public, and anyone can access them using the module. Any definitions that are not in the signature file are private and can be used only inside the module itself. The typical way to create a signature file is to generate it from the module source, and then go through and erase any values and functions that you want to be private.

The signature file name must be the same as the name of the module with which it is paired. It must have the extension .fsi or .mli, and you must specify the signature file to the compiler. On the command line, you must give it directly before the source file for its module. In Visual Studio, the signature file must appear before the source file in Solution Explorer.

For example, assume you have the following in the file Lib.fs:

```
// define a function to be exposed
let funkyFunction x =
    x + ": keep it funky!"

// define a function that will be hidden
let notSoFunkyFunction x = x + 1
```

Now assume you want to create a library that exposes funkyFunction but not notSoFunkyFunction. You would use the signature code like this and save it as Lib.fsi:

```
// expose a function
val funkyFunction: string -> string
```

Next, you would use the command line like this:

```
fsc -a Lib.fsi Lib.fs
```

This gives you an assembly named Lib.dll with one class named Lib, one public function named funkyFunction, and one private function named notSoFunkyFunction.

Private and Internal let Bindings and Members

F# supports another way of controlling the visibility of a value or type. You can use the private or internal keywords directly after the let of a let binding to make it private or internal, as the following example demonstrates:

```
let private aPrivateBinding = "Keep this private"
let internal aInternalBinding = "Keep this internal"
```

The private keyword makes the value or type visible only within the current module, and the internal keyword makes the value or type visible only within the current assembly. The private and internal keywords have roughly the same meaning as the private and internal keywords in C#. The internal keyword is particularly useful to make types that are specific to F# invisible outside the assembly, while allowing them to be shared between modules within the assembly. The following example shows how to hide a union type using the internal keyword:

```
// This type will not be visible outside the current assembly
type internal MyUnion =
    | String of string
    | TwoStrings of string * string
```

You see this style of programming frequently when programming in the object-oriented style. To support this, you can also hide members of objects using the private or internal keywords. Doing this is as simple as placing the private or internal keywords directly after the member keyword, as shown in the following example:

```
namespace Strangelight.Beginning

type Thing() =
    member private x.PrivateThing() =
        ()
    member x.ExternalThing() =
        ()
```

The private and internal keywords offer similar functionality to interface files, so you might wonder which one you should use in real-world programming. The answer is not clear-cut: interface files provide a nice overview of a module and an excellent place to keep the documentation of the interface. They also help you to avoid littering the source code with extra keywords. However, interface files can get a little annoying because every external definition is repeated to some extent. This means that you must update the definitions in two places when you refactor code. Given the double update problem, I generally prefer to use the private and internal keywords; however, I think either choice is valid, and it's much more important to be consistent throughout your project.

Module Scope

The order that you pass modules to the compiler is important because it affects the scope of identifiers within the modules, as well as the order in which you execute the modules. I cover scope in this section and execution order in the next.

Values and types within a module cannot be seen from another module unless the module they're in appears on the command line before the module that refers to them. This is probably easier to understand with an example. Suppose you have a source file, ModuleOne.fs, that contains the following:

```
module ModuleOne
// some text to be used by another module
let text = "some text"
```

And let's assume that you have another module, ModuleTwo.fs, that contains the following:

```
module ModuleTwo
// print out the text defined in ModuleOne
printfn "ModuleOne.text: %s" ModuleOne.text
```

You can compile these two modules successfully with the following code:

```
fsc ModuleOne.fs ModuleTwo.fs -o ModuleScope.exe
```

However, you would face a complication with the following command:

```
fsc ModuleTwo.fs ModuleOne.fs -o ModuleScope.exe
```

The preceding command would result in this error message:

```
ModuleTwo.fs(3,17): error: FS0039: The namespace or module 'ModuleOne' is not defined.
```

This error occurs because ModuleOne is used in the definition of ModuleTwo, so ModuleOne must appear before ModuleTwo in the command line, or else ModuleOne will not be in scope for ModuleTwo.

Files are passed to the compiler in the same order that files appear in Solution Explorer. This means you must sometimes spend a few moments rearranging the order of the files when you add a new file to a project. Visual Studio allows you to change the file order using the context menu of the Solution Explorer (see Figure 6-2) or, in recent versions of Visual Studio, using Alt+Up and Alt+Down. In Xamarin Studio and MonoDevelop you can drag files up and down to order them.

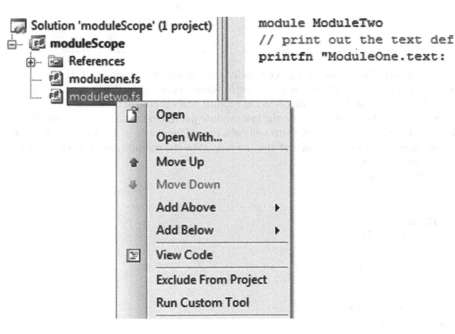

Figure 6-2. *Visual Studio's file reordering context menu*

Module Execution

Roughly speaking, execution in F# starts at the top of a module and works its way down to the bottom. Any values that are not functions are calculated, and any statements at the top level or any top-level do statements are executed. Consider the following code:

```
module ModuleOne
// statements at the top level
printfn "This is the first line"
printfn "This is the second"

// a value defined at the top level
let file =
    let temp = new System.IO.FileInfo("test.txt") in
    printfn "File exists: %b" temp.Exists
    temp
```

Executing the preceding code gives the following results:

```
This is the first line

This is the second

File exists: false
```

This is all as you might expect. When a source file is compiled into an assembly, none of the code in it will execute until a value from it is used by a currently executing function. Then, when the first value in the file is touched, all the let expressions and do statements in the module will execute in their lexical order. When you split a program over more than one module, the last module passed to the compiler is special. All the items in this module will execute, and the other items will behave as if they were in an assembly. Items in other modules will execute only when a value from that module is used by the module currently executing. Suppose you create a program with two modules.

This code is placed in ModuleOne.fs:

```
module ModuleOne
// then this one should be printed
printfn "This is the third and final"
```

This code is placed in ModuleTwo.fs:

```
module ModuleTwo
// these two lines should be printed first
printfn "This is the first line"
printfn "This is the second"
```

Now assume you compile the preceding code with the following command:

```
fsc ModuleOne.fs ModuleTwo.fs -o ModuleExecution.exe
```

Doing this gives you the following results:

```
This is the first line
This is the second
```

This might not be what you expected, but it is important to remember that ModuleOne was the not the last module passed to the compiler, so nothing in it will execute until a value from it is used by a function currently executing. In this case, no value from ModuleOne is ever used, so it never executes. Taking this into account, you can fix your program so it behaves more as you expect.

This code is placed in ModuleOne.fs:

```
module ModuleOne
// this will be printed when the module
// member n is first accessed
printfn "This is the third and final"

let n = 1
```

And this code is placed in ModuleTwo.fs:

```
module ModuleTwo
// these two lines should be printed first
printfn "This is the first line"
printfn "This is the second"

// function to access ModuleOne
let funct() =
    printfn "%i" ModuleOne.n

funct()
```

You can compile the preceding example with the following command:

```
fsc ModuleOne.fs ModuleTwo.fs -o ModuleExecution.exe
```

This gives the following result:

```
This is the first line

This is the second

This is the third and final

1
```

However, using this sort of trick to get the results you want is not recommended. It is generally best to use only statements at the top level in the last module passed to the compiler. In fact, the typical form of an F# program is to have one statement at the top level at the bottom of the last module that is passed to the compiler.

Optional Compilation

Optional compilation is a technique where the compiler can ignore various bits of text from a source file. Most programming languages support some kind of optional compilation. It can be handy, for example, if you want to build a library that supports both .NET 1.1 and 2.0, and you want to include extra values and types that take advantage of the new features of version 2.0. However, you should use the technique sparingly and with great caution because it can quickly make code difficult to understand and maintain.

In F#, optional compilation is supported by the compiler switch `--define FLAG` and the command `#if FLAG` in a source file. In Visual Studio, you can also set these by right-clicking on the project, choosing Properties, and going to the Build tab (see Figure 6-3).

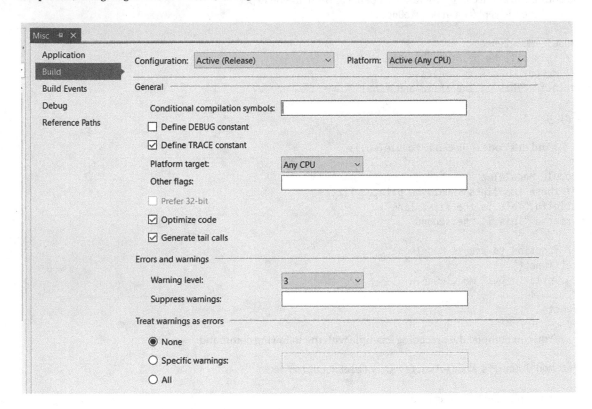

Figure 6-3. *Visual Studio's Build configuration dialog*

In MonoDevelop and Xamarin Studio, you can set conditional compilation symbols by right-clicking the project and going to Options ➤ Build ➤ Compiler (see Figure 6-4). In this screen, the relevant field is called "Defined symbols" in MonoDevelop and "Define symbols" in Xamarin Studio.

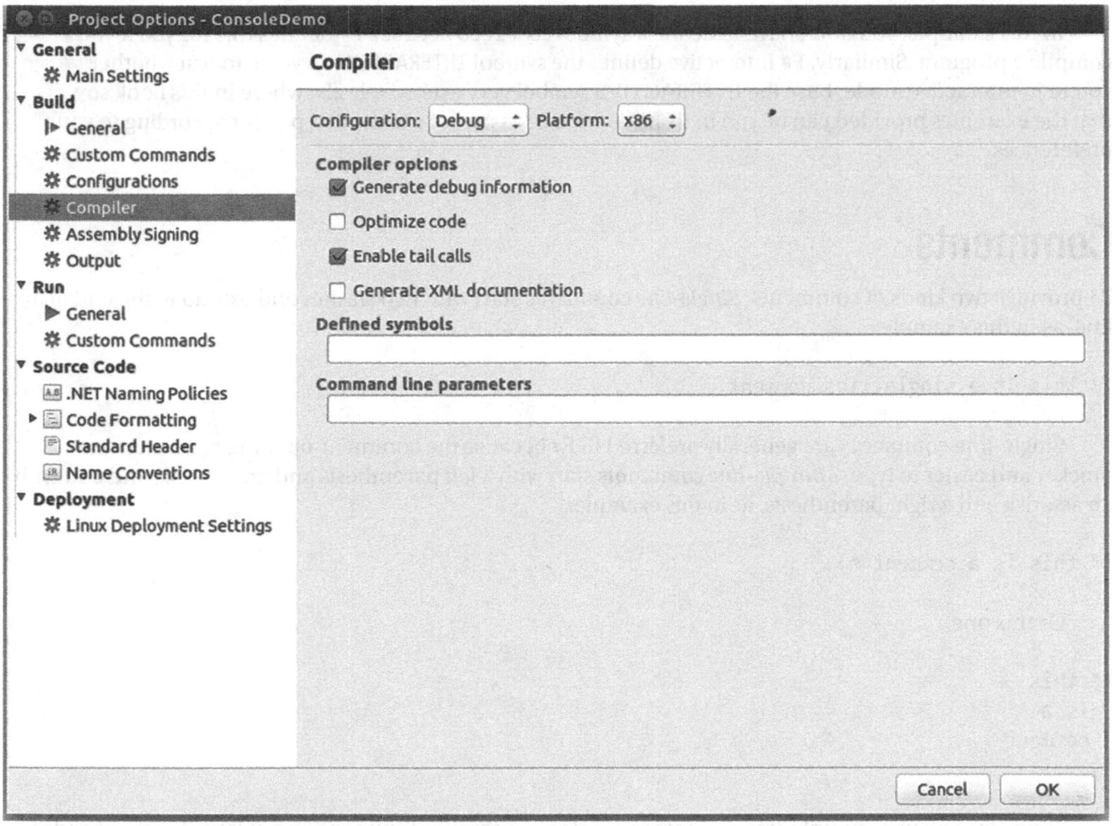

Figure 6-4. *MonoDevelop's compiler configuration dialog*

Notice that Visual Studio lets you add two predefined switches: DEBUG and TRACE. (MonoDevelop and Xamarin Studio have just DEBUG). These switches are special because they affect some framework methods; for example, assertions via a call to Assert.Debug only fire when the DEBUG symbol is defined.

The following example shows how to define two different versions of statements that execute at the top level, one for when the code is compiled, and the other for when the code is running as a script in F# Interactive (if you wish to compile this code, you also need to add a reference to System.Windows.Forms.dll):

```
open System.Windows.Forms

// define a form
let form = new Form()

// do something different depending if we're runing
// as a compiled program of as a script
#if COMPILED
```

```
Application.Run form
#else
form.Show()
#endif
```

In this example, you don't have to define a symbol COMPILED because F# defines this for you if you compile a program. Similarly, F# Interactive defines the symbol INTERACTIVE so you can test whether you're in interactive mode. I use the INTERACTIVE symbol very extensively elsewhere in this book so that the examples provided can be run in F# Interactive or as part of a compiled project according to your preferences.

Comments

F# provides two kinds of comments. *Single-line* comments start with two slashes and extend to the end of a line, as in this example:

```
// this is a single-line comment
```

Single-line comments are generally preferred in F# because the comment-opening characters are quicker and easier to type. *Multiple-line* comments start with a left parenthesis and an asterisk, and end with an asterisk and a right parenthesis, as in this example:

```
(* this is a comment *)
```

Or this one:

```
(* this
   is a
   comment
*)
```

Typically, you use multiple-line comments only for temporarily commenting out large blocks of code. Unlike a lot of other languages, F# lets you can nest multiline comments; this is the same behavior you see in OCaml comments. You get a compile error if you leave a multiple-line comment unclosed.

At the time of writing, MonoDevelop's code editor doesn't support multi-line comments, though hopefully this will be fixed at some point.

Doc Comments

Doc comments allow you to extract comments from the source file in the form of XML or HTML. This is useful because it allows programmers to browse code comments without having to browse the source. This is especially convenient for the vendors of APIs because it allows them to provide documentation about the code without having to provide the source itself. This approach also makes it more convenient to browse the docs without having to open the source. In addition, the documentation is stored alongside the source where it has more chance of being updated when code changes. Another big advantage is that IDEs like Visual Studio and Xamarin Studio will show the doc comments for functions and types in tool tips when you hover over the item name.

Doc comments start with three slashes instead of two. They can be associated only with top-level values or type definitions and are associated with the value or type they appear immediately before. The following code associates the comment this is an explanation with the value myString:

```
/// this is an explanation
let myString = "this is a string"
```

To extract doc comments into an XML file, you use the –doc compiler switch. For example, assume you were to run this command in a source file:

```
fsc -doc doc.xml Prog.fs
```

Doing this would produce the following XML:

```
<?xml version="1.0" encoding="utf-8"?>
<doc>
<assembly><name>Prog</name></assembly>
<members>
<member name="F:Prog.myString">
<summary>
 this is an explanation
</summary>

</member>
<member name="T:Prog">

</member>
</members>
</doc>
```

You can then process the XML using various open source tools to transform it into a number of more readable formats. The compiler also supports the direct generation of HTML from doc comments. This is less flexible than XML, but it can produce usable documentation with less effort. It can also produce better results under some circumstances because notations such as generics and union types are not always well supported by documentation-generation tools.

In F#, you don't need to add any XML tags explicitly; for example, the <summary> and </summary> tags were added automatically. This is useful because it saves you a lot of typing and avoids wasted space in the source file; however, you can take control and write out the XML tags explicitly if you want. The following is a doc comment where the tags have been explicitly written out:

```
/// <summary>
/// divides the given parameter by 10
/// </summary>
/// <param name="x">the thing to be divided by 10</param>
let divTen x = x / 10
```

The preceding code produces the following XML:

```
<?xml version="1.0" encoding="utf-8"?>
<doc>
<assembly><name>AnotherProg</name></assembly>
<members>
<member name="M:AnotherProg.divTen (System.Int32)">
<summary>
divides the given parameter by 10
</summary>
<param name="x">the thing to be divided by 10</param>

</member>
<member name="T:AnotherProg">

</member>
</members>
</doc>
```

If no signature file exists for the module file, then the doc comments are taken directly from the module file itself. However, if a signature file exists, then doc comments come from the signature file. This means that even if doc comments exist in the module file, they will not be included in the resulting XML or HTML if the compiler is given a signature file for the module.

Comments for Cross-Compilation

To enable easier cross-compilation between F# and OCaml, F# supports some optional compilation flags disguised as comment tags. Any code you place between these comment tags (*F# F#*) will be compiled as if the comment tags were not there. This code will appear as a normal comment to the OCaml compiler, so it will be ignored. Similarly, the F# compiler will ignore any code placed between the comments (*IF-OCAML*) (*ENDIF-OCAML*) as if it were a comment. However, the code between these two comment tags will be treated as normal code by the OCaml compiler. This provides a simple but effective mechanism for working around small differences in the two languages to make cross-compilation easier. The following sample shows these comments in action. If you use the OCaml-compatible version of the F# syntax, then you should save your file with the extension .ml instead of .fs.

```
(*F#
printfn "This will be printed by an F# program"
F#*)

(*IF-OCAML*)
Format.printf "This will be printed by an OCaml program"
(*ENDIF-OCAML*)
```

You'll get the following results when F# compiles the preceding code:

```
This will be printed by an F# program
```

Custom Attributes

Custom attributes add information to your code that will be compiled into an assembly and stored alongside your values and types. This information can then be read programmatically via reflection or by the runtime itself.

Attributes can be associated with types, members of types, and top-level values. They can also be associated with do statements. You specify an attribute in brackets, with the attribute name in angle brackets, as in this example:

```
[<Obsolete>]
```

By convention, attribute names end with the string Attribute, so the actual name of the Obsolete attribute is ObsoleteAttribute.

An attribute must immediately precede what it modifies. The following code marks the function, functionOne, as obsolete:

```
open System
[<Obsolete>]
let functionOne () = ()
```

An attribute is essentially a class; using an attribute basically makes a call to its constructor. In the previous example, Obsolete has a parameterless constructor, and you can call it with or without parentheses. In this case, you called it without parentheses. If you want to pass arguments to an attribute's constructor, then you must use parentheses and separate arguments with commas, as in this example:

```
open System
[<Obsolete("it is a pointless function anyway!")>]
let functionOne () = ()
```

Sometimes an attribute's constructor does not expose all the properties of the attribute. If you want to set such a property, you need to specify the property and a value for it. You specify the property name, an equals sign, and the value after the other arguments to the constructor. The following example sets the Unrestricted property of the PrintingPermission attribute to true:

```
open System.Drawing.Printing
open System.Security.Permissions

[<PrintingPermission(SecurityAction.Demand, Unrestricted = true)>]
let functionThree () = ()
```

You can use two or more attributes by separating the attributes with semicolons:

```
open System
open System.Drawing.Printing
open System.Security.Permissions

[<Obsolete; PrintingPermission(SecurityAction.Demand)>]
let functionFive () = ()
```

So far, you've used attributes only with values, but using them with type or type members is just as straightforward. The following example marks a type and all its members as obsolete:

```
open System

[<Obsolete>]
type OOThing = class
    [<Obsolete>]
    val stringThing : string
    [<Obsolete>]
    new() = {stringThing = ""}
    [<Obsolete>]
    member x.GetTheString () = x.stringThing
end
```

If you intend to use WinForms or Windows Presentation Foundation (WPF) graphics in your program, you must ensure that the program is a *single-thread apartment*. This is because the libraries that provide the graphical components use *unmanaged* code (not compiled by the CLR) under the covers. The easiest way to do this is by using the STAThread attribute. This must modify the first do statement in the last file passed to the compiler–that is, the first statement that will execute when the program runs.

```
open System
open System.Windows.Forms

let form = new Form()

[<STAThread>]
Application.Run(form)
```

Once you attach attributes to types and values, it's possible to use reflection to find which values and types are marked with which attributes. You usually do this with the IsDefined or GetCustomAttributes methods of the System.Reflection.MemberInfo class, which means these methods are available on most objects used for reflection, including System.Type. The next example shows you how to look for all types that are marked with the Obsolete attribute:

```
open System

// create a list of all obsolete types
let obsolete = AppDomain.CurrentDomain.GetAssemblies()
                 |> List.ofArray
                 |> List.map (fun assm -> assm.GetTypes())
                 |> Array.concat
                 |> List.ofArray
                 |> List.filter (fun m ->
                  m.IsDefined(typeof<ObsoleteAttribute>, true))

// print the lists
printfn "%A" obsolete
```

Executing the preceding code produces something like the following results:

```
[System.ContextMarshalException;( System.Collections.IHashCodeProvider;

 System.Collections.CaseInsensitiveHashCodeProvider;

 System.Runtime.InteropServices.IDispatchImplType;

 System.Runtime.InteropServices.IDispatchImplAttribute;

 System.Runtime.InteropServices.SetWin32ContextInIDispatchAttribute;

 System.Runtime.InteropServices.BIND_OPTS;

 System.Runtime.InteropServices.UCOMIBindCtx;

 System.Runtime.InteropServices.UCOMIConnectionPointContainer;

...
```

You've seen how you can use attributes and reflection to examine code; now let's look at a similar, but more powerful technique for analyzing compiled code, called *quotation*.

Quoted Code

Quotations give you a way to tell the compiler, "Don't generate code for this section of the source file; turn it into a data structure, or an *expression tree*, instead." You can then interpret this expression tree in a number of ways, transform or optimize it, compile it into another language, or even ignore it.

To quote an expression, place it between the <@ @> operators:

```
// quote the integer one
let quotedInt = <@ 1 @>

// print the quoted integer
printfn "%A" quotedInt
```

Executing the preceding code produces this result:

```
Value (1)
```

The following example defines an identifier and uses it in a quotation:

```
// define an identifier n
let n = 1
// quote the identifier
let quotedId = <@ n @>

// print the quoted identifier
printfn "%A" quotedId
```

Executing the preceding code produces the following results:

```
val n : int = 1

val quotedId : Quotations.Expr<int> = PropertyGet (None, n, [])
```

Next, you can quote a function applied to a value. Notice that you are quoting two items, so the result of this quotation is split into two parts. The first part represents the function, and the second part represents the value to which it is applied.

```
// define a function
let inc x = x + 1
// quote the function applied to a value
let quotedFun = <@ inc 1 @>

// print the quotation
printfn "%A" quotedFun
```

Executing the preceding code produces the following results:

```
val inc : x:int -> int

val quotedFun : Quotations.Expr<int> = Call (None, inc, [Value (1)])
```

The next example shows how to apply an operator to two values. Notice how you return an expression that is similar to the function call; this is because operators are basically function calls.

```
open Microsoft.FSharp.Quotations

// quote an operator applied to two operands
let quotedOp = <@ 1 + 1 @>

// print the quotation
printfn "%A" quotedOp
```

Executing the preceding code produces the following results:

```
Call (None, op_Addition, [Value (1), Value (1)])

val quotedOp : Quotations.Expr<int> =

   Call (None, op_Addition, [Value (1), Value (1)])
```

The next example quotes an anonymous function. Note how now the resulting expression is a Lambda.

```
open Microsoft.FSharp.Quotations

// quote an anonymous function
let quotedAnonFun = <@ fun x -> x + 1 @>
```

144

```
// print the quotation
printfn "%A" quotedAnonFun
```

When you execute the preceding code, you get the following result:

```
Lambda (x, Call (None, op_Addition, [x, Value (1)]))
```

Quotations are simply a discriminated union of Microsoft.FSharp.Quotations.Expr; working with them is as simple as pattern matching over the quotation. The next example defines a function, interpretInt, that queries the expression passed to it to see whether it is an integer. If it is, it prints the value of that integer; otherwise, it prints the string, "not an int".

```
open Microsoft.FSharp.Quotations.Patterns

// a function to interpret very simple quotations
let interpretInt exp =
    match exp with
    | Value (x, typ) when typ = typeof<int> -> printfn "%d" (x :?> int)
    | _ -> printfn "not an int"

// test the function
interpretInt <@ 1 @>
interpretInt <@ 1 + 1 @>
```

Executing the preceding code produces the following results:

```
1
```

```
not an int
```

You printed two expressions with interpretInt. The first was an integer value, so it printed out the value of that integer. The second was not an integer, although it contained integers. Pattern matching over quotations like this can be a bit tedious, so the F# libraries define a number of active patterns to help you do this. You can find these active patterns defined in the Microsoft.FSharp.Quotations.DerivedPatterns namespace. The following example shows how to use the SpecificCall active pattern to recognize a call to the plus operator:

```
open Microsoft.FSharp.Quotations.Patterns
open Microsoft.FSharp.Quotations.DerivedPatterns

// a function to interpret very simple quotations
let rec interpret exp =
    match exp with
    | Value (x, typ) when typ = typeof<int> -> printfn "%d" (x :?> int)
    | SpecificCall <@ (+) @> (_, _, [l;r])  -> interpret l
                                               printfn "+"
                                               interpret r
    | _ -> printfn "not supported"

// test the function
interpret <@ 1 @>
interpret <@ 1 + 1 @>
```

Executing the preceding code produces the following results:

```
1

1

+

1
```

Note that you can use the `SpecificCall` active pattern to recognize function calls, as well as operators.

No library functions exist to compile a quotation back into F# and execute it, although there have been some open source efforts made in this direction. Instead, you can mark any top-level function with the `ReflectedDefinition` attribute. This attribute tells the compiler to generate the function or value, as well as to generate an expression tree. You can then retrieve the quotation using the `<@@ @@>` operator, which is similar to the quotation operator (note the double @ sign). The following example demonstrates the use of the `ReflectedDefinition` attribute; notice how you have the quote for `inc` available, but you can also use the function inc directly:

```
// this defines a function and quotes it
[<ReflectedDefinition>]
let inc n = n + 1

// fetch the quoted defintion
let incQuote = <@@ inc @@>

// print the quotation
printfn "%A" incQuote
// use the function
printfn "inc 1: %i" (inc 1)
```

Executing this code produces the following results:

```
Lambda (n@5, Call (None, Int32 inc(Int32), [n@5]))

inc 1: 2
```

Quotations are a huge topic, and it would be impossible to cover them completely in this section (or even in this book). You will, however, learn more about them in Chapter 11.

Summary

In this chapter, you saw how to organize code in F#. You also saw how to comment, annotate, and quote code, but you have only scratched the surface of both annotating and quoting.

This concludes the tour of the F# core language. The rest of the book will focus on how to use F#, from working with relational databases to creating user interfaces. You will begin this process with a look at the F# core libraries in the next chapter.

CHAPTER 7

■ ■ ■

The F# Libraries

Although F# can use all the classes available in the .NET BCL, it also ships with its own set of libraries, which can be found under the FSharp namespace. The objective of this chapter is not to completely document every nuance of every F# library type and function. It is to give you an overview of what the modules can do, with a particular focus on features that aren't readily available in the BCL. The F# online documentation (https://msdn.microsoft.com/en-us/library/ee353413.aspx) is the place to find detailed documentation about each function.

The Native F# Library FSharp.Core.dll

The native F# library contains all the classes that you need to make the compiler work, such as the definition of the type into which F#'s list literal compiles. I'll cover the following modules:

- FSharp.Core.Operators is a module containing functions that are mathematical operators.

- FSharp.Reflection is a module containing functions that supplement the .NET Framework's reflection classes to give a more accurate view of F# types and values.

- FSharp.Collections.Seq is a module containing functions for any type that supports the IEnumerable interface.

- FSharp.Core.Printf is a module for formatting strings.

- FSharp.Control.Event is a module for working with events in F#.

The FSharp.Core.Operators Module

In F#, operators are defined by libraries rather than built into the language. The FSharp.Core.Operators module contains some of the language's operators. It also contains some useful operators, such as functions, and it is these that I will cover here. The module is open by default, which means the user can use these functions with no prefix. Specifically, I will cover the following types of functions:

- *Arithmetic operators*: Operators for basic arithmetic operations such as addition and subtraction.

- *Floating-point arithmetic functions*: More advanced arithmetic functions including logarithms and trigonometry.

- *Mutable integer functions*: Functions on mutable integers.

- *Tuple functions*: Functions on tuples.

- *Conversion functions*: Functions for converting between primitive types, such as strings, floats, and integers.

© Robert Pickering and Kit Eason 2016
R. Pickering and K. Eason, *Beginning F# 4.0*, DOI 10.1007/978-1-4842-1374-2_7

Arithmetic Operators

As already covered in Chapter 2, F# operators can be defined by the programmer, so all of the arithmetic operators are defined in the Operators module rather than built into the language. Therefore, the majority of operators that you will use in your day-to-day programming in F# are defined in the Operators module. I imagine that operators such as + and – need little explanation, since their usage is straightforward:

```
let x1 = 1 + 1
let x2 = 1 - 1
```

By default, F# operators are unchecked, which means that if a value is too big, it will wrap, rather than causing an error. If you prefer to use checked operators that raise an exception when a value overflows, you can do so by opening the module FSharp.Core.Operators.Checked:

```
open FSharp.Core.Operators.Checked
let x = System.Int32.MaxValue + 1
```

The above example will now throw an error when executed, whereas if the module FSharp.Core. Operators.Checked was not open, the value in x would simply be wrapped to -2147483648.

The F# equality operator is a bit more subtle than most of the other arithmetic operators. This is because for F# *record*, *struct*, and *discriminated union* types, default equality is *structural* equality, meaning that the contents of the instances are compared to check whether the items that make up the object are the same. This is opposed to *referential* equality, which determines whether two identifiers are bound to the same object or the same physical area of memory. For OO-style types, the default equality remains *referential* as in C#.

The structural equality operator is =, and the structural inequality operator is <>. The next example demonstrates this. The records robert1 and robert2 are equal because even though they are separate record instances, their contents are the same. On the other hand, robert1 and robert3 are not equal because their contents are different.

```
type person = { name : string ; favoriteColor : string }

let robert1 = { name = "Robert" ; favoriteColor = "Red" }
let robert2 = { name = "Robert" ; favoriteColor = "Red" }
let robert3 = { name = "Robert" ; favoriteColor = "Green" }

printfn "(robert1 = robert2): %b" (robert1 = robert2)
printfn "(robert1 <> robert3): %b" (robert1 <> robert3)
```

When you compile and execute this example, you get the following results:

```
(robert1 = robert2): true

(robert1 <> robert3): true
```

Structural comparison is also used to implement the > and < operators, which means they too can be used to compare F#'s record types. This is demonstrated here:

```
type person = { name : string ; favoriteColor : string }

let robert2 = { name = "Robert" ; favoriteColor = "Red" }
let robert3 = { name = "Robert" ; favoriteColor = "Green" }

printfn "(robert2 > robert3): %b" (robert2 > robert3)
```

When you compile and execute this example, you get the following result:

```
(robert2 > robert3): true
```

If you need to determine whether two records, structs, or discriminated union instances are physically equal, you can use the PhysicalEquality function available in the LanguagePrimitives module, as in the following example:

```
type person = { name : string ; favoriteColor : string }

let robert1 = { name = "Robert" ; favoriteColor = "Red" }
let robert2 = { name = "Robert" ; favoriteColor = "Red" }

printfn "(LanguagePrimitives.PhysicalEquality robert1 robert2): %b"
    (LanguagePrimitives.PhysicalEquality robert1 robert2)
```

From F# 4.0 onwards, you can override structual equality behavior for records by simply opening the FSharp.Core.NonStructuralOperators namespace. This namespace contains versions of the = and <> operators, which use referential equality. Thus, if you simply add

```
open FSharp.Core.Operators.NonStructuralComparison
```

the results of executing the same code become

```
(robert1 = robert2): false
(robert1 <> robert3): true
```

Alternatively, you can force reference equality for a particular type by adding the [<ReferenceEquality>] attribute to the type.

Floating-Point Arithmetic Functions

The Operators module also offers a number of functions (see Table 7-1) specifically for floating-point numbers, some of which are used in the following sample:

```
printfn "(sqrt 16.0): %f" (sqrt 16.0)
printfn "(log 160.0): %f" (log 160.0)
printfn "(cos 1.6): %f" (cos 1.6)
```

When you compile and execute this example, you get the following results:

```
(sqrt 16.0): 4.000000
(log 160.0): 5.075174
(cos 1.6): -0.029200
```

Table 7-1. *Arithmetic Functions for Floating-Point Numbers*

Function	Description
abs	Returns the absolute value of the argument.
acos	Returns the inverse cosine (arccosine) of the argument, which should be specified in radians.
asin	Returns the inverse sine (arcsine) of the argument, which should be specified in radians.
atan	Returns the inverse tangent (arctangent) of the argument, which should be specified in radians.
atan2	Returns the inverse tangent (arctangent) of the two arguments, which should both be specified in radians.
ceil	Returns the next highest integer value by rounding up the value if necessary; the value returned is still of type float.
floor	Returns the next lowest integer value by rounding up the value if necessary; the value returned is still of type float.
exp	Returns the exponential.
infinity	Returns the floating-point number that represents infinity.
Log	Returns the natural log of the floating-point number.
log10	Returns the base 10 log of the floating-point number.
Nan	Returns the floating-point number that represents "not a number".
Sqrt	Returns the square root of the number.
Cos	Returns the cosine of the parameter, which should be specified in radians.
Cosh	Returns the hyperbolic cosine of the parameter, which should be specified in radians.
Sin	Returns the sine of the parameter, which should be specified in radians.
Sinh	Returns the hyperbolic sine of the parameter, which should be specified in radians.
Tan	Returns the tangent of the parameter, which should be specified in radians.
Tanh	Returns the hyperbolic tangent of the parameter, which should be specified in radians.
truncate	Returns the parameter converted to an integer.
Float	Takes an integer and returns it as a float.
float32	Takes an integer and returns it as a float32.

Tuple Functions

The Operators module also offers two useful functions that operate on tuples. You can use the functions fst and snd to break up a tuple with two items in it. The following example demonstrates their use:

```
printfn "(fst (1, 2)): %i" (fst (1, 2))
printfn "(snd (1, 2)): %i" (snd (1, 2))
```

The results are as follows:

```
(fst (1, 2)): 1

(snd (1, 2)): 2
```

The Conversion Functions

The Operators module offers a number of overload functions for converting between the primitive types. For example, the function float is overloaded to convert from a string or integer type to a floating point number, a System.Double. The following example shows how to convert from an enumeration to an integer and then convert it back to an enumeration. Converting from an enumeration to an integer is straightforward; you just use the int function. Converting back is slightly more complicated; you use the enum function, but you must provide a type annotation so that the compiler knows which type of enumeration to convert it to. You can see this in the following example where you add the annotation DayOfWeek to the identifier dayEnum:

```
open System

let dayInt = int DateTime.Now.DayOfWeek
let (dayEnum : DayOfWeek) = enum dayInt

printfn "%i" dayInt
printfn "%A" dayEnum
```

When you compile and execute this example, you get the following results:

```
0

Sunday
```

The Bitwise Or and And Operators

The other common tasks that you need to perform with enumerations are to combine them using a bitwise "or" and "and" operations. Enum types marked with the System.Flags attribute support the use of the &&& and ||| operators to perform these operations directly. For example, you can use the ||| operator to combine several enum values. You can test to see if value is part of an enum using the &&& operators in the form v1 &&& v2 <> enum 0:

```
open System.Windows.Forms

let anchor = AnchorStyles.Left ||| AnchorStyles.Left

printfn "test AnchorStyles.Left: %b"
    (anchor &&& AnchorStyles.Left <> enum 0)
printfn "test AnchorStyles.Right: %b"
    (anchor &&& AnchorStyles.Right <> enum 0)
```

The FSharp.Reflection Module

This module contains F#'s own version of reflection. F# contains some types that are 100 percent compatible with the CLR type system, but aren't precisely understood with .NET reflection. For example, F# uses some sleight of hand to implement its union type, and this is transparent in 100 percent F# code. It can look a little strange when you use the BCL to reflect over it. The F# reflection system addresses this kind of problem. But, it blends with the BCL's System.Reflection namespace, so if you are reflecting over an F# type that uses BCL types, you will get the appropriate object from the System.Reflection namespace.

In F#, you can reflect over types or over values. The difference is a bit subtle and is best explained with an example. Those of you familiar with .NET reflection might like to think of reflection over types as using the Type, EventInfo, FieldInfo, MethodInfo, and PropertyInfo types, and reflections over values as calling their members, such as GetProperty or InvokeMember, to get values dynamically. Yet reflection over values offers a high-level, easy-to-use system.

- *Reflection over types* lets you examine the types that make up a particular value or type.

- *Reflection over values* lets you examine the values that make up a particular composite value.

Reflection Over Types

The following example shows a function that will print the type of any tuple:

```
open FSharp.Reflection

let printTupleTypes (x: obj) =
    let t = x.GetType()
    if FSharpType.IsTuple t then
        let types = FSharpType.GetTupleElements t
        printf "("
        types
        |> Seq.iteri
```

```
                (fun i t ->
                if i <> Seq.length types - 1 then
                    printf " %s * " t.Name
                else
                    printf "%s" t.Name)
        printfn " )"
    else
        printfn "not a tuple"

printTupleTypes ("hello world", 1)
```

First, you use the object's GetType method to get the System.Type that represents the object. You can then use this value with the function FSharpType.IsTuple to test if it is a tuple. You then use function FSharpType.GetTupleElements to get an array of System.Type that describes the elements that make up the tuple. These could represent F# types, so you could recursively call the function to investigate what they are. In this case, you know they are types from the BCL, so you simply print out the type names. This means that, when compiled and run, the sample outputs the following:

```
( String * Int32 )
```

Reflection Over Values

Imagine, instead of displaying the types of a tuple, that you want to display the values that make up the tuple. To do this, you use reflection over values, and you need to use the function FSharpValue.GetTupleFields to get an array of objects that are the values that make up the tuple. These objects can be tuples, or other F# types, so you can recursively call the function to print out the values of the objects. However, in this case, you know there are fundamental values from the BCL library, so you simply use the F# printfn function to print them out. The F# Printf module is described later in the chapter. The following example implements such a function:

```
open FSharp.Reflection
let printTupleValues (x: obj) =
    if FSharpType.IsTuple(x.GetType()) then
        let vals = FSharpValue.GetTupleFields x
        printf "("
        vals
        |> Seq.iteri
            (fun i v ->
                if i <> Seq.length vals - 1 then
                    printf " %A, " v
                else
                    printf " %A" v)
        printfn " )"
    else
        printfn "not a tuple"

printTupleValues ("hello world", 1)
```

When you compile and execute this example, you get the following result:

```
( "hello world", 1 )
```

Reflection is used both within the implementation of fsi, the interactive command-line tool that is part of the F# tool suite, and within the F# library's printf function family. If you want to learn more about the way you can use reflection, take a look at the source for printf, available in on GitHub (https://github.com/fsharp/fsharp/blob/master/src/fsharp/FSharp.Core/printf.fs).

The FSharp.Collections.Seq Module

The FSharp.Collections.Seq module contains functions that work with any collection that supports the IEnumerable interface, which is most of the collections in the BCL. The module is called Seq (short for "sequence") because F# gives the alias seq to the IEnumerable interface to shorten it and make it easier to type and read. This alias is used when type definitions are given.

■ **Note** Microsoft.FSharp.Collections contains several modules designed to work with various types of collections. These include Array, Array2D (two-dimensional arrays), Array3D (three-dimensional arrays), IEnumerable (Seq), List, Map, and Set. I'll cover only Seq, but all of the basic operations (iteration, mapping, filtering, and so on) are implemented for each of the different collection types and work in a similar, often identical, way.

Some of these functions can be replaced by the list comprehension syntax covered in Chapters 3 and 4. For simple tasks and working with untyped collections, it's generally easier to use list comprehension, but for more complicated tasks you will want to stick to these functions. You will take a look at the following functions:

- map and iter: These two functions let you apply a given function to every item in the collection.

- concat: This function lets you concatenate a collection of collections into one collection.

- fold: This function lets you create a summary of a collection by folding the items in the collection together.

- exists and forall: These functions let you make assertions about the contents of a collection.

- filter, find and tryFind: These functions let you pick elements in the list that meet certain conditions.

- choose: This function lets you perform a filter and map at the same time.

- init and initInfinite: These functions let you initialize collections.

- unfold: This provides a more flexible way to initialize collections.

- cast: This is a way to convert from the nongeneric version of IEnumerable, rather than IEnumerable<T>.

The map and iter Functions

Let's look at map and iter first. These apply a function to each element in a collection. The difference between them is that map is designed to create a new collection by transforming each element in the collection, while iter is designed to apply an operation that has a side effect to each item in the collection. A typical example of a side effect is writing the element to the console. The following example shows both map and iter in action:

```
let myArray = [|1; 2; 3|]

let myNewCollection =
    myArray |>
    Seq.map (fun x -> x * 2)

printfn "%A" myArray

myNewCollection |> Seq.iter (fun x -> printf "%i ... " x)
```

When you compile and execute this example, you get the following results:

```
[|1; 2; 3|]
2 ... 4 ... 6 ...
```

The concat Function

The previous example used an array because it was convenient to initialize this type of collection, but you could use any of the collection types available in the BCL. The next example uses the List type provided in the System.Collections.Generic namespace (i.e. not an "F# list" but a ".NET" or "C#" list) and demonstrates how to use the concat function, which has type #seq< #seq<'a> > -> seq<'a> and which collects IEnumerable values into one IEnumerable value:

```
open System.Collections.Generic

let myList =
    let temp = new List<int[]>()
    temp.Add([|1; 2; 3|])
    temp.Add([|4; 5; 6|])
    temp.Add([|7; 8; 9|])
    temp

let myCompleteList = Seq.concat myList

myCompleteList |> Seq.iter (fun x -> printf "%i ... " x)
```

When you compile and execute this example, you get the following results:

```
1 ... 2 ... 3 ... 4 ... 5 ... 6 ... 7 ... 8 ... 9 ...
```

The fold Function

The next example demonstrates the fold function, which has type ('b -> 'a -> 'b) -> 'b -> #seq<'a> -> 'b. This is a function for creating a summary of a collection by threading an accumulator value through each function call. The function takes two parameters. The first of these is an accumulator, which is the result of the previous function, and the second is an element from the collection. The function body should combine these two values to form a new value of the same type as the accumulator. In the next example, the elements of myPhrase are concatenated to the accumulator so that all the strings end up combined into one string:

```
let myPhrase = [|"How"; "do"; "you"; "do?"|]

let myCompletePhrase =
    myPhrase |>
    Seq.fold (fun acc x -> acc + " " + x) ""

printfn "%s" myCompletePhrase
```

When you compile and execute this example, you get the following result:

```
How do you do?
```

The exists and forall Functions

The next example demonstrates two functions that you can use to determine facts about the contents of collections. These functions are exists and forall, which both have the type ('a -> bool) -> #seq<'a> -> bool. You can use the exists function to determine whether any element in the collection exists that meets certain conditions. The conditions that must be met are determined by the function passed to exists, and if any of the elements meet this condition, then exists will return true. The function forall is similar except that all the elements in the collection must meet the condition before it will return true. The following example first uses exists to determine whether there are any elements in the collections that are multiples of 2 and then uses forall to determine whether all items in the collection are multiples of 2:

```
let intArray = [|0; 1; 2; 3; 4; 5; 6; 7; 8; 9|]

let existsMultipleOfTwo =
    intArray |>
    Seq.exists (fun x -> x % 2 = 0)

let allMultipleOfTwo =
    intArray |>
    Seq.forall (fun x -> x % 2 = 0)

printfn "existsMultipleOfTwo: %b" existsMultipleOfTwo
printfn "allMultipleOfTwo: %b" allMultipleOfTwo
```

When you compile and execute this example, you get the following results:

```
existsMultipleOfTwo: true
allMultipleOfTwo: false
```

The filter, find, and tryFind Functions

The next example looks at three functions that are similar to exists and forall. These functions are filter of type ('a -> bool) -> #seq<'a> -> seq<'a>, find of type ('a -> bool) -> #seq<'a> -> 'a, and tryFind of type ('a -> bool) -> #seq<'a> -> 'a option. They are similar to exists and forall because they use functions to examine the contents of a collection. Instead of returning a Boolean, these functions actually return the item or items found. The function filter uses the function passed to it to check every element in the collection. The filter function then returns a list that contains all the elements that have met the condition of the function. If no elements meet the condition, then an empty list is returned. The functions find and tryFind both return the first element in the collection to meet the condition specified by the function passed to them. Their behavior is altered when no element in the collection meets the condition. find throws an exception, whereas tryFind returns an option type that will be None if no element is found. Since exceptions are relatively expensive in .NET, you should prefer tryFind over find.

In the following example, you look through a list of words. First, you use filter to create a list containing only the words that end in *at*. Then you use find to find the first word that ends in *ot*. Finally, you use tryFind to check whether any of the words end in *tt*.

```
let shortWordList = [|"hat"; "hot"; "bat"; "lot"; "mat"; "dot"; "rat";|]

let atWords =
    shortWordList
    |> Seq.filter (fun x -> x.EndsWith("at"))

let otWord =
    shortWordList
    |> Seq.find (fun x -> x.EndsWith("ot"))

let ttWord =
    shortWordList
    |> Seq.tryFind (fun x -> x.EndsWith("tt"))

atWords |> Seq.iter (fun x -> printf "%s ... " x)
printfn ""
printfn "%s" otWord
printfn "%s" (match ttWord with | Some x -> x | None -> "Not found")
```

When you compile and execute this example, you get the following results:

```
hat ... bat ... mat ... rat ...

hot

Not found
```

The choose Function

The next Seq function you'll look at is a clever function that allows you to do a filter and a map at the same time. This function is called choose and has the type ('a -> 'b option) -> #seq<'a> -> seq<'b>. To do this, the function that is passed to choose must return an option type. If the element in the list can be transformed into something useful, the function should return Some containing the new value. When the element is not wanted, the function returns None.

In the following example, you take a list of floating-point numbers and multiply them by 2. If the value is an integer, it is returned. Otherwise, it is filtered out. This leaves you with just a list of integers.

```
let floatArray = [|0.5; 0.75; 1.0; 1.25; 1.5; 1.75; 2.0 |]

let integers =
    floatArray |>
    Seq.choose
        (fun x ->
            let y = x * 2.0
            let z = floor y
            if y - z = 0.0 then
                Some (int z)
            else
                None)

integers |> Seq.iter (fun x -> printf "%i ... " x)
```

When you compile and execute this example, you get the following results:

```
1 ... 2 ... 3 ... 4 ...
```

The init and initInfinite Functions

Next, you'll look at two functions for initializing collections, init of type int -> (int -> 'a) -> seq<'a> and initInfinite of type (int -> 'a) -> seq<'a>. You can use the function init to make a collection of a finite size. It does this by calling the function passed to it the number of times specified by the number passed to it. You can use the function initInfinite to create a collection of an unbounded size. It does this by calling the function passed to it each time it is asked for a new element this way. In theory, a list of unlimited size can be created, but in reality you are constrained by the limits of the machine performing the computation. Typically initInfinite will fail once the value of the integer that it sends into the generator function exceeds the maximum integer size for .NET.

The following example shows init being used to create a list of ten integers, each with the value 1. It also shows a list being created that should contain all the possible 32-bit integers and demonstrates using the function take to create a list of the first ten.

```
let tenOnes = Seq.init 10 (fun _ -> 1)
let allIntegers = Seq.initInfinite (fun x -> System.Int32.MinValue + x)
let firstTenInts = Seq.take 10 allIntegers

tenOnes |> Seq.iter (fun x -> printf "%i ... " x)
printfn ""
printfn "%A" firstTenInts
```

When you compile and execute this example, you get the following results:

```
1 ... 1 ... 1 ... 1 ... 1 ... 1 ... 1 ... 1 ... 1 ... 1 ...
[-2147483648; -2147483647; -2147483646; -2147483645; -2147483644; -2147483643;
 -2147483642; -2147483641; -2147483640; -2147483639]
```

The unfold Function

You already met unfold in Chapter 3. It is a more flexible version of the functions init and initInfinite. The first advantage of unfold is that it can be used to pass an accumulator through the computation, which means you can store some state between computations and don't simply have to rely on the current position in the list to calculate the value, like you do with init and initInfinite. The second advantage is that it can be used to produce a list that is either finite or infinite. Both of these advantages are achieved by using the return type of the function passed to unfold. The return type of the function is 'a * 'b option, meaning an option type that contains a tuple of values. The first value in the option type is the value that will be placed in the list, and the second is the accumulator. If you want to continue the list, you return Some with this tuple contained within it. If want to stop it, you return None.

The following example, repeated from Chapter 2, shows unfold being used to compute the Fibonacci numbers. You can see the accumulator being used to store a tuple of values representing the next two numbers in the Fibonacci sequence. Because the list of Fibonacci numbers is infinite, you never return None.

```
let fibs =
    (1,1) |> Seq.unfold
        (fun (n0, n1) ->
            Some(n0, (n1, n0 + n1)))

let first20 = Seq.take 20 fibs
printfn "%A" first20
```

When you compile and execute this example, you get the following results:

```
[1; 1; 2; 3; 5; 8; 13; 21; 34; 55; 89; 144; 233; 377; 610; 987;
1597; 2584; 4181; 6765]
```

This example demonstrates using unfold to produce a list that never terminates. Now imagine you want to calculate a sequence of numbers where the value decreases by half its current value, such as a nuclear source decaying. Imagine that beyond a certain limit the number becomes so small that you are no longer interested in it. You can model such a sequence in the following example by returning None when the value has reached its limit:

```
let decayPattern =
    Seq.unfold
        (fun x ->
            let limit = 0.01
            let n = x - (x / 2.0)
            if n > limit then
```

```
            Some(x, n)
        else
            None)
    10.0

decayPattern |> Seq.iter (fun x -> printf "%f ... " x)
```

When you compile and execute this example, you get the following results:

```
10.000000 ... 5.000000 ... 2.500000 ... 1.250000 ...

0.625000 ... 0.312500 ... 0.156250 ... 0.078125 ... 0.039063 ...
```

The cast Function

The BCL contains two versions of the IEnumerable interface, one defined in System.Collections.Generic and an older one defined in System.Collections. All the samples shown so far have been designed to work with the new generic version from System.Collections.Generic. However, sometimes it might be necessary to work with collections that are not generic, so the F# IEnumerable module also provides a function to work with that converts from nongeneric collections to a generic one.

Before using this function, I strongly recommend that you see whether you can use the list comprehension syntax covered in Chapters 3 and 4 instead. This is because the list comprehension syntax can infer the types of many untyped collections, usually by looking at the type of the Item indexer property, so there is less need for type annotations, which generally makes programming easier.

If for any reason you prefer not to use the list comprehension syntax, you can convert a non-generic collection to a generic one using the function cast, which is demonstrated in the following example:

```
open System.Collections

let floatArrayList =
    let temp = new ArrayList()
    temp.AddRange([| 1.0; 2.0; 3.0 |])
    temp

let (typedFloatSeq: seq<float>) = Seq.cast floatArrayList
```

Using the cast function often requires using type annotations to tell the compiler what type of list you are producing. Here you have a list of floats, so you use the type annotation IEnumerable<float> to tell the compiler it will be an IEnumerable collection containing floating-point numbers.

The FSharp.Text.Printf Module

The Printf module provides functions for formatting strings in a type-safe way. The functions in the Printf module take a string with placeholders for values as their first argument. This returns another function that expects values for the placeholders. You form placeholders by using a percentage sign and a letter representing the type that they expect. Table 7-2 shows the full list.

Table 7-2. *Printf Placeholders and Flags*

Flag	Description
%b	bool, formatted as "true" or "false".
%c	Any character.
%s	string, formatted as its unescaped contents.
%d, %i	Any basic integer type (that is, sbyte, byte, int16, uint16, int32, uint32, int64, uint64, nativeint, or unativeint) formatted as a decimal integer, signed if the basic integer type is signed.
%u	Any basic integer type formatted as an unsigned decimal integer.
%x, %X, %o	Any basic integer type formatted as an unsigned hexadecimal, (a-f)/Hexadecimal (A-F)/ Octal integer.
%e, %E	Any basic floating-point type (that is, float or float32), formatted using a C-style floating-point format specification, signed value having the form [-]d.dddde[sign]ddd where *d* is a single decimal digit, *dddd* is one or more decimal digits, *ddd* is exactly three decimal digits, and *sign* is + or -.
%f	Any basic floating-point type, formatted using a C-style floating-point format specification, signed value having the form [-]dddd.dddd, where *dddd* is one or more decimal digits. The number of digits before the decimal point depends on the magnitude of the number, and the number of digits after the decimal point depends on the requested precision.
g, %G	Any basic floating-point type, formatted using a C-style floating-point format specification, signed value printed in f or e format, whichever is more compact for the given value and precision.
%M	System.Decimal value.
%O	Any value, printed by boxing the object and using its ToString method(s).
%A	Any value; values will be pretty printed, allowing the user to see the values of properties and fields.
%a	A general format specifier that requires two arguments. A function that accepts two arguments: a context parameter of the appropriate type for the given formatting function (such as a System.IO.TextWriter) and a value to print that either outputs or returns appropriate text. The second argument is the particular value to print.
%t	A general format specifier that requires one argument. A function that accepts a context parameter of the appropriate type for the given formatting function (such as a System.IO.TextWriter) and that either outputs or returns appropriate text.
0	A flag that adds zeros instead of spaces to make up the required width.
-	A flag that left-justifies the result within the width specified.
+	A flag that adds a + character if the number is positive (to match the - sign for negatives).
' '	Adds an extra space if the number is positive (to match the - sign for negatives).

The following example shows how to use the printf function. It creates a function that expects a string and then passes a string to this function.

```
Printf.printf "Hello %s" "Robert"
```

When you compile and execute this example, you get the following result:

```
Hello Robert
```

The significance of this might not be entirely obvious, but the following example will probably help explain it. If a parameter of the wrong type is passed to the printf function, then it will not compile.

```
Printf.printf "Hello %s" 1
```

This code will not compile, giving the following error:

```
Prog.fs(4,25): error: FS0001: This expression has type
    int
but is here used with type
    string
```

This also has an effect on type inference. If you create a function that uses printf, then any arguments that are passed to printf will have their types inferred from this. For example, the function myPrintInt, shown here, has the type int -> unit because of the printf function contained within it:

```
let myPrintInt x =
    Printf.printf "An integer: %i" x
```

The basic placeholders in a Printf module function are %b for a Boolean; %s for a string; %d or %i for an integer; %u for an unsigned integer; and %x, %X, or %o for an integer formatted as a hexadecimal. It is also possible to specify the number of decimal places that are displayed in numeric types. The following example demonstrates this:

```
let pi = System.Math.PI

Printf.printfn "%f" pi
Printf.printfn "%1.1f" pi
Printf.printfn "%2.2f" pi
Printf.printfn "%2.8f" pi
```

The results of this code are as follows:

```
3.141593

3.1

3.14

3.14159265
```

The Printf module (which is automatically opened for you) also contains a number of other functions that allow a string to be formatted in the same ways as printf itself, but allow the result to be written to a different destination. The following example shows some of the different versions available:

```
// write to a string
let s = Printf.sprintf "Hello %s\r\n" "string"
printfn "%s" s
// prints the string to a .NET TextWriter
fprintf System.Console.Out "Hello %s\r\n" "TextWriter"
// create a string that will be placed
// in an exception message
failwithf "Hello %s" "exception"
```

The results of this code are as follows:

```
Hello string

Hello TextWriter

Microsoft.FSharp.FailureException: Hello exception

    at Microsoft.FSharp.Text.Printf.failwithf@60.Invoke(String s)

    at Microsoft.FSharp.Text.PrintfImpl.Make@188.Invoke(A inp))

    at <StartupCode>.FSI_0003._main()

stopped due to error
```

The FSharp.Control.Event Module

You can think of an event in F# as a collection of functions that can be triggered by a call to a function. The idea is that functions will register themselves with the event, the collection of functions, to await notification that the event has happened. The trigger function is then used to give notice that the event has occurred, causing all the functions that have added themselves to the event to be executed.

I will cover the following features of the Event module:

- *Creating and handling events*: The basics of creating and handling events using the create and add functions.

- *The* filter *function*: A function to filter the data coming into events.

- *The* partition *function*: A function that splits the data coming into events into two.

- *The* map *function*: A function that maps the data before it reaches the event handler.

Creating and Handling Events

The first example looks at a simple event being created using a call to the constructor of the Event object. You should pass a type parameter to the constructor representing the type of event you want. This object contains a Trigger function and a property that represents the event itself called Publish. You use the event's Publish property's Add function to add a handler method, and finally you trigger the event using the trigger function.

```
let event = new Event<string>()
event.Publish.Add(fun x -> printfn "%s" x)
event.Trigger "hello"
```

The result of this code is as follows:

```
hello
```

In addition to this basic event functionality, the F# Event module provides a number of functions that allow you to filter and partition events to give fine-grained control over which data is passed to which event handler.

The filter Function

The following example demonstrates how you can use the Event module's filter function so that data being passed to the event is filtered before it reaches the event handlers. In this example, you filter the data so that only strings beginning with H are sent to the event handler:

```
let event = new Event<string>()
let newEvent = event.Publish |> Event.filter (fun x -> x.StartsWith("H"))

newEvent.Add(fun x -> printfn "new event: %s" x)

event.Trigger "Harry"
event.Trigger "Jane"
event.Trigger "Hillary"
event.Trigger "John"
event.Trigger "Henry"
```

When you compile and execute this example, you get the following results:

```
new event: Harry

new event: Hillary

new event: Henry
```

The partition Function

The Event module's partition function is similar to the filter function except two events are returned, one where data caused the partition function to return false and one where data caused the partition function to return true. The following example demonstrates this:

```
let event = new Event<string>()
let hData, nonHData = event.Publish |> Event.partition (fun x -> x.StartsWith "H")

hData.Add(fun x -> printfn "H data: %s" x)
nonHData.Add(fun x -> printfn "None H data: %s" x)
```

```
event.Trigger "Harry"
event.Trigger "Jane"
event.Trigger "Hillary"
event.Trigger "John"
event.Trigger "Henry"
```

The results of this code are as follows:

```
H data: Harry

None H data: Jane

H data: Hillary

None H data: John

H data: Henry
```

The map Function

It is also possible to transform the data before it reaches the event handlers. You do this using the map function provided in the Event module. The following example demonstrates how to use it:

```
let event = new Event<string>()
let newEvent = event.Publish |> Event.map (fun x -> "Mapped data: " + x)
newEvent.Add(fun x -> printfn "%s" x)

event.Trigger "Harry"
event.Trigger "Sally"
```

The results of this code are as follows:

```
Mapped data: Harry

Mapped data: Sally
```

This section has just provided a brief overview of events in F#. You will return to them in more detail in Chapter 8 when I discuss user interface programming, because that is where they are most useful.

Summary

We covered a lot of ground in this chapter, since the F# libraries have a diverse range of functionalities. First, you looked through the FSharp.Core.dll library with its useful operators, and its Collections and Reflection modules. In particular, the Seq module is something that any nontrivial F# program would not be able to do without since it provides invaluable functions such as iter, map, and concat. You looked at the significance of structural versus reference equality, and how you can override the default behaviors. You tried out the Printf module and the corresponding format strings, which give you strongly typed string formatting. Finally, you learned to define, raise, and filter events.

The next three chapters will look at how you can use F# with various .NET APIs for common programming tasks. You'll look at data access in Chapter 8, parallel programming in Chapter 9, and distributed applications in Chapter 10.

CHAPTER 8

■ ■ ■

Data Access

Computers are designed to process data, so it's a rare program that doesn't require some form of data access, whether it's reading a small configuration file or an enterprise application that accesses a full-scale relational database management system. In this chapter, you will learn about F#'s wide range of data access options.

In F#, data access relies heavily on tools and libraries within, or built upon, the .NET BCL. This means that a lot of the data access code you write in F# will resemble data access code in C# or VB.NET, although the F# code will often be more concise than in those other languages.

Although it's important to understand the way basic data access works in F#, you should bear in mind that *type providers* can take away much of the pain of accessing external data sources. These are covered in Chapter 13.

The System.Configuration Namespace

Whenever you execute any program written in any .NET language, the .NET runtime will automatically check whether a configuration file is available. This is a file with the same name as the executable, plus the extension .config, which must exist in the same directory as the executable. Visual Studio will normally create this file for you when you create a project. In Xamarin Studio and MonoDevelop, you have to add a configuration file to your project explicitly. In the Solution Explorer, right-click the project and select Add ➤ New File. In the Misc tab, select Application Configuration File and name the file App.config. The App.config (or for web projects, Web.config) file will be renamed and placed alongside the .exe or .dll file during the build process. Thus, after building, the configuration file for MyApp.exe would be MyApp.exe.config. These files are useful for storing settings that you want to be able to change without recompiling the application; a classic example of this is a connection string to a database. You should be careful not to store values that are specific to a user in the configuration file because any changes to the file will affect all users of the application. The best place to store user-specific settings is often in a relational database. You'll learn more about relational database access later in this chapter.

The System.Configuration namespace provides an easy way to access configuration values; the simplest way of accessing configuration data is with ConfigurationManager. The following example shows how to load a simple key-value pair from a configuration file. Imagine you have the following configuration file, and you want to read "MySetting" from the file:

```
<configuration>
    <appSettings>
        <add key="MySetting" value="An important string" />
    </appSettings>
</configuration>
```

The following code loads the setting by using `ConfigurationManager`'s static `AppSettings` property:

```
open System.Configuration

// read an application setting
let setting = ConfigurationManager.AppSettings.["MySetting"]

// print the setting
printfn "%s" setting
```

Executing the preceding code produces the following result:

```
An important string
```

■ **Note** To compile this example, you need to add a reference to `System.Configuration.dll`.

Typically, you use these name-value pairs to store connection strings. It is customary to use a separate section specifically for this purpose, which can help you separate them from other configuration settings. The providerName property allows you to store information about which database provider the connection string should be used with. The following example shows how to load the connection string "MyConnectionString" from a configuration file:

```
<configuration>
        <connectionStrings>
                <add
                        name="MyConnectionString"
                        connectionString=" Data Source=server;
                                Initial Catalog=pubs;
                                Integrated Security=SSPI;"
                        providerName="System.Data.SqlClient" />
        </connectionStrings>
</configuration>
```

The following example loads the connection string via another static property in the `ConfigurationManager` class, the `ConnectionStrings` property. This is a collection that gives access to a type called `ConnectionStringSettings`, which has a `ConnectionString` property that gives access to the connection string, as well as a `ProviderName` property that gives access to the provider name string:

```
open System.Configuration

// get the connection string
let connectionStringDetails =
    ConfigurationManager.ConnectionStrings.["MyConnectionString"]

// print the details
printfn "%s\r\n%s"
    connectionStringDetails.ConnectionString
    connectionStringDetails.ProviderName
```

Executing this code gives you the following results:

```
Data S
ource=server;
Initial Catalog=pubs;
Integrated Security=SSPI;
System.Data.SqlClient
```

■ **Caution**   Notice that I added spaces and newline characters to the configuration file to improve the formatting. This meant that I also had to add them to the connection string, which you can see when output to the console. Most libraries consuming the connection string will correct for this, but some might not, so be careful when formatting your configuration file.

It's also possible to load configuration files associated with other programs, web applications, and even machine.config, which contains the default settings for .NET on a particular machine. You can query, update, and save these files. The following code shows how to open machine.config and enumerate the various sections within it:

```
open System.Configuration

// open the machine config
let config =
    ConfigurationManager.OpenMachineConfiguration()

// print the names of all sections
for x in config.Sections do
    printfn "%s" x.SectionInformation.Name
```

When I execute this code on my machine, I get the following results:

```
system.data
windows
system.webServer
mscorlib
system.data.oledb
system.data.oracleclient
system.data.sqlclient
configProtectedData
satelliteassemblies
```

```
system.data.dataset

startup

system.data.odbc

system.diagnostics

runtime

system.codedom

system.runtime.remoting

connectionStrings

assemblyBinding

appSettings

system.windows.forms
```

This section showed you how to work with configuration files, a particular kind of XML file. A later section, "The System.Xml Namespace," will show you how to use the System.Xml namespace to work with any kind of XML file. In the next section, you'll take a general look at accessing files using the System.IO namespace.

The System.IO Namespace

The main purpose of the System.IO namespace is to provide types that give easy access to the files and directories of the operating system's file store, although it also provides ways of writing to memory and network streams.

The namespace offers two main ways to deal with files and directories. You can use FileInfo and DirectoryInfo objects to get or alter information about a file or directory. You can also find File and Directory classes that offer the same functionality, but which are exposed as static members that require the filename to be passed to each method. Generally, you use the File and Directory classes if you want a single piece of information about a file system object, and you use the FileInfo and DirectoryInfo classes if you need lots of information about a single file system object. The two techniques are complementary; for example, you might use the Directory type to get information about all of the files in a directory, and then use the FileInfo object to find out the name and other information about the file. Here's an example of how to do this:

```
open System.IO

// list all the files in the root of C: drive
let files = Directory.GetFiles(@"c:\")

// write out various information about the file
for filepath in files do
    let file = new FileInfo(filepath)
    printfn "%s\t%d\t%O"
        file.Name
        file.Length
        file.CreationTime
```

When I execute the preceding code on my machine, I get the following results:

.rnd	1024	07/03/2015 14:02:23
autoexec.bat	24	02/11/2014 11:23:09
bootmgr	333203	21/01/2014 09:36:26
BOOTSECT.BAK	8192	21/01/2014 09:36:28
config.sys	10	02/11/2014 07:25:08
hiberfil.sys	2143363072	06/09/2015 06:49:56
ImageUploader4.ocx	2663944	13/11/2014 17:42:08
IO.SYS	0	22/12/2014 14:44:31
MSDOS.SYS	0	22/12/2014 14:44:31
pagefile.sys	2459238400	18/12/2014 07:21:04
trace.ini	11	22/12/2015 14:41:28

The namespace also provides an extremely convenient way to work with the contents of files. For example, opening a file and reading text from it could not be simpler—just call the `File.ReadAllLines` method, and you return an array that contains all the lines in a file. The following example demonstrates how to read a comma-separated file that contains three columns of data:

```
open System.IO
//test.csv:
//Apples,12,25
//Oranges,12,25
//Bananas,12,25

// open a test file and print the contents
let readFile() =
    let lines = File.ReadAllLines("test.csv")
    let printLine (line: string) =
        let items = line.Split([|',','|])
        printfn "%O %O %O"
            items.[0]
            items.[1]
            items.[2]
    Seq.iter printLine lines

do readFile()
```

When you execute this code with the text file in the comments, you get the following results:

Apples	12	25
Oranges	12	25
Bananas	12	25

■ **Note** The File.ReadAllLines method assumes your file has a UTF-8 encoding. If your file does not use this text encoding, you can use another overload of the method that allows you to pass in the appropriate encoding object. For example, if your file uses the encoding Windows-1252 for Western languages, you should open it using this line of code: File.ReadAllLines("accents.txt", Encoding.GetEncoding(1252)).

Using Sequences with System.IO

One interesting aspect of F# is its ability to generate lazy sequences (you learned about this originally in Chapter 3). You can use lazy sequences when working with large files to avoid the overhead of allocating all the memory for the file up front. This can potentially allow you to work with files that would otherwise be too large to fit into memory.

Generating a sequence is straightforward. You simply read the file using File.ReadLines() instead of File.ReadAllLines().

Let's look at a quick test that demonstrates how this improves memory performance, by measuring the memory consumed using performance counters. Performance counters are the standard way to measure and tune a program's performance in Windows. Windows includes a tool called Performance Monitor (perfmon.exe) that allows you to view performance counter values, or you can access their values in code using a class in the .NET Framework, as you'll learn how to do in this test.

Begin by creating a Console program and adding the following code to its source file. Change the line containing a ReadAllLines call to use the path of a large text file. You can download interesting text files from Project Gutenberg (www.gutenberg.org). See how the code measures the memory performance of the File.ReadAllLines method, as demonstrated in the previous section. To do this, you use PerformanceCounter class to create an instance of the Process, Private Bytes counter, like so:

■ **Note** It's important that you create the counter before the test because creating it afterwards could cause a garbage collection that would destroy your test results.

```
open System
open System.IO
open System.Diagnostics

let wordCount() =
    // Get the "Private Bytes" performance counter
    let proc = Process.GetCurrentProcess()
    let counter = new PerformanceCounter("Process",
                                         "Private Bytes",
                                         proc.ProcessName)
    // Read the file
    let lines = File.ReadAllLines(@"C:\Data\Gutenberg\TomJones\TomJones.txt")
    // Do a very naive unique-word count (to prove we get
    // the same results whichever way we access the file)
    let wordCount =
        lines
        |> Seq.map (fun line -> line.Split([|' '|]))
        |> Seq.concat
```

```
    |> Seq.distinct
    |> Seq.length
  printfn "Private bytes: %f" (counter.NextValue())
  printfn "Word count: %i" wordCount

[<EntryPoint>]
let main argv =
  wordCount ()
  Console.ReadKey() |> ignore
  0
```

The following results are from a test I ran using a file that is about 1.9MB (I compiled the program in Release mode):

```
Private bytes: 37158910.000000

Word count: 27768
```

Now change the program so that it uses `File.ReadLines` instead `File.ReadAllLines` and run it again.

```
Private bytes: 29212670.000000

Word count: 27768
```

The version where you use `File.ReadAllLines` takes about 8MB more space than the version that uses a sequence via `File.ReadLines`. In fact, the sequence version hardly uses any additional memory because an empty .NET program, containing just the counter, takes about 26MB of memory.

So it's fine (and very convenient) for you to use `File.ReadAllLines` when you know that the contents of the file will be reasonably small or that memory performance is not an issue. However, using F#'s sequences to lazy load a file line by line will give great memory performance in situations where you need it.

■ **Note**   Measuring memory consumption is a complex topic, but often just measuring the `Process, Private Byte` counter is enough to give you a good indication of your current memory consumption.

The System.Xml Namespace

XML has become a popular data format for a number of reasons, probably because it gives most people a convenient format to represent their data and because the resulting files tend to be reasonably human readable. Programmers tend to like that you can have files be unstructured, which means your data doesn't follow a set pattern; or you can have the files be structured, which means you can have the data conform to a contract defined by an XSD schema. Programmers also like the convenience of being able to query the data using XPath, which means that writing custom parsers for new data formats is rarely necessary, and files can quickly be converted between different XML formats using the powerful XSLT language to transform data.

■ **Note**   You can also access XML data using a *type provider*. See Chapter 13 for information on type providers.

The System.Xml namespace contains classes for working with XML files using all the different technologies I have described and more. You'll look at the most common way to work with XML files—the .NET implementation of the W3C recommendation for the XML Document Object Model (DOM), which is generally represented by the class XmlDocument. The first example in this section reads information from the following short XML file, fruits.xml:

```
<fruits>
  <apples>2</apples>
  <oranges>3</oranges>
  <bananas>1</bananas>
</fruits>
```

The following code loads fruits.xml, binds it to the identifier fruitsDoc, and then uses a loop to display the data:

```
open System.Xml

// create an xml dom object
let fruitsDoc =
    let temp = new XmlDocument()
    temp.Load("fruits.xml")
    temp

// select a list of nodes from the xml dom
let fruits = fruitsDoc.SelectNodes("/fruits/*")

// print out the name and text from each node
for x in fruits do
    printfn "%s = %s " x.Name x.InnerText
```

Executing this code produces the following results:

```
apples = 2

oranges = 3

bananas = 1
```

The next example looks at how to build up an XML document and then write it to disk. Assume you have a set of data, bound to the identifier animals, and you'd like to write it as XML to the file animals.xml. You start by creating a new XmlDocument object, and then you build the document by creating the root node via a call to XmlDocument.CreateElement, and appending to the document object using its AppendChild method. You build up the rest of the document by enumerating over the animals list and creating and appending nodes.

```
open System.Xml

let animals =
    [
        "ants", 6
```

```
        "spiders", 8
        "cats", 4
    ]

// create an xml dom object
let animalsDoc = new XmlDocument()

// create the root element and append it to the doc
let rootNode = animalsDoc.CreateElement("animals")
animalsDoc.AppendChild(rootNode) |> ignore

// add each animal to the document
for animal in animals do
    let name, legs = animal
    let animalElement = animalsDoc.CreateElement(name)
    // set the leg-count as the inner text of the element
    animalElement.InnerText <- legs.ToString()
    rootNode.AppendChild(animalElement) |> ignore

// save the document
animalsDoc.Save(@"c:\temp\animals.xml")
```

Running this code creates a file, animals.xml, that contains the following XML document:

```
<animals>

  <ants>6</ants>

  <spiders>8</spiders>

  <cats>4</cats>

</animals>
```

The System.Xml namespace is large, and it includes many interesting classes to help you work with XML data. Table 8-1 describes some of the most useful classes.

Table 8-1. *Summary of Useful Classes from the System.XML Namespace*

Class	Description
System.Xml.XmlDocument	This class is the Microsoft .NET implementation of the W3C's XML DOM.
System.Xml.XmlNode	This class can't be created directly, but it's often used; it is the result of the XmlDocument's SelectSingle node method.
System.Xml.XmlNodeList	This class is a collection of nodes; it's the result of the XmlDocument's SelectNode method.
System.Xml.XmlTextReader	This provides forward-only, read-only access to an XML document. It isn't as easy to use as the XmlDocument class, but it doesn't require the whole document to be loaded into memory. When working with big documents, you can often use this class to provide better performance than the XmlDocument.
System.Xml.XmlTextWriter	This class provides a forward-only way to write to an XML document. If you must start your XML document from scratch, this is often the easiest way to create it.
System.Xml.Schema.XmlSchema	This class provides a way of loading an XML schema into memory and then allows the user to validate XML documents with it.
System.Xml.Serialization. XmlSerializer	This class allows a user to serialize .NET objects directly to and from XML. However, unlike the BinarySerializer available elsewhere in the framework, this class serializes only public fields.
System.Xml.XPath.XPathDocument	This class is the most efficient way to work with XPath expressions. Note that this class is only the wrapper for the XML document; the programmer must use XPathExpression and XPathNavigator to do the work.
System.Xml.XPath.XPathExpression	This class represents an XPath expression to be used with an XPathDocument; it can be compiled to make it more efficient when used repeatedly.
System.Xml.XPath.XPathNavigator	Once an XPathExpression has been executed against the XPathDocument, this class can be used to navigate the results; the advantage of this class is that it pulls only one node at a time into memory, making it efficient in terms of memory.
System.Xml.Xsl.XslTransform	This class can be used to transform XML using XSLT style sheets.

ADO.NET

Relational database management systems (RDBMSs) are the most pervasive form of data storage. ADO.
NET—and its System.Data and associated namespaces—make it easy to access relational data. In this
section, you'll look at various ways you can use F# with ADO.NET. As with XML, an alternative to the
techniques detailed in this section is to access a relational database using a type provider, which is covered
in Chapter 13.

■ **Note**   All database providers use a connection string to specify the database to connect to. You can find a nice summary of the connection strings you need to know at www.connectionstrings.com.

All examples in this section use the AdventureWorks sample database and SQL Server 2014 Express Edition; you can download both for free at www.microsoft.com and http://msftdbprodsamples.codeplex.com/releases/view/125550. It should be easy to port these samples to other relational databases. To use this database with SQL Server 2014 Express Edition, you can use the following connection settings (or an adaptation of them appropriate to your system):

```
<connectionStrings>
  <add
      name="MyConnection"
      connectionString="
            Data Source=.\SQLEXPRESS;
            Initial Catalog=AdventureWorks2014;
            Integrated Security=True"
      providerName="System.Data.SqlClient"/>
</connectionStrings>
```

I'll discuss options for accessing other relational databases in the "ADO.NET Extensions" section. The following example shows a simple way of accessing a database. This example is best created and run as a Console project due to the complications of accessing .config files from F# Interactive. You will also need to add references to System.Data and System.Configuration.

```
open System.Configuration
open System.Data
open System.Data.SqlClient

// get the connection string
let connectionString =
    let connectionSetting =
        ConfigurationManager.ConnectionStrings.["MyConnection"]
    connectionSetting.ConnectionString

[<EntryPoint>]
let main argv =
    // create a connection
    use connection = new SqlConnection(connectionString)

    // create a command
    let command =
        connection.CreateCommand(CommandText = "select * from Person.Contact", CommandType =
        CommandType.Text)

    // open the connection
    connection.Open()

    // open a reader to read data from the DB
    use reader = command.ExecuteReader()
```

```
// fetch the column-indexes of the required columns
let title = reader.GetOrdinal("Title")
let firstName = reader.GetOrdinal("FirstName")
let lastName = reader.GetOrdinal("LastName")

// function to read strings from the data reader
let getString (r: #IDataReader) x =
    if r.IsDBNull(x) then ""
    else r.GetString(x)

// read all the items
while reader.Read() do
    printfn "%s %s %s"
        (getString reader title )
        (getString reader firstName)
        (getString reader lastName)
0
```

Executing the preceding code produces the following results:

```
Mr. Gustavo Achong

Ms. Catherine Abel

Ms. Kim Abercrombie

Sr. Humberto Acevedo

Sra. Pilar Ackerman

Ms. Frances Adams

Ms. Margaret Smith

Ms. Carla Adams

Mr. Jay Adams

Mr. Ronald Adina

Mr. Samuel Agcaoili

Mr. James Aguilar

Mr. Robert Ahlering

Mr. François Ferrier

Ms. Kim Akers

...
```

In this example, you begin by finding the connection string you will use; after this, you create the connection:

```
use connection = new SqlConnection(connectionString)
```

Notice how you use the use keyword instead of let to ensure it is closed after you finish what you're doing. The use keyword ensures that the connection's Dispose method is called when it goes out of scope. You use the connection to create a SqlCommand class, and you use its CommandText property to specify which command you want to execute:

```
let command =
    connection.CreateCommand(CommandText = "select * from Person.Contact",
    CommandType = CommandType.Text)
```

Next, you execute the command to create a SqlDataReader class; you use this class to read from the database:

```
use reader = command.ExecuteReader()
```

This too is bound with the use keyword, instead of let, to ensure it is closed promptly.

The # symbol in the #IDataReader parameter of the getString() function indicates a "flexible type." This means that that the function can take any input value that can be cast into an IDataReader.

You probably wouldn't write data access code in F# if you had to write this amount of code for every query. One way to simplify things is to create a library function to execute commands for you. Doing this allows you to parameterize which command to run and which connection to use.

The following example shows you how to write such a function:

```
open System.Configuration
open System.Collections.Generic
open System.Data
open System.Data.SqlClient
open System

/// create and open an SqlConnection object using the connection string
/// found in the configuration file for the given connection name
let openSQLConnection (connName:string) =
    let connSetting = ConfigurationManager.ConnectionStrings.[connName]
    let conn = new SqlConnection(connSetting.ConnectionString)
    conn.Open()
    conn

/// create and execute a read command for a connection using
/// the connection string found in the configuration file
/// for the given connection name
let openConnectionReader connName cmdString =
    let conn = openSQLConnection(connName)
    let cmd = conn.CreateCommand(CommandText=cmdString,
                                 CommandType = CommandType.Text)
    let reader = cmd.ExecuteReader(CommandBehavior.CloseConnection)
    reader
```

```
/// read a row from the data reader
let readOneRow (reader: SqlDataReader) =
    if reader.Read() then
        let dict = new Dictionary<string, obj>()
        for x in [ 0 .. (reader.FieldCount - 1) ] do
            dict.Add(reader.GetName(x), reader.[x])
        Some(dict)
    else
        None

/// execute a query using a recursive list comprehension
let execQuery (connName: string) (cmdString: string) =
    use reader = openConnectionReader connName cmdString
    let rec read() =
        [
            let row = readOneRow reader
            match row with
            | Some r ->
                yield r
                // call same function recursively and add
                // all the elements returned, one-by-one
                // to the list
                yield! read()
            | None -> ()
        ]
    read()

let printRows() =
    /// open the people table
    let peopleTable =
        execQuery
            "MyConnection"
            "select top 1000 * from Person.Person"
    /// print out the data retrieved from the database
    for row in peopleTable do
        for col in row.Keys do
            printfn "%s = %O" col (row.Item(col))

[<EntryPoint>]
let main argv =
    printRows()
    Console.ReadKey() |> ignore
    0
```

See how in the execQuery function, you define an inner recursive function named read() which actually does the work. The read() function reads one row, and if a row is returned, yields it into the resulting list. It then calls itself recursively and uses yield! to return all the resulting rows into the final list. The yield! keyword takes a collection-in this case, the results of all the "lower" recursive calls-and adds them individually to the final output collection. This is a common pattern-yield at "this" level, then recurse and yield! the results of the recursion. When readOneRow returns None you end the recursion by returning *unit* ('()').

After you define a function such as execQuery, it becomes easy to access a database. You call execQuery, passing it the chosen connection and command, and then enumerate the results, as in the printRows() function:

```
let printRows() =
    /// open the people table
    let peopleTable =
        execQuery
            "MyConnection"
            "select top 1000 * from Person.Person"
    /// print out the data retrieved from the database
    for row in peopleTable do
        for col in row.Keys do
            printfn "%s = %O" col (row.Item(col))
```

Executing this code produces the following results:

```
...

PersonType = EM

NameStyle = False

Title =

FirstName = Patrick

MiddleName = M

LastName = Cook

Suffix =

EmailPromotion = 0

AdditionalContactInfo =

Demographics = <IndividualSurvey xmlns="http://schemas.microsoft.com/sqlserver/2004/07/
adventure-works/IndividualSurvey"><TotalPurchaseYTD>0</TotalPurchaseYTD></
IndividualSurvey>

rowguid = f03e1512-0dc2-4329-8f21-6c5dbb9996f3

ModifiedDate = 05/02/2010 00:00:00

BusinessEntityID = 84

...
```

Here's an important caveat you should keep in mind when dealing with relational databases. You need to ensure that the connection is closed in a timely manner. Closing the connection quickly makes the connection available to other database users, which improves concurrent access. This is why you create the reader using the use keyword, which ensures that the reader and the associated connection are closed and disposed of promptly when they go out of scope:

```
use reader = openConnectionReader connName cmdString
```

This in turn has an important consequence for how you generate the collection of results. Syntactically you could have generated a sequence instead of a list in the read() function. The only change you have to make to do this is to replace the square brackets with seq { ... }.

```
let execQuerySeq (connName: string) (cmdString: string) =
    use reader = openConnectionReader connName cmdString
    // return a sequence instead of a list - this will
    // cause an error at run time!
    let rec read() = seq {
            let row = readOneRow reader
            match row with
            | Some r ->
                yield r
                yield! read()
            | None -> ()
        }
    read()
```

But if you run this version you will get an exception saying that the connection has already been closed. This is because sequences are lazily evaluated, and by the time your code gets around to retrieving the results, the connection has indeed been closed and disposed. Generally, you should prioritize prompt disposal of connections over any wish to generate database results lazily. If your results are potentially so large that lazy evaluation might be beneficial, consider filtering them to the client side by changing the SQL query that you run.

Closing connections promptly is important. Yes, connections will be closed when the cursors are garbage collected, but this process usually takes too long, especially if a system is under stress. For example, if the code you are writing will run in a server application that will handle lots of concurrent users, then not closing connections will cause errors because the server will run out of database connections.

Data Binding

Data binding is the process of mapping a value or set of values to a user interface control. The data does not need to be from a relational database, but it is generally from some system external to the program. The process of accessing this data and transforming it into a state where it can be bound is more complicated than the binding itself, which is straightforward. The next example shows how to bind data from a database table to a combo box. To set up this example, create a new Console project and add references to System. Data, System.Configuration, and System.Windows.Forms. You also need to add the same connection string to App.config as for the previous example. Then add the following code to Program.fs:

```
open System.Configuration
open System.Collections.Generic
open System.Data
open System.Data.SqlClient
open System.Windows.Forms

/// create and open an SqlConnection object using the connection string
/// found in the configuration file for the given connection name
let openSQLConnection (connName:string) =
```

```fsharp
    let connSetting = ConfigurationManager.ConnectionStrings.[connName]
    let conn = new SqlConnection(connSetting.ConnectionString)
    conn.Open()
    conn

/// create and execute a read command for a connection using
/// the connection string found in the configuration file
/// for the given connection name
let openConnectionReader connName cmdString =
    let conn = openSQLConnection(connName)
    let cmd = conn.CreateCommand(CommandText=cmdString,
                                    CommandType = CommandType.Text)
    let reader = cmd.ExecuteReader(CommandBehavior.CloseConnection)
    reader

/// read a row from the data reader
let readOneRow (reader: SqlDataReader) =
    if reader.Read() then
        let dict = new Dictionary<string, obj>()
        for x in [ 0 .. (reader.FieldCount - 1) ] do
            dict.Add(reader.GetName(x), reader.[x])
        Some(dict)
    else
        None

/// execute a query using a recursive list comprehension
let execQuery (connName: string) (cmdString: string) =
    use reader = openConnectionReader connName cmdString
    let rec read() =
        [
            let row = readOneRow reader
            match row with
            | Some r ->
                yield r
                yield! read()
            | None -> ()
        ]
    read()

// get the contents of the person table
let peopleTable =
    execQuery "MyConnection"
        "select top 10 * from Person.Person"

// create an array of first and last names
let contacts =
    [| for row in peopleTable ->
        Printf.sprintf "%O %O"
            (row.["FirstName"])
            (row.["LastName"]) |]
```

```
// create form containing a ComboBox with results list
let form =
    let frm = new Form()
    let combo = new ComboBox(Top=8, Left=8, DataSource=contacts)
    frm.Controls.Add(combo)
    frm

[<EntryPoint>]
let main argv =
    // show the form
    Application.Run(form)
        0
```

You can see the form that results from running this code in Figure 8-1.

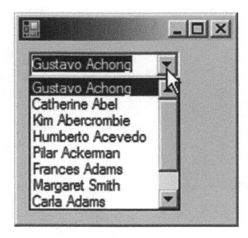

Figure 8-1. *A data-bound combo box*

Let's break the previous example down a bit. You begin by executing the query:

```
let peopleTable =
    execQuery "MyConnection"
        "select top 10 * from Person.Person"
```

Next, you need to turn the resulting IEnumerable collection into something suitable that you can bind to the combo box. You do this by yielding a string containing appropriate values from the peopleTable row collection, inside an array comprehension:

```
let contacts =
    [| for row in peopleTable ->
        Printf.sprintf "%O %O"
            (row.["FirstName"])
            (row.["LastName"]) |]
```

Then you must bind the resulting string array to the control that will display it; you do this by setting the control's DataSource property, which is the last named argument here:

```
let combo = new ComboBox(Top=8, Left=8, DataSource=contacts)
```

The examples in this chapter cover only the ComboBox class, but most Windows and web controls can be data bound in a similar way. These include the ListBox and CheckListBox classes. Next, you'll look at binding data to a more complicated control, the DataGridView class.

Data Binding and the DataGridView Control

Unlike the controls you saw in the previous section, the DataGridView control can display more than one column; however, you must format the data in such a way that the data grid knows which columns to display. You can achieve this in two ways. First, you can bind the DataGridView to a DataTable. Second, you can bind the grid to a list of objects that have properties; the various properties will become the grid's columns.

Binding to a DataSet is the simpler solution, as in the next example. As before, you need to paste this code into a console project; add references to System.Data, System.Configuration, and System.Windows. Forms; and add a connection string to App.config:

```
open System
open System.Collections.Generic
open System.Configuration
open System.Data
open System.Data.SqlClient
open System.Windows.Forms

// creates a connections then executes the given command on it
let createDataSet commandString =
    // read the connection string
    let connectionSetting =
        ConfigurationManager.ConnectionStrings.["MyConnection"]

    // create a data adapter to fill the dataset
    let adapter = new SqlDataAdapter(commandString, connectionSetting.ConnectionString)

    // create a new data set and fill it
    let ds = new DataSet()
    adapter.Fill(ds) |> ignore
    ds

// create the data set that will be bound to the form
let dataSet = createDataSet "select top 10 * from Person.Person"

// create a form containing a data bound data grid view
let form =
    let frm = new Form()
    let grid = new DataGridView(Dock = DockStyle.Fill)
    frm.Controls.Add(grid)
    grid.DataSource <- dataSet.Tables.[0]
    frm
```

```
[<EntryPoint>]
let main args =
  // show the form
  Application.Run(form)
  0
```

You can see the results of running this code in Figure 8-2.

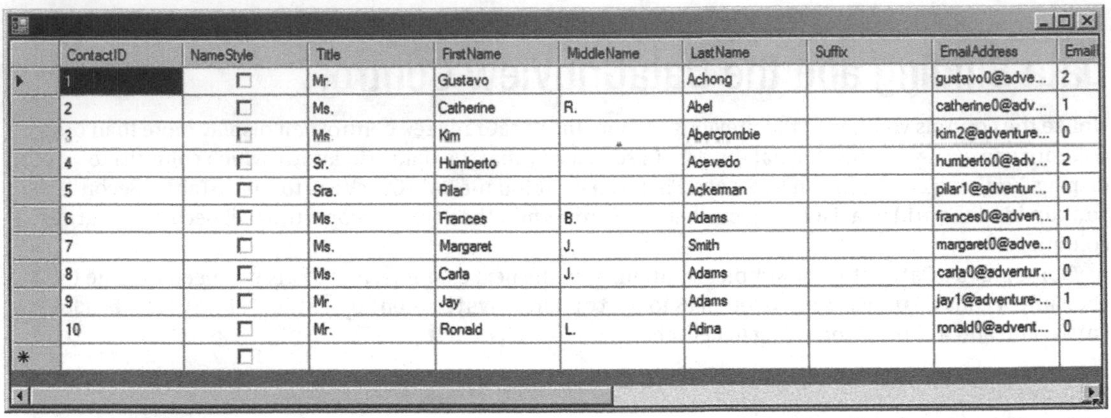

ContactID	NameStyle	Title	FirstName	MiddleName	LastName	Suffix	EmailAddress	Email
1	☐	Mr.	Gustavo		Achong		gustavo0@adve...	2
2	☐	Ms.	Catherine	R.	Abel		catherine0@adv...	1
3	☐	Ms.	Kim		Abercrombie		kim2@adventure...	0
4	☐	Sr.	Humberto		Acevedo		humberto0@adv...	2
5	☐	Sra.	Pilar		Ackerman		pilar1@adventur...	0
6	☐	Ms.	Frances	B.	Adams		frances0@adven...	1
7	☐	Ms.	Margaret	J.	Smith		margaret0@adve...	0
8	☐	Ms.	Carla	J.	Adams		carla0@adventur...	0
9	☐	Mr.	Jay		Adams		jay1@adventure-...	1
10	☐	Mr.	Ronald	L.	Adina		ronald0@advent...	0
*	☐							

Figure 8-2. *A data-bound data grid*

Using Dapper to Access Relational Data

What if you want to work in a more strongly-typed way–in other words, to have query arguments populated from native F# types, and query results returned to you also as native F# types? A great solution to this requirement is the open source package named *Dapper*. Dapper is a super-lightweight *object relational mapper* (ORM) that allows C# and F# programs to interact with SQL databases in exactly this strongly typed way.

To try out Dapper, create a console program and, as before, add references to System.Data, System. Windows.Forms, and System.Configuration. Now use NuGet (or the package manager of your choice) to install the package "Dapper." Next, add the following code to Program.fs, replacing its existing contents:

```
open System.Configuration
open System.Data.SqlClient
open System.Windows.Forms
open Dapper

// a record containing some of the Person fields
type Contact =
  {
    FirstName : string
    LastName : string
    Title : string
    PhoneNumber : string
  }
```

```fsharp
// a record for any arguments we want to send to the query
type GetContactsArgs =
    {
        LastNamePattern : string
    }

// the SQL we want to run
let sql =
    """
    SELECT
            P.FirstName,
            P.LastName,
            P.Title,
            PP.PhoneNumber
    FROM
            Person.Person P
    JOIN
            Person.PersonPhone PP
    ON
            P.BusinessEntityID = PP.BusinessEntityID
    WHERE
        P.LastName LIKE @LastNamePattern
    """

// get all the contacts whose last name matches a search pattern
// and return them as F# Contact records
let getContacts pattern =
    let connString =
        ConfigurationManager
            .ConnectionStrings.["MyConnection"]
            .ConnectionString
    use conn = new SqlConnection(connString)
    conn.Open()
    // use Dapper's Query extension method to run the query, supplying
    // the query argument through the args record and automatically
    // transforming the query results to Contact records
    let args = { LastNamePattern = pattern }
    let contacts = conn.Query<Contact>(sql, args)
    contacts |> Seq.toArray

let form =
    let frm = new Form()
    let grid = new DataGridView(Dock = DockStyle.Fill)
    frm.Controls.Add(grid)
    // get all the contacts with "smi" in the last name
    let contacts = getContacts "%smi%"
    grid.DataSource <- contacts
    frm
```

```
[<EntryPoint>]
let main argv =
    // show the form
    Application.Run(form)
    0
```

To use Dapper, you need to do two more things in addition to the usual plumbing of creating a SQL connection. First, you need a record type to carry any arguments into the query. Here, you declare the record type, which in this case happens to have just one field:

```
type GetContactsArgs =
    {
        LastNamePattern : string
    }
```

And here you create an instance of that record and supply it to the Query method:

```
let args = { LastNamePattern = pattern }
let contacts = conn.Query<Contact>(sql, args)
```

When Dapper runs the query, it will look for fields in the arguments record that match, by name, the @ variables in the query, and populate the query variables with the field values.

The second thing you need to do is define a type for the results, and specify that type as a type parameter in the call to the Query method. Here you define a record for the results:

```
type Contact =
    {
        FirstName : string
        LastName : string
        Title : string
        PhoneNumber : string
    }
```

And here you specify that Dapper should try to map the rows returned by the query into instances of that type:

```
let contacts = conn.Query<Contact>(sql, args)
```

Dapper will try to match query result fields with fields in the specified type by name, and create instances of the type populated with the field values.

Finally, you run the query for a particular last name pattern, and bind the resulting array to the data grid:

```
let contacts = getContacts "%smi%"
grid.DataSource <- contacts
```

ADO.NET Extensions

ADO.NET has been successful at providing a set of bases classes and interfaces that others have used to provide access to their relational database of choice. The result: you can access most relational databases from F# with little effort. You have already seen most of these classes (or at least classes that implement the functionality they are intended to provide). Table 8-2 summarizes the key classes.

Table 8-2. *The Key Classes in ADO.NET*

Class	Description
System.Data.Common.DbConnection	This class represents a connection to a particular instance of a relational database; you use classes derived from this class to specify which database you want the query to be executed against.
System.Data.Common.DbCommand	Classes derived from this base class can be used to configure what query you want to execute against the database, whether it's an actual SQL query or a stored procedure.
System.Data.Common.DbParameter	This class represents the parameters of a query; typically, parameterized queries promote reuse in the relational database, so they execute more efficiently.
System.Data.Common.DbDataReader	Classes derived from this class allow you to access the results of a query in a linear manner; you use this class for fast access to your results.
System.Data.Common.DbDataAdapter	This class is used to fill a DataSet class with data from a relational database.
System.Data.DataSet	This class provides an in-memory representation of a database that can contain tables and relationships between them; unlike the other class in this table, this class is concrete, and you can use it directly.

With the exception of System.Data.DataSet, the classes in Table 8-2 are abstract classes, so you must use concrete implementations of them. For example, the following code shows you how to create an instance of System.Data.SqlClient.SqlConnection, which is an implementation of System.Data.Common. DbConnection. Doing this gives you access to a SQL Server database.

```
use connection = new SqlConnection(connectionString)
```

If you want to access an Oracle database, you replace the SqlConnection class with the OracleConnection class. Table 8-3 summarizes some of the most popular libraries and namespaces that implement these classes; note that this table is incomplete because the range of providers is quite large.

Table 8-3. *Database Providers for .NET*

Namespace	DLL	Description
System.Data.Odbc	System.Data.dll	This namespace allows you to connect to any database that provides drivers that support the Open Database Connectivity standard. Most databases provide drivers that support this standard, but typically you should avoid using them in favor of a more specific driver, which will probably be more efficient.
System.Data.OleDb	System.Data.dll	OleDb is a COM-based standard for database drivers; again, a huge number of relational databases provide drivers that support this standard, but where possible, you should use something more specific. This namespace is often used to connect to Access databases or Excel spreadsheets, which do not have .NET drivers of their own.
System.Data. SqlClient	System.Data.dll	This is the native .NET Microsoft SQL Server driver. It will work with all supported versions of SQL Server, and it is the *de facto* choice when working with SQL Server. The examples in this book use this namespace.
System.Data. OracleClient	System.Data. OracleClient.dll	This is the native .NET provider for the Oracle database created by Microsoft; it is distributed with the .NET Framework.
IBM.Data.DB2	IBM.Data.DB2.dll	This is the native .NET provider developed by IBM; it is provided with the distribution of the database.
MySql.Data. MySqlClient	MySql.Data.dll	This is the open source native .NET provider created by the MySQL team. You can download it from dev.mysql.com/downloads/connector/net.
FirebirdSql.Data. FirebirdClient	FirebirdSql.Data. FirebirdClient.dll	This is the native provider for the open source database Firebird; you can download it from www.firebirdsql.org/index.php?op=files&id=netprovider.

Introducing LINQ

Language-Integrated Query (LINQ) is another useful.NET data access technology. It borrows heavily from functional programming, so it fits nicely with F#.

At its heart, LINQ is a set of libraries for manipulating collections that implement the IEnumerable<T> interface; in this respect, it is a lot like F#'s Seq module, which you learned about in Chapter 7. The idea is that you can use this library to query any in-memory collection, whether the data comes from a database, an XML file, or objects returned from another API.

Although the concepts implemented in the LINQ library will be familiar to you by now, they follow a slightly different naming convention, based on SQL. For instance, the equivalent of Seq.map is called Enumerable.Select, and the equivalent Seq.filter is called Enumerable.Where. The following example shows how to use this library. The first step is to import the methods exposed by the LINQ library into a more usable form:

```
module Strangelights.LinqImports
open System
open System.Linq
open System.Reflection

// define easier access to LINQ methods
let select f s = Enumerable.Select(s, new Func<_,_>(f))
let where f s = Enumerable.Where(s, new Func<_,_>(f))
let groupBy f s = Enumerable.GroupBy(s, new Func<_,_>(f))
let orderBy f s = Enumerable.OrderBy(s, new Func<_,_>(f))
let count s = Enumerable.Count(s)
```

Once you import these functions, you can apply them easily, typically by using the pipe-forward operator. The following example demonstrates how to do this. It uses the LINQ library to query the string class and group the overloads of its nonstatic methods together:

```
open System
open Strangelights.LinqImports

// query string methods using functions
let namesByFunction =
    (typeof<string>).GetMethods()
    |> where (fun m -> not m.IsStatic)
    |> groupBy (fun m -> m.Name)
    |> select (fun m -> m.Key, count m)
    |> orderBy (fun (_, m) -> m)

// print out the data we've retrieved from about the string class
namesByFunction
|> Seq.iter (fun (name, count) -> printfn "%s - %i" name count)
```

Executing this code produces the following results:

```
ToLowerInvariant - 1

get_Chars - 1

CopyTo - 1

GetHashCode - 1

get_Length - 1

TrimStart - 1

TrimEnd - 1

Contains - 1
```

```
ToLowerInvariant - 1
ToUpperInvariant - 1
Clone - 1
Insert - 1
GetTypeCode - 1
GetEnumerator - 1
GetType - 1
ToCharArray - 2
Substring - 2
Trim - 2
IsNormalized - 2
Normalize - 2
CompareTo - 2
PadLeft - 2
PadRight - 2
ToLower - 2
ToUpper - 2
ToString - 2
Replace - 2
Remove - 2
Equals - 3
EndsWith - 3
IndexOfAny - 3
LastIndexOfAny - 3
StartsWith - 3
Split - 6
IndexOf - 9
LastIndexOf - 9
```

Using LINQ to XML

The goal of LINQ to XML is to provide an XML object model that works well with LINQ's functional style of programming. Table 8-4 summarizes the important classes within this namespace.

Table 8-4. *A Summary of the Classes Provided by LINQ to XML*

Class Name	Parent Class	Description
XNode		This class provides the basic functionality that applies to all nodes in an XML document.
XContainer	XNode	This class provides the functionality for XML nodes that can contain other nodes.
XDocument	XContainer	This class represents the XML document as a whole.
XElement	XContainer	This class represents an element in the XML document; that is, it represents a regular XML node that can be a tag (such as <myTag />) or can contain other tags or an attribute, such as myAttribute="myVal".
XDocumentType	XNode	This class represents a document type tag.
XProcessInstruction	XNode	This class represents a processing instruction, which is a tag of the form <? name instruction ?>.
XText	XNode	This class represents text contained within the XML document.
XName		This class represents the name of a tag or an attribute.

You can see this object model in action by revising the example from the previous section to output XML instead of plain text. LINQ to XML makes this easy to do; begin by adding references to System.Xml and System.Xml.Linq, and opening the System.Xml.Linq namespace. Then modify the select statement to return an XElement instead of a tuple:

```
|> select (fun m -> new XElement(XName.Get(m.Key), count m))
```

This gives you an array of XElements that you can then use to initialize another XElement, which provides the root of the document. At that point, it is a simple matter of calling the root XElement's ToString method, which will provide the XML in the form of a string:

```
open System
open System.Linq
open System.Reflection
open System.Xml.Linq

// define easier access to LINQ methods
let select f s = Enumerable.Select(s, new Func<_,_>(f))
let where f s = Enumerable.Where(s, new Func<_,_>(f))
let groupBy f s = Enumerable.GroupBy(s, new Func<_,_>(f))
let orderBy f s = Enumerable.OrderBy(s, new Func<_,_>(f))
let count s = Enumerable.Count(s)
```

```
// query string methods using functions
let namesByFunction =
    (typeof<string>).GetMethods()
    |> where (fun m -> not m.IsStatic)
    |> groupBy (fun m -> m.Name)
    |> select (fun m -> new XElement(XName.Get(m.Key), count m))
    |> orderBy (fun e -> int e.Value)

// create an xml document with the overloads data
let overloadsXml =
    new XElement(XName.Get("MethodOverloads"), namesByFunction)

// print the xml string
printfn "%s" (overloadsXml.ToString())
```

Compiling and executing this code produces the following results (line breaks added):

```
<MethodOverloads>
(get_Chars, 1)
(CopyTo, 1)
(GetHashCode, 1)
(get_Length, 1)
(TrimStart, 1)
(TrimEnd, 1)
(Contains, 1)
(ToLowerInvariant, 1)
(ToUpperInvariant, 1)
(Clone, 1)
(Insert, 1)
(GetTypeCode, 1)
(GetEnumerator, 1)
(GetType, 1)
(ToCharArray, 2)
(Substring, 2)
(Trim, 2)
(IsNormalized, 2)
(Normalize, 2)
(CompareTo, 2)
(PadLeft, 2)
```

```
(PadRight, 2)
(ToLower, 2)
(ToUpper, 2)
(ToString, 2)
(Replace, 2)
(Remove, 2)
(Equals, 3)
(EndsWith, 3)
(IndexOfAny, 3)
(LastIndexOfAny, 3)
(StartsWith, 3)
(Split, 6)
(IndexOf, 9)
(LastIndexOf, 9)
</MethodOverloads>
```

Summary

This chapter looked at the options for data access in F#. It showed how the combination of F# with .NET libraries is powerful yet straightforward, regardless of data source. The next chapter will walk you through the emerging topic of how to parallelize applications.

CHAPTER 9

■ ■ ■

Parallel Programming

Parallel programming has recently moved from being a relatively obscure topic, practiced only by specialist developers, to a more mainstream endeavor. This is due to the increasing prevalence of multicore processors. At the time of writing, it is almost impossible buy a PC with a single core processor, and machines with four, eight, or more processers are readily available. It is fully expected that this trend will continue in the years to come.

To a certain extent, this interest in parallel programming has driven the renewed interest in functional programming. Functional programming is certainly not a silver bullet for all parallel programming problems, but it can help you design your software so it executes in parallel. In this chapter, you will learn about some of the simpler techniques to help your software execute in parallel, as well as how to take advantage of several processors.

It's often helpful to break down parallel programming into several smaller subtopics, all of which you'll learn about this chapter:

- *Threads, memory, locking, and blocking*: You'll learn about basic techniques for creating and controlling threads in .NET programming. You'll also take a quick look at how to share resources (such as memory) between threads, as well as how to control access to these shared resources.

- *Reactive programming*: It's often important to the user experience that programs remain reactive to input. To do this, it's important that you avoid doing too much processing on the thread responsible for reacting to user input. This is particularly relevant to GUI programming, but it can also apply to a server that needs to stay responsive to incoming requests.

- *Data parallelism*: This term refers to executing one piece of code concurrently on several processors with varying input data. This is a good way to parallelize the processing of large data structures such as collections. It's often possible to apply a transformation to several items in a collection in parallel, which will generally speed up the overall execution time. The classic example of this is the parallel map, which provides one of the simplest ways to parallelize a functional program.

- *Asynchronous programming*: Some tasks, particularly I/O, need to happen asynchronously to make program execution efficient. It is important that threads are not blocked for long periods while I/O takes place.

- *Message passing*: This technique is more formally referred to as the actor model. You use it to coordinate tasks that execute in parallel. This is the most advanced parallel-programming topic covered in this chapter.

Parallel programming is a large topic, so this chapter won't be exhaustive, but it will provide some straightforward ways to help you get started with parallel programming in F#.

© Robert Pickering and Kit Eason 2016
R. Pickering and K. Eason, *Beginning F# 4.0*, DOI 10.1007/978-1-4842-1374-2_9

Threads, Memory, Locking, and Blocking

If you are serious about parallel programming, it's worth investing time to understand threads and memory. In this section, you'll take a look at explicitly creating threads and how to control their access to shared resources, such as memory. My advice is to avoid explicitly creating and managing threads like this; however, when using the other parallel programming techniques, it's useful to understand the underlying threading concepts.

When a program is executed, the operating system creates a *process* to execute it. The process represents the resources that are allocated to the program, most notably the memory allocated to it. A process has one or more *threads* that are responsible for executing the program's instructions and share the process memory. In .NET, a program starts with one thread to execute the program's code. To create an extra thread in F#, you use the System.Threading.Thread class. The Thread class's constructor takes a delegate that represents the function the thread will start executing. Once a Thread class has been constructed, it does not start executing automatically: you must call its Start method. The following example demonstrates how to create and start a new thread:

```
open System.Threading

let main() =
    // create a new thread passing it a lambda function
    let thread = new Thread(fun () ->
        // print a message on the newly created thread
        printfn "Created thread: %i" Thread.CurrentThread.ManagedThreadId)
    // start the new thread
    thread.Start()
    // print an message on the original thread
    printfn "Orginal thread: %i" Thread.CurrentThread.ManagedThreadId
    // wait for the created thread to exit
    thread.Join()

do main()
```

Compiling and executing the preceding program will output results similar to this:

```
Orginal thread: 1
Created thread: 3
```

You should look at a couple of important things in this example. First, notice that the original thread prints its message before the second thread does. This is because calling a thread's Start method does not immediately start the thread; rather, it schedules a new thread for execution and the operating system chooses when to start it. Normally, the delay will be short, but as the original thread will continue to execute, it's probable that the original thread will execute a few instructions before the new thread starts executing. Second, notice how you use the thread's Join function to wait for it to exit. If you did not do this, it is highly probable that the original thread would finish executing before the second thread had a chance to start. While the original thread is waiting for the create thread to do its work, you say that it is *blocked*. Threads can become blocked for a number of reasons. For example, they might be waiting on a *lock*, or might be waiting for I/O to complete. When a thread becomes blocked, the operating system switches to the next runnable thread; this is called a *context switch*. You'll learn about locking in the next section; in this section, you'll look at blocking I/O operations in asynchronous programming.

Any resource that can be updated by two different threads at the same time is at risk of being corrupted. This is because a thread can context switch at any time, leaving operations that should have been atomic half done. To avoid corruption, you need to use locks. A lock, sometimes referred to as a *monitor*, is a section of code where only one thread can pass through it at a time. In F#, you use the lock function to create and control locking. You do this by locking on an object; the idea is that, as soon as the lock is taken, any thread attempting to enter the section of code will be blocked until the lock is released by the thread that holds it. Code protected in this way is sometimes called a *critical section*. You achieve this by calling System.Threading.Monitor.Enter at the start of the code that you want to protect and System.Threading. Monitor.Exit at the end of that code. You must guarantee that Monitor.Exit is called, or this could lead to threads being locked forever. The lock function is a nice way to ensure that Monitor.Exit is always called if Monitor.Enter has been called. This function takes two parameters: the first is the object you want to lock on, while the second is a function that contains the code you want to protect. This function should take unit as its parameter, and it can return any value.

The following example demonstrates the subtle issues involved in locking. The code to accomplish the lock needs to be quite long, and this example has been deliberately written to exaggerate the problem of context switching. The idea behind this code is this: if two threads run at the same time, both try to write the console. The aim of the sample is to write the string "One ... Two ... Three ... " to the console atomically; that is, one thread should be able to finish writing its message before the next one starts. The example has a function, called makeUnsafeThread, that creates a thread that won't be able to write to the console atomically, and a second thread, makeSafeThread, that writes to the console atomically by using a lock.

```fsharp
open System
open System.Threading

// function to print to the console character by character
// this increases the chance of there being a context switch
// between threads.
let printSlowly (s : string) =
    s.ToCharArray()
    |> Array.iter (printf "%c")
    printfn ""

// create a thread that prints to the console in an unsafe way
let makeUnsafeThread() =
    new Thread(fun () ->
    for x in 1 .. 100 do
        printSlowly "One ... Two ... Three ... ")

// the object that will be used as a lock
let lockObj = new Object()

// create a thread that prints to the console in a safe way
let makeSafeThread() =
    new Thread(fun () ->
        for x in 1 .. 100 do
            // use lock to ensure operation is atomic
            lock lockObj (fun () ->
                printSlowly "One ... Two ... Three ... "))
```

```
// helper function to run the test
let runTest (f: unit -> Thread) message =
    printfn "%s" message
    let t1 = f()
    let t2 = f()
    t1.Start()
    t2.Start()
    t1.Join()
    t2.Join()

// runs the demonstrations
let main() =
    runTest
        makeUnsafeThread
        "Running test without locking ..."
    runTest
        makeSafeThread
        "Running test with locking ..."

do main()
```

The part of the example that uses the lock is repeated next to highlight the important points. You should note a couple of important factors. First, you use the declaration of the lockObj to create the critical section. Second, you embed your use of the lock function in the makeSafeThread function. The most important thing to notice is how, when printing the functions you want to be atomic, you place them inside the function you want to pass to lock.

```
// the object that will be used as a lock
let lockObj = new Object()

// create a thread that prints to the console in a safe way
let makeSafeThread() =
    new Thread(fun () ->
        for x in 1 .. 100 do
            // use lock to ensure operation is atomic
            lock lockObj (fun () ->
                printSlowly "One ... Two ... Three ... "))
```

The results of the first part of the test will vary each time it runs because it depends on when a thread context switches. It might also vary based on the number of processors because multiple threads can run at the same time if a machine has two or more processors, so the messages will be more tightly packed together. On a single-processor machine, the output will be less tightly packed together because printing a message will go wrong only when a content switch takes place. The results of the first part of the sample, run on a dual-processor machine, look like this:

```
Running test without locking ...
...
One ... Two ... Three ...
One One ... Two ... Three ...
One ... Two ... Three ...
...
```

The lock means that the results of the second half of the example will not vary at all, so they will always look like this:

```
Running test with locking ...
One ... Two ... Three ...
One ... Two ... Three ...
One ... Two ... Three ...
...
```

Locking is an important aspect of concurrency. You should lock any resource that you write to and share between threads. A resource is often a variable, but it can also be a file or even the console, as shown in this example. Although locks can provide a solution to concurrency, they also can also create problems of their own because they can create a deadlock. A deadlock occurs when two or more different threads lock resources that the other thread needs and so neither can advance. The simplest solution to concurrency is often to avoid sharing a resource that different threads can write to. In the rest of this chapter you'll look at solutions for creating parallel programs that do not rely on explicitly creating locks.

■ **Note** This book provides an extremely brief introduction to threading. You will need to learn much more about threading if you want to become good at parallel programming. A good place to start is the MSDN section on managed threads: `https://msdn.microsoft.com/en-us/library/3e8s7xdd(v=vs.110).aspx`.

Reactive Programming

Reactive programming refers to the practice of ensuring your programs react to events or input. In this section, you'll concentrate on reactive programming in terms of GUI programming; GUIs should always be reactive. However, other styles of programming also need to take reactive programming into account. For example, programs running on servers often need to stay reactive to input, even as they process other, longer running tasks.

Most GUI libraries use an event loop to handle drawing the GUI and the interactions with the user. This means that one thread takes care of drawing the GUI and raising all the events on it. This thread is referred to as the GUI thread. Another consideration: you should update GUI objects only with the GUI thread; you want to avoid creating situations where other threads can corrupt the state of GUI objects. This means that computations or I/O operations that take a significant amount of time should not take place on the GUI thread. If the GUI thread is involved with a long-running computation, it cannot process interactions from the user, nor can it draw the GUI. This is the number one cause of unresponsive GUIs.

You can see this in action in the following example that creates a GUI that could easily become unreactive because it tries to do too much computation on the GUI thread. This example also illustrates how to ensure your GUI remains reactive by making a few simple changes. You will look primarily at a useful abstraction called the BackgroundWorker class, which you find in the System.ComponentModel namespace. This useful class allows you to run some work, raising a notification event when this work is complete. This is especially useful for GUI programming because the completed notification is raised on the GUI thread. This helps you enforce the rule that GUI objects should only be altered from the thread that created them.

Specifically, the example creates a GUI for calculating the Fibonacci numbers using the simple Fibonacci calculation algorithm you saw in Chapter 7. To simplify your setup, this code is designed so that you can place it all in the same .fs file, do a select-all, and it send to F# Interactive.

```
#if INTERACTIVE
#r "System.Windows.Forms.dll"
#else
module ThreadingDemo
#endif

let fibs =
    (1I,1I) |> Seq.unfold
        (fun (n0, n1) ->
            Some(n0, (n1, n0 + n1)))

let fib n = Seq.item n fibs
```

Creating a simple GUI for this calculation is straightforward; you can do it using WinForms:

```
open System
open System.Windows.Forms

let form =
    let form = new Form()
    // input text box
    let input = new TextBox()
    // button to launch processing
    let button = new Button(Left = input.Right + 10, Text = "Go")
    // label to display the result
    let output = new Label(Top = input.Bottom + 10, Width = form.Width,
                            Height = form.Height - input.Bottom + 10,
                            Anchor = (AnchorStyles.Top
                                        ||| AnchorStyles.Left
                                        ||| AnchorStyles.Right
                                        ||| AnchorStyles.Bottom))

    // do all the work when the button is clicked
    button.Click.Add(fun _ ->
        output.Text <- Printf.sprintf "%A" (fib (Int32.Parse(input.Text))))
    // add the controls
    let dc c = c :> Control
    form.Controls.AddRange([|dc input; dc button; dc output |])
    // return the form
    form

// run the form
#if INTERACTIVE
form.ShowDialog() |> ignore
#else
Application.Run()
#endif
```

Running this example in F# Interactive creates the GUI you see in Figure 9-1.

Figure 9-1. *A GUI for the Fibonacci numbers*

This GUI lets you display the results of your calculation in a reasonable way; unfortunately, your GUI becomes unreactive as soon as the calculation starts to take a long time. You may need to enter inputs of six or even seven digits to see this, depending on the speed of your computer. The following code is responsible for the unresponsiveness:

```
// do all the work when the button is clicked
button.Click.Add(fun _ ->
    output.Text <- Printf.sprintf "%A" (fib (Int32.Parse(input.Text))))
```

This code means that you do all the calculation on the same thread that raised the click event: the GUI thread. The GUI thread is responsible for making the calculations, and it cannot process other events while it performs the calculation.

It's fairly easy to fix this using the background worker:

```
open System
open System.ComponentModel
open System.Windows.Forms

let form =
    let form = new Form()
    // input text box
    let input = new TextBox()
    // button to launch processing
```

203

```
    let button = new Button(Left = input.Right + 10, Text = "Go")
    // label to display the result
    let output = new Label(Top = input.Bottom + 10, Width = form.Width,
                           Height = form.Height - input.Bottom + 10,
                           Anchor = (AnchorStyles.Top
                                          ||| AnchorStyles.Left
                                          ||| AnchorStyles.Right
                                          ||| AnchorStyles.Bottom))

    // create and run a new background worker
    let runWorker() =
        let background = new BackgroundWorker()
        // parse the input to an int
        let input = Int32.Parse(input.Text)
        // add the "work" event handler
        background.DoWork.Add(fun ea ->
            ea.Result <- fib input)
        // add the work completed event handler
        background.RunWorkerCompleted.Add(fun ea ->
            output.Text <- Printf.sprintf "%A" ea.Result)
        // start the worker off
        background.RunWorkerAsync()

    // hook up creating and running the worker to the button
    button.Click.Add(fun _ -> runWorker())
    // add the controls
    let dc c = c :> Control
    form.Controls.AddRange([|dc input; dc button; dc output |])
    // return the form
    form

// run the form
#if INTERACTIVE
form.ShowDialog() |> ignore
#else
Application.Run()
#endif
```

Using the background worker imposes few changes on the code. You do need to split what the code does between the DoWork and the RunWorkerCompleted events, and this means you need to write slightly more code, but this will never require more than a few extra lines. Let's step though the required code changes. Begin by creating a new instance of the background worker class:

```
let background = new BackgroundWorker()
```

You place the code that you need to happen in the background on a different thread—in the DoWork event. You also need to be careful that you extract any data you need from controls outside of the DoWork event. Because this code happens on a different thread, letting that code interact with the GUI objects would break the rule that they should only be manipulated by the GUI thread. You can see the code you use to read the integer and wire up the DoWork event here:

```
// parse the input to an int
let input = Int32.Parse(input.Text)
// add the "work" event handler
background.DoWork.Add(fun ea ->
    ea.Result <- fib input)
```

In this example, you extract the input integer from the text box and parse it just before adding the event handler to the DoWork event. Next, the lambda function you added to the DoWork event captures the resulting integer. You should place the result that interests you in the DoWork event's Result property of the event argument. You can then recover the value in this property in the RunWorkerCompleted event. It too has a result property, which you can see in the following code:

```
// add the work completed event handler
background.RunWorkerCompleted.Add(fun ea ->
    output.Text <- Printf.sprintf "%A" ea.Result)
```

You can be certain that the RunWorkerCompleted event runs on the GUI thread, so it is fine to interact with GUI objects. You've wired up the events, but you have a couple of tasks remaining. First, you need to start the background worker:

```
// start the worker off
background.RunWorkerAsync()
```

Second, you need to add all of this code to the button's Click event. You've wrapped the preceding code in a function called runWorker(), so it's a simple matter of calling this code in the event handler:

```
// hook up creating and running the worker to the button
button.Click.Add(fun _ -> runWorker())
```

Notice how this means you create a new background worker each time the button is clicked. This happens because a background worker cannot be reused once it's in use.

Now the GUI remains reactive no matter how many times someone clicks the Go button. This does lead to some other problems; for example, it's fairly easy to set off two calculations that will take some time to complete. If this happens, the results of both are placed in the same result label, so the user might have no idea which one finished first and is being displayed at the time she sees it. Your GUI remains reactive, but it's not well adapted to this multithreaded style of programming. One option is to disable all of the controls while the calculation takes place. This might be appropriate for a few case, but it's not a great option overall because it means the user can take little advantage of your reactive GUI. A better option is to create a system capable of displaying multiple results, along with their initial parameters to ensure that the user knows what a given result means. This example uses a data grid view to display the results:

```
open System
open System.ComponentModel
open System.Windows.Forms
open System.Numerics

// define a type to hold the results
type Result =
    { Input: int;
      Fibonacci: BigInteger; }
```

```fsharp
let form =
    let form = new Form()
    // input text box
    let input = new TextBox()
    // button to launch processing
    let button = new Button(Left = input.Right + 10, Text = "Go")
    // list to hold the results
    let results = new BindingList<Result>()
    // data grid view to display multiple results
    let output = new DataGridView(Top = input.Bottom + 10, Width = form.Width,
                                  Height = form.Height - input.Bottom + 10,
                                  Anchor = (AnchorStyles.Top
                                            ||| AnchorStyles.Left
                                            ||| AnchorStyles.Right
                                            ||| AnchorStyles.Bottom),
                                  DataSource = results)

    // create and run a new background worker
    let runWorker() =
        let background = new BackgroundWorker()
        // parse the input to an int
        let input = Int32.Parse(input.Text)
        // add the "work" event handler
        background.DoWork.Add(fun ea ->
            ea.Result <- (input, fib input))
        // add the work completed event handler
        background.RunWorkerCompleted.Add(fun ea ->
            let input, result = ea.Result :?> (int * BigInteger)
            results.Add({ Input = input; Fibonacci = result; }))
        // start the worker off
        background.RunWorkerAsync()

    // hook up creating and running the worker to the button
    button.Click.Add(fun _ -> runWorker())
    // add the controls
    let dc c = c :> Control
    form.Controls.AddRange([|dc input; dc button; dc output |])
    // return the form
    form

// run the form
#if INTERACTIVE
form.ShowDialog() |> ignore
#else
Application.Run()
#endif
```

You can see this new GUI in Figure 9-2.

Figure 9-2. *A GUI that is better adapted to multi-threaded programming*

Data Parallelism

Data parallelism relies on executing a single function in parallel with varying data inputs. This breaks work into discrete units so it can be processed in parallel, on separate threads, ensuring that work can be partitioned between the available processors.

Typically this means processing a collection of data in parallel. This method takes advantage of the fact that the items in the collection provide a natural way to partition the work. In the simplest case, a parallel map function, you apply a transformation to each item in the collection, and the results form a new collection. This simple case generally works because each item in the collection can typically be processed independently and in any order. It's also possible to use this technique to handle more complex scenarios, such as summing all the items in a list; however, it can also prove tricky for some complex cases, and the processing order can take on added significance.

Data parallelism typically relies on libraries and frameworks to provide parallel processing. Although they use multiple threads or processes to provide the parallelism, parallelism doesn't typically require the user to create or control these threads explicitly; instead, it's the job of the library or framework to do this. In many such environments, work units can be distributed between different physical machines that form a computing grid; for the sake of simplicity and because multicore systems are becoming more common and powerful, this chapter will concentrate on systems where work is distributed between multiple processors of a single physical machine.

There are two straightforward ways of implementing data-parallel processing in F#. You can use the Array.Parallel module that comes with F#. This approach is simple and can cover a great many practical requirements. Beyond this, you can use the FSharp.Collections.ParallelSeq library available on NuGet.

The Array.Parallel Module

The simplest approach for many data-parallel problems is to use the collection functions such as map and iter available in the Array.Parallel module. You don't have to add any references, download any NuGet packages, or even open any namespaces to use Array.Parallel.

Let's say you want to compute the MD5 hashes of every file in a folder. Computing such hashes can be quite expensive, particularly if the files are large. Here's how you'd do it without using parallel processing:

```
open System.IO
open System.Security.Cryptography

let Hashes path =
   Directory.EnumerateFiles(path)
   |> Array.ofSeq
   |> Array.map (fun name ->
      use md5 = MD5.Create()
      use stream = File.OpenRead(name)
      let hash = md5.ComputeHash(stream)
      path, hash)
```

Note incidentally that `Directory.Enumerate` returns an `IEnumerable` or "sequence," so you have to use `Array.ofSeq` to translate this into an array.

This works; on my machine, it took 11 seconds of real time to run on the contents of the `c:\temp` folder.

You can parallelize this simply by adding the word "Parallel" to the `Array.map` call, like so:

```
open System.IO
open System.Security.Cryptography

let Hashes path =
   Directory.EnumerateFiles(path)
   |> Array.ofSeq
   |> Array.Parallel.map (fun name ->
      use md5 = MD5.Create()
      use stream = File.OpenRead(name)
      let hash = md5.ComputeHash(stream)
      path, hash)
```

On my machine, this runs in 6 seconds of real time.

Using `Array.Parallel` can be an incredibly easy shortcut to performance gains in your code. However, there are two gotchas to be aware of. Firstly, you will only see gains if the computation you are doing is relatively heavy in relation to the overhead of .NET splitting up the dataset for you, and assigning it for processing to multiple threads. You can really only determine the cost/benefit by experimentation. Secondly, you need to ensure that any resources that will be accessed by multiple threads are themselves thread safe. You can observe the importance of thread safety by moving the creation of the md5 instance outside the mapping operation, thus

```
let Hashes path =
   use md5 = MD5.Create()
   Directory.EnumerateFiles(path)
   |> Array.ofSeq
   |> Array.Parallel.map (fun name ->
      use stream = File.OpenRead(name)
      let hash = md5.ComputeHash(stream)
      path, hash)
```

Run this and you will immediately get

```
System.AggregateException: One or more errors occurred. ---> System.Security.Cryptography.
CryptographicException: Hash not valid for use in specified state.
```

Clearly ComputeHash() is not thread safe, so you need to create one MD5 instance per hash computation.

The FSharp.Collections.ParallelSeq Module

The previous examples focused on the built-in Array.Parallel module, and got around the fact that System.IO.EnumerateFiles returns an IEnumerable by converting it to an array first. However, you can skip this conversion stage by installing the NuGet package FSharp.Collections.ParallelSeq. To install the package, go into the NuGet package manager console and use Install-Package:

```
PM> Install-Package FSharp.Collections.ParallelSeq
```

Now you can process the files "natively" as a sequence:

```
open System.IO
open System.Security.Cryptography
open FSharp.Collections.ParallelSeq

let Hashes3 path =
   Directory.EnumerateFiles(path)
   |> PSeq.map (fun name ->
      use md5 = MD5.Create()
      use stream = File.OpenRead(name)
      let hash = md5.ComputeHash(stream)
      path, hash)
```

Again, this took about 6 seconds on my machine, versus 12 seconds for a non-parallel version.

Asynchronous Programming

Asynchronous programming is slightly different from the other forms of parallel programming you've seen so far. The other topics covered allow a number of threads to execute work in parallel, taking advantage of all available processors in a system. In asynchronous programming, you want to avoid blocking threads. You're already familiar with the concept of blocked threads from this chapter's first section, "Threads, Memory, Locking, and Blocking." A blocked thread is one that can do no work because it is waiting for some task to finish; commonly the task a thread is waiting for is the operating system performing I/O, but sometimes it might also be waiting for a lock so it can enter a critical section. Threads are relatively expensive resources; each thread is allocated a 1MB stack by default, and there are other expenses concerning how the operating system kernel handles a large number of threads. In performance-critical code, it's important to keep the number of blocked threads low. Ideally, you will only have as many threads as you have processors, and you will have no blocked threads.

■ **Note**   For an overview of the kind of results that you can achieve using these techniques, see Amanda Laucher's 2009 QCon talk in which she describes using F# asynchronous workflows to parallelize a C# program and achieves some impressive results: `www.infoq.com/presentations/Concurrent-Programming-with-Microsoft-F-Amanda-Laucher`.

In this section, you will look at how to use the .NET Framework's asynchronous programming model to avoid blocking threads during I/O. The asynchronous programming model means using the pairs of `Begin/End`, such as the `BeginRead/EndRead`, on the `Stream` class. Typically you use these pairs of methods to perform some kind of I/O task, such as reading from a file. This method of programming has acquired a reputation for being difficult, mainly because you need to find a good way to store state between the `Begin/End` calls. This section will not cover the asynchronous programming model directly; instead, you'll look at how to use a feature of F# called *asynchronous workflows* to avoid some of the work associated with asynchronous programming model in other .NET languages.

Asynchronous workflows are not exclusively for use with the .NET asynchronous programming model. In the next section, "Message Passing," you'll see how to use these workflows with F#'s *mailboxes* to coordinate a number of different tasks. This will allow you to wait for tasks to complete without blocking threads.

The first step in understanding asynchronous workflows in F# is to understand the syntax itself. To create an asynchronous workflow, you use a computation expression, similar to the sequence expressions you saw in Chapter 3. The basic syntax is the keyword `async` with the workflow expression surrounded by curly brackets: `async { ... }`. A simple workflow program that uses workflows looks like this:

```
open System.IO

// a function to read a text file asynchronusly
let readFile file =
    async { let! stream = File.AsyncOpenText(file)
            let! fileContents = stream.AsyncReadToEnd()
            return fileContents }

// create an instance of the workflow
let readFileWorkflow = readFile "mytextfile.txt"

// invoke the workflow and get the contents
let fileContents = Async.RunSynchronously readFileWorkflow
```

To compile this program, you need to use NuGet to install the package named `FSPowerPack.Community`. This program shows a function named `readFile` that creates a workflow that reads a file asynchronously and then returns its contents. Next, you create an instance of the workflow called `readFileWorkflow`, and finally, you execute the workflow to get the file's contents. It's important to understand that simply calling the `readFile` function won't actually read the file. Instead, it creates a new instance of the workflow, and you can then execute the workflow to perform the task of reading the file. The `Async.RunSynchronously` function is actually responsible for executing the workflow. A workflow instance is a small data structure, rather like a small program, that can be interpreted to do some work.

The most important thing to notice about this example is the `let` followed by an exclamation mark (`let!`), often pronounced *let bang*. The workflow or "computation expression" syntax allows library writers to give different meanings to `let!`. In the case of asynchronous workflows, it means that an asynchronous operation will take place, during which the workflow itself will stop executing. A callback will be placed in the thread pool, and it will be invoked when the operation has completed, possibly on a different thread if the thread making the original call is not free. After the async call, the original thread is free to carry on doing other work.

You've probably also noticed that the let! is used with some special methods prefixed with Async. These functions are defined as type augmentations, which are F#'s equivalent of C#'s extension methods, in FSharp.PowerPack.dll. These methods handle the calling of the Begin/End method pairs. If no Async method is available, it's fairly easy to create your own using the Async.Primitive function and the Begin/End method pairs.

The execution flow of your simple example would follow these steps.

- *Step 1*: The main program thread starts the process of opening the file stream, and a callback is placed in the thread pool that can be used when this completes. This thread is now free to continue doing other work.

- *Step 2*: A thread pool thread will activate when the file stream has opened. It will then start reading the contents of the file and place a callback in the thread pool that can be used when this completes. Because it is a thread pool thread, it will return to the thread pool.

- *Step 3*: A thread pool thread will activate when the file has been completely read. It will return the text data that has been read from the file and return to the thread pool.

- *Step 4*: Because you used the Async.RunSynchronously function, the main program thread is waiting for the results of the workflow. It will receive the file contents.

You have probably spotted the flaw in this simple example. You do not block the main program thread waiting for I/O, but as you wait for the asynchronous workflow to complete, you do block the main program thread until the I/O has completed. To put this another way, there's little or no advantage to executing one asynchronous workflow on its own and waiting for the result. However, it's fairly simple to execute several workflows in parallel. Executing several workflows at once does have a distinct advantage because the original thread is not blocked after it starts executing the first Async task; this means it is free to go on and start executing more asynchronous tasks.

It's fairly easy to illustrate this using a slightly modified version of the original example where, instead of reading one file, you read three of them. Let's compare this to a synchronous version of the program, which will help demonstrate the differences. First, take a look at the synchronous version:

```
open System
open System.IO
open System.Threading

let print s =
    let tid = Thread.CurrentThread.ManagedThreadId
    Console.WriteLine(sprintf "Thread %i: %s" tid s)

let readFileSync file =
    print (sprintf "Beginning file %s" file)
    let stream = File.OpenText(file)
    let fileContents = stream.ReadToEnd()
    print (sprintf "Ending file %s" file)
    fileContents

// invoke the workflow and get the contents
let filesContents =
    [| readFileSync "text1.txt";
       readFileSync "text2.txt";
       readFileSync "text3.txt"; |]
```

This program is fairly straightforward. Note that the preceding code includes some debugging code to show when you begin and end processing a file. Now look at the asynchronous version:

```
open System
open System.IO
open System.Threading

let print s =
    let tid = Thread.CurrentThread.ManagedThreadId
    Console.WriteLine(sprintf "Thread %i: %s" tid s)

// a function to read a text file asynchronusly
let readFileAsync file =
    async { do print (sprintf "Beginning file %s" file)
            let! stream = File.AsyncOpenText(file)
            let! fileContents = stream.AsyncReadToEnd()
            do print (sprintf "Ending file %s" file)
            return fileContents }

let filesContents =
    Async.RunSynchronously
        (Async.Parallel [ readFileAsync "text1.txt";
                          readFileAsync "text2.txt";
                          readFileAsync "text3.txt"; ])
```

Again, this version incorporates some debugging code so you can see how the program executes. The biggest change is that you now use the Async.Parallel function to compose several workflows into a single workflow. This means that when the first thread finishes processing the first asynchronous call, it will be free to carry on processing the other workflows. This is probably easiest to see when you look at the results of the two programs:

Synchronous results

```
Thread 1: Beginning file text1.txt
Thread 1: Ending    file text1.txt
Thread 1: Beginning file text2.txt
Thread 1: Ending    file text2.txt
Thread 1: Beginning file text3.txt
Thread 1: Ending    file text3.txt
```

Asynchronous results

```
Thread 3: Beginning file text1.txt
Thread 4: Beginning file text2.txt
Thread 3: Beginning file text3.txt
Thread 4: Ending    file text2.txt
Thread 4: Ending    file text1.txt
Thread 4: Ending    file text3.txt
```

The two sets of results look quite different. For synchronous results, you see that each *Beginning file* is followed by an *Ending file*, and they all occur on the same thread. In the second case, you can see that all instances of the *Beginning file* occur at once, on two different threads. This occurs because once the first thread comes to an asynchronous operation, it is free to carry on and start another operation. The ending files occur later, once the I/O has completed.

Message Passing

It's often useful to think of a parallel program as a series of independent components that send and receive messages. This is often referred to as the actor model; you can find a more formal description of the actor model on Wikipedia at http://en.wikipedia.org/wiki/Actor_model. Although the scenarios in which you would use message passing tend to be quite complex, the ideas behind it are relatively simple, as you'll see in a handful of straightforward examples.

The basic idea behind message passing is that a system is composed of agents, or actors. They can both send and receive messages. When an agent receives a message, the message is placed in a queue until the agent is ready to process it. When an agent processes a message, it makes a decision about what to do with it based on its internal state and the contents of the message. The agent has a number of possibilities open to it in response to an incoming message: it might send a reply to the agent that initiated the exchange, create a new message for a different agent, create a new agent, or perhaps update some internal data structure.

F# provides the generic `MailboxProcessor` class as its implementation of message passing and the actor model. When a `MailboxProcessor` is created, it has (as the name suggests) a message queue that it can use to receive messages. `MailboxProcessor` is responsible for deciding what it will do with the message once it receives it. The implementation of a `MailboxProcessor` tends to follow a few simple patterns. The following example illustrates the simplest pattern for a `MailboxProcessor`:

```
open System

let mailbox =
    MailboxProcessor.Start(fun mb ->
        let rec loop x =
            async { let! msg = mb.Receive()
                    let x = x + msg
                    printfn "Running total: %i - new value %i" x msg
                    return! loop x }
        loop 0)

mailbox.Post(1)
mailbox.Post(2)
mailbox.Post(3)

Console.ReadLine() |> ignore
```

Executing this code produces the following results:

```
Running total: 1 - new value 1
Running total: 3 - new value 2
Running total: 6 - new value 3
```

In the first part of the example, you create a mailbox that receives messages of type int. When the mailbox receives a message, it adds it to a running total and then displays the running total, along with the value received. Let's take a closer look at how you achieve this. The MailboxProcessor has a static start method that receives a function as a parameter. The function the start method receives has an instance of the new MailboxProcessor, and it must return an asynchronous workflow. You should use the asynchronous workflow to read messages from the queue. You make it an asynchronous workflow because messages need to be read asynchronously; this ensures that a mailbox is not tied to a single thread, which would cause scalability issues if you were using lots of mailboxes. You need to keep checking the queue for new messages that arrive; typically, you do this by using an infinite loop to keep checking the queue. In this case, you define a recursive function called loop, which reads from the queue by calling the Receive function, processes the message, and then calls itself to start the process again. This is an infinite recursion, but there's no danger of the stack overflowing because the function is *tail recursive*. The loop function takes a single parameter, which you use to store the mailbox's state: an integer that represents the running total, in this case.

It's also worth noting that Console.ReadLine() at the end of this example is important. This is because the message queue is processed in a separate thread. Once you finish posting messages to the mailbox using the Post method, the main thread has no more work to do, so it exits, causing the process to exit. In this case, the process will probably exit before the mailbox has had chance to process the messages in its queue. Calling Console.ReadLine() provides a simple way to block the main thread until the user has had chance to see the results of the mailbox processing the messages.

One final detail about this example: the mailbox's Post member function is safe to call from any thread because of the mailbox's work queue that ensures each message is processed in turn in an atomic way. The current example does not take advantage of this, but you will see this used in the next two examples.

This particular asynchronous workflow isn't that useful; however, it does represent the simplest usage pattern of workflow: receive a message, update some internal state, and then react to the message. In this case, reacting to the message means writing to the console, which probably is too simplistic to be of much use. However, you can find more realistic scenarios for this usage pattern. A good example of this is using a mailbox to gather up a number of values, and then marshal to the GUI thread so the values can be viewed. You'll learn more about this technique in the next pair of examples.

Begin by looking at the problem you're trying to solve in a bit more detail. If you have a simulation that generates data, you might want to be able to see this data in real time, as it is generated. When working with GUIs, you face two related constraints that make this quite challenging. First, the GUI must run on its own thread, and this thread must not be occupied for a long time or the GUI will become unresponsive. This makes it impossible to execute a long-running simulation on the GUI thread. Second, you can only access GUI objects from the thread that created them: the GUI thread. If your simulation is running on anther thread, then it cannot write directly to the GUI. Fortunately, GUI objects provide an Invoke method that allows you to invoke a function on the GUI thread and safely update the GUI with the generated data. Calling the invoke function too often can have a negative impact on performance because marshalling data to the GUI thread is fairly expensive. If your simulation outputs a small amount of data frequently, it's often a good idea to batch up the results, so you can print them to the screen 12 to 20 times a second to get a smooth animation effect. You'll begin by learning how to use mailboxes to solve a specific instance of this problem; next, you'll see a second example where you tidy this up into a more generic example.

F#'s mailboxes can help here by providing an elegant way to buffer the data before you print it to the screen. The basics of the algorithm are fairly simple. The thread running the simulation posts messages to the mailbox; when the mailbox has received enough messages, it notifies the GUI of the new updates to be drawn. This programming style also provides a neat way of separating the logic for generating the data from the logic presenting the data in the UI. Let's have a look at the whole code example, and then step through and examine the how it all works. As with the Fibonacci example above, this code has been arranged so that you can run it by selecting all the code and sending to F# Interactive.

```fsharp
#if INTERACTIVE
#r "System.Windows.Forms.dll"
#r "System.Drawing.dll"
#else
module MailboxProcessorSimulation
#endif

open System
open System.Threading
open System.Windows.Forms
open System.Drawing.Imaging
open System.Drawing
// the width & height for the simulation
let width, height = 500, 600

// the bitmap that will hold the output data
let bitmap = new Bitmap(width, height, PixelFormat.Format24bppRgb)

// a form to display the bitmap
let form = new Form(Width = width, Height = height,
                    BackgroundImage = bitmap)

// the function which recieves that points to be plotted
// and marshals to the GUI thread to plot them
let printPoints points =
    form.Invoke(new Action(fun () ->
        List.iter bitmap.SetPixel points
        form.Invalidate()))
    |> ignore

// the mailbox that will be used to collect the data
let mailbox =
    MailboxProcessor.Start(fun mb ->
        // main loop to read from the message queue
        // the parameter "points" holds the working data
        let rec loop points =
            async { // read a message
                    let! msg = mb.Receive()
                    // if we have over 100 messages write
                    // message to the GUI
                    if List.length points > 100 then
                        printPoints points
                        return! loop []
                    // otherwise append message and loop
                    return! loop (msg :: points) }
        loop [])

// start a worker thread running our fake simulation
let startWorkerThread() =
    // function that loops infinitely generating random
    // "simulation" data
```

```fsharp
    let fakeSimulation() =
        let rand = new Random()
        let colors = [| Color.Red; Color.Green; Color.Blue |]
        while true do
            // post the random data to the mailbox
            // then sleep to simulate work being done
            mailbox.Post(rand.Next(width),
                rand.Next(height),
                colors.[rand.Next(colors.Length)])
            Thread.Sleep(rand.Next(100))
    // start the thread as a background thread, so it won't stop
    // the program exiting
    let thread = new Thread(fakeSimulation, IsBackground = true)
    thread.Start()

// start 6 instances of our simulation
for _ in 0 .. 5 do startWorkerThread()

// run the form
#if INTERACTIVE
form.ShowDialog() |> ignore
#else
Application.Run()
#endif
```

This example has three key parts: how the simulation posts data to the mailbox, how the mailbox buffers points to be sent to the GUI, and how the GUI receives the points. Let's examine each of these in turn. Posting data to the mailbox remains simple; you continue to call the Post method on the mailbox. Two important differences exist between this example and the previous one. First, you pass a different data structure; however, the Post method is generic, so you remain strongly typed. Second, you call the Post method from six different threads. The message queue enables this to work just fine, so everything just works. You use a simple technique to buffer data, which means you can simply count the number of messages received. When you receive 100, you send them to the GUI.

```fsharp
async { // read a message
        let! msg = mb.Receive()
        // if we have over 100 messages write
        // message to the GUI
        if List.length points > 100 then
            printPoints points
            return! loop []
        // otherwise append message and loop
        return! loop (msg :: points) }
```

The number 100 is fairly arbitrary; it was chosen because it seemed to work well for this particular simulation. It's also worth noting that you count the number of messages you receive at each iteration by calling the List.length function. This is suboptimal from a performance point of view because the List.length function will traverse the list each time you call it. This won't matter much in the current example because it uses a fairly small list; however, if you increase the buffer size, this approach could become a bottleneck. A better approach is to store a separate parameter that you increment during each iteration of the function; however, this example avoids doing that for the sake of maintaining simplicity. Another alternative is to store the time of the previous update, updating again only if the previous update was more than a twentieth of a second ago. This approach works well because it allows you to aim for the correct number of frames per second required to achieve a smooth animation effect. Again, this book's examples don't rely on this approach because adopting it would add an unnecessary element of complexity to the examples. The example includes one more technique worth mentioning, which is how you write the data to the screen:

```
let printPoints points =
    form.Invoke(new Action(fun () ->
        List.iter bitmap.SetPixel points
        form.Invalidate()))
    |> ignore
```

This is fairly straightforward. The `printPoints` function takes a `points` parameter, and then invokes a delegate in the context of the form and allows you to write the points to the bitmap. Finally, you need to call the form's `Invalidate` function to ensure the points are displayed correctly.

The previous example provides a nice demonstration of how to use mailboxes, but the main problem with it is that the code is not reusable. It would be better if you could wrap your mailbox into a reusable component. F#'s object-oriented features provide a great way of doing this. This following example also demonstrates a couple of other important concepts, such as how you can support messages of different types within the same mailbox, as well as how you can return messages to a client of the mailbox. Again, you can send all this code to F# Interactive for execution.

```
#if INTERACTIVE
#r "System.Windows.Forms.dll"
#r "System.Drawing.dll"
#else
module MailboxProcessorSimulationGeneric
#endif

open System
open System.Threading
open System.ComponentModel
open System.Windows.Forms
open System.Drawing.Imaging
open System.Drawing

// type that defines the messages types our updater can handle
type Updates<'a> =
    | AddValue of 'a
    | GetValues of AsyncReplyChannel<list<'a>>
    | Stop

// a generic collecter that receives a number of post items and
// once a configurable limit is reached fires the update event
type Collector<'a>(?updatesCount) =
    // the number of updates to count to before firing the update even
    let updatesCount = match updatesCount with Some x -> x | None -> 100
```

```
    // Capture the synchronization context of the thread that creates this object. This
    // allows us to send messages back to the GUI thread painlessly.
    let context = AsyncOperationManager.SynchronizationContext
    let runInGuiContext f =
        context.Post(new SendOrPostCallback(fun _ -> f()), null)

    // This events are fired in the synchronization context of the GUI (i.e. the thread
    // that created this object)
    let event = new Event<list<'a>>()

    let mailboxWorkflow (inbox: MailboxProcessor<_>) =
        // main loop to read from the message queue
        // the parameter "curr" holds the working data
        // the parameter "master" holds all values received
        let rec loop curr master =
            async { // read a message
                    let! msg = inbox.Receive()
                    match msg with
                    | AddValue x ->
                        let curr, master = x :: curr, x :: master
                        // if we have over 100 messages write
                        // message to the GUI
                        if List.length curr > updatesCount then
                            do runInGuiContext(fun () -> event.Trigger(curr))
                            return! loop [] master
                        return! loop curr master
                    | GetValues channel ->
                        // send all data received back
                        channel.Reply master
                        return! loop curr master
                    | Stop -> () } // stop by not calling "loop"
        loop [] []

    // the mailbox that will be used to collect the data
    let mailbox = new MailboxProcessor<Updates<'a>>(mailboxWorkflow)

    // the API of the collector

    // add a value to the queue
    member w.AddValue (x) = mailbox.Post(AddValue(x))
    // get all the values the mailbox stores
    member w.GetValues() = mailbox.PostAndReply(fun x -> GetValues x)
    // publish the updates event
    [<CLIEvent>]
    member w.Updates = event.Publish
    // start the collector
    member w.Start() = mailbox.Start()
    // stop the collector
    member w.Stop() = mailbox.Post(Stop)

// create a new instance of the collector
let collector = new Collector<int*int*Color>()
```

```fsharp
// the width & height for the simulation
let width, height = 500, 600

// a form to display the updates
let form =
    // the bitmap that will hold the output data
    let bitmap = new Bitmap(width, height, PixelFormat.Format24bppRgb)
    let form = new Form(Width = width, Height = height, BackgroundImage = bitmap)
    // handle the collector's update event and use it to post
    collector.Updates.Add(fun points ->
        List.iter bitmap.SetPixel points
        form.Invalidate())
    // start the collector when the form loads
    form.Load.Add(fun _ -> collector.Start())
    // when the form closes get all the values that were processed
    form.Closed.Add(fun _ ->
        let vals = collector.GetValues()
        MessageBox.Show(sprintf "Values processed: %i" (List.length vals))
        |> ignore
        collector.Stop())
    form

// start a worker thread running our fake simulation
let startWorkerThread() =
    // function that loops infinitely generating random
    // "simulation" data
    let fakeSimulation() =
        let rand = new Random()
        let colors = [| Color.Red; Color.Green; Color.Blue |]
        while true do
            // post the random data to the collector
            // then sleep to simulate work being done
            collector.AddValue(rand.Next(width),
                rand.Next(height),
                colors.[rand.Next(colors.Length)])
            Thread.Sleep(rand.Next(100))
    // start the thread as a background thread, so it won't stop
    // the program exiting
    let thread = new Thread(fakeSimulation, IsBackground = true)
    thread.Start()

// start 6 instances of our simulation
for _ in 0 .. 5 do startWorkerThread()

// run the form
#if INTERACTIVE
form.ShowDialog() |> ignore
#else
Application.Run()
#endif
```

The output of this example is exactly the same as that of the previous example, and the code base follows largely the same pattern; however, you can see several important differences in the two examples. Perhaps the most noticeable one is that the mailbox is now wrapped in an object that provides a strongly typed interface. The class you have created is called a Collector<'a>; its interface looks like this:

```
type Collector<'a> =
  class
    new : ?updatesCount:int -> Collector<'a>
    member AddValue : x:'a -> unit
    member GetValues : unit -> 'a list
    member Start : unit -> unit
    member Stop : unit -> unit
    member Updates : IEvent<'a list>
  end
```

The class is generic in terms of the type of values that it collects. It has an AddValue method to post a value to the internal mailbox and a GetValues method to get all the messages that have been passed to the mailbox so far. The collector must now be explicitly started and stopped by its Start and Stop methods. Finally, the collector has an Update event that is raised when enough messages have been collected. The number of messages collected is configurable by an optional integer that you can pass to the class constructor. The fact that you use an event is an important design detail. Using an event to notify clients that updates exist means that your Collector<'a> needs no knowledge of the clients it uses, which greatly improves its reusability.

You now use a union type to represent your messages; this gives you the flexibility to have different types of messages. Clients of the Collector<'a> don't deal with it directly, but instead use the member methods it provides. The member methods have the job of creating the different types of messages. In addition to providing a value to the message queue, you can also send a message to retrieve all the current messages, as well as a message to stop the mailbox from reading new messages.

```
type Updates<'a> =
    | AddValue of 'a
    | GetValues of AsyncReplyChannel<list<'a>>
    | Stop
```

Next, you implement these different types of messages by pattern matching over the received messages.

```
let! msg = inbox.Receive()
match msg with
| AddValue x ->
    let curr, master = x :: curr, x :: master
    // if we have over 100 messages write
    // message to the GUI
    if List.length curr > updatesCount then
        do runInGuiCtxt(fun () -> fireUpdates(curr))
        return! loop [] master
    return! loop curr master
| GetValues channel ->
    // send all data received back
    channel.Reply master
    return! loop curr master
| Stop -> ()
```

The AddValue union case is basically what you did in the previous example, except that this time you add the values to both the curr and master lists. The curr list stores the current values you will pass to the GUI on the next update, while the mast list provides a list of all the values that you've received. The master list enables you to accommodate any client that requests all the values.

For the union case GetValues, it's worth spending some time looking at how a client can return values. You start this process by calling the mailbox's PostAndReply method rather than its Post method; you can see this at work in the GetValues member method implementation:

```
// get all the values the mailbox stores
member w.GetValues() = mailbox.PostAndReply(fun x -> GetValues x)
```

The PostAndReply method accepts a function that is passed an AsyncReplyChannel<'a> type. You can use this AsyncReplyChannel<'a> type to send a message back to the call via its Reply member. This is what you see in the GetValues case of your union. Users of this method should be careful because it blocks until the message is returned, which means the message won't be processed until it reaches the front of the queue. This can take a long time if you have a long queue. In practice, you should use the AsyncPostAndReply approach because it enables you to avoid blocking a thread while waiting for the reply; however, this example doesn't do this for the sake of keeping the example simple.

The Stop union case is the simplest way to stop reading messages from the queue; all you need to do is avoid calling the loop method recursively. That's not an issue in this case, but you still need to return a value, which you do by returning the unit type, which is represented by empty parentheses, (). The only subtlety you need to be careful of here is that calling the Stop method will not stop the mailbox immediately; it will stop the mailbox only when the stop message reaches the front of the queue.

You've seen how the Collector<'a> type handles messages; now let's look at how the Collector<'a> raises the Update event so that it runs on the GUI thread. You create the Update event using new Event, just as you create any other event in F#. You use the function runInGuiContext to make this event run in the context of the GUI:

```
let context = AsyncOperationManager.SynchronizationContext
let runInGuiContext f =
    context.Post(new SendOrPostCallback(fun _ -> f()), null)
```

First, you store the SynchronizationContext of the thread that created the object. You do this by using a static property on the AsyncOperationManager available in the System.ComponentModel namespace. The SynchronizationContext enables you to marshal to the thread that created it using its Post member method. The only thing you need to be careful about is that the thread that creates the collector object becomes the GUI thread; however, typically you'll use the main program thread to do both things, so this won't be a problem. This technique where you capture the synchronization context is also used in the BackgroundWorker class from the "Reactive Programming" section of this chapter.

The definition of the form is now somewhat simpler because you no longer need to provide a function for the mailbox to call. You simply handle the Updates event instead:

```
// handle the collector's update event and use it to post
collector.Updates.Add(fun points ->
    List.iter bitmap.SetPixel points
    form.Invalidate())
```

You can also now take advantage of the form's Closed event to stop the mailbox processor and obtain a list of all the messages processed when a user closes the form:

```
// when the form closes get all the values that were processed
form.Closed.Add(fun _ ->
    let vals = collector.GetValues()
    MessageBox.Show(sprintf "Values processed: %i" (List.length vals))
    |> ignore
    collector.Stop())
```

You haven't changed the behavior of your example, but these additions greatly improved the design of the code by decoupling the code for the mailbox from the GUI code, which improves the reusability of the Collector<'a> class tremendously.

Summary

This chapter covered quite a lot of ground. You saw five different concurrency techniques, all of which have their place in certain kinds of applications.

In the next chapter, you'll see how some of these techniques, especially asynchronous workflows, can be used to make programming *distributed applications* easier.

CHAPTER 10

■ ■ ■

Distributed Applications

Applications that use networks, called distributed applications, become more important every day. Fortunately, the .NET BCL and other libraries offer many constructs that make communicating over a network easy, which in turn makes creating distributed applications in F# straightforward.

Networking Overview

Several types of distributed applications exist; they're generally classified into either *client-server* applications, in which clients make requests to a central server, or *peer-to-peer* applications, in which computers exchange data among themselves. In this chapter, you'll focus on building client-server applications because these applications are currently more common. Whichever type of distributed application you want to build, the way computers exchange data is controlled by a protocol. A protocol is a standard that defines the rules for communication over a network.

Building a network-enabled application is generally considered one of the most challenging tasks a programmer can undertake, with good reason. When building a network application, you must consider three important requirements:

- *Scalability*: The application must remain responsive when used by many users concurrently; typically this means you must perform extensive testing and profiling of your server code to ensure that it performs when a high load is placed on it.

- *Fault tolerance*: Networks are inherently unreliable, and you shouldn't write code that assumes that the network will always be there. If you do, your applications will be frustrating to end users. Every application should go to great lengths to ensure communication failures are handled smoothly, which means giving the user appropriate feedback, displaying error messages, and perhaps offering diagnostic or retry facilities. Do not let your application crash because of a network failure. You should also consider data consistency (that is, can you be sure that all updates necessary to keep data consistent reached the target computer or store?). Using transactions and a relational database as a data store can help with this. Depending on the type of application, you might also want to consider building an offline mode where the user can access locally stored data, and network requests are queued up until the network comes back online. A good example of this kind of facility is the offline mode that most email clients offer.

© Robert Pickering and Kit Eason 2016
R. Pickering and K. Eason, *Beginning F# 4.0*, DOI 10.1007/978-1-4842-1374-2_10

- *Security*: Security should be a concern for every application you write, but it becomes a hugely important issue in network programming. This is because, when you expose your application to a network, you open it up to attack from any other user of the network; therefore, if you expose your application to the Internet, you might be opening it up to thousands or even millions of potential attackers. Typically you need to think about whether data traveling across the network needs to be secured, whether signed to guarantee it has not been tampered with or encrypted to guarantee only the appropriate people can read it. You also need to ensure that the people connecting to your application are who they say they are, and that they are authorized to do what they are requesting to do.

Fortunately, modern programmers don't have to tackle these problems on their own; network protocols can help you tackle these problems. For example, if it is important that no one else on the network can read the data you are sending, you should not attempt to encrypt the data yourself. Instead, you should use a network protocol that offers this facility. These protocols are exposed through components from libraries that implement them for you. The type of protocol, and the library used, is dictated by the requirements of your applications. Some protocols offer encryption and authentication, and others don't. Some are suitable for client-server applications, and others are suitable for peer-to-peer applications. You'll look at the following components and libraries, along with the protocols they implement, in this chapter:

- *HTTP/HTTPS requests* support requests from web pages to servers, typically only for client-server applications.

- *Web services* expose applications so other applications can request services, typically used only for client-server applications.

Despite the inherent challenge of distributed programming, it is generally worth the effort because it enables you to access interesting data and share the results of your programs with others. By the end of this chapter, you will be able to access data stored in Google spreadsheets, and use two different web-development paradigms to write a simple URL shortening service.

Using HTTP

The Web uses Hypertext Transfer Protocol (HTTP) to communicate, typically with web browsers, but you might want to make web requests from a script or a program for several reasons. For example, you might use this to aggregate site content through RSS or Atom feeds.

To make an HTTP request, you use the static method `Create` from the `System.Net.WebRequest` class. This creates a `WebRequest` object that represents a request to the uniform resource locator (URL, an address used to address a resource on a network uniquely) that was passed to the `Create` method. You then use the `GetResponse` method to get the server's response to your request, which is represented by the `System.Net.WebResponse` class.

Listing 10-1 illustrates how to call an RSS on the British Broadcasting Corporation's web site. The core of the example is the function `getUrlAsXml`, which does the work of retrieving the data from the URL and loading the data into an `XmlDocument`. The rest of the example illustrates the kind of post-processing you might want to do on the data; in this case, it displays the title of each item on the console, allowing users to choose which item to display. You can run the example in F# Interactive.

Listing 10-1. Using HTTP

```
#if INTERACTIVE
#r "System.Xml.dll"
#else
module Rss
#endif
```

```fsharp
open System
open System.Diagnostics
open System.Net
open System.Xml

/// makes a http request to the given url
let getUrlAsXml (url: string) =
    let request = WebRequest.Create(url)
    let response = request.GetResponse()
    let stream = response.GetResponseStream()
    let xml = new XmlDocument()
    xml.Load(stream)
    xml

/// the url we interested in
let url = "http://newsrss.bbc.co.uk/rss/newsonline_uk_edition/sci/tech/rss.xml"

/// main application function
let main() =
    // read the rss fead
    let xml = getUrlAsXml url

    // write out the tiles of all the news items
    let nodes = xml.SelectNodes("/rss/channel/item/title")
    for i in 0 .. (nodes.Count - 1) do
        printf "%i. %s\r\n" (i + 1) (nodes.[i].InnerText)

    // read the number the user wants from the console
    let item = int(Console.ReadLine())

    // find the new url
    let newUrl =
        let xpath = sprintf "/rss/channel/item[%i]/link" item
        let node = xml.SelectSingleNode(xpath)
        node.InnerText

    // start the url using the shell, this automatically opens
    // the default browser
    let procStart = new ProcessStartInfo(UseShellExecute = true,
                                         FileName = newUrl)
    let proc = new Process(StartInfo = procStart)
    proc.Start() |> ignore

do main()
```

The results of this example at the time of writing were as follows (your results will vary):

```
1. Korean leader for UN climate panel
2. Neutrino 'flip' wins physics Nobel
3. Homo naledi was 'jack of all trades'
4. Plant uses raindrops to eat ants
5. Wild mammals 'return to Chernobyl'
6. New rat discovered in Indonesia
7. Cacti facing extinction, study warns
8. Nobel Prize for anti-parasite drugs
9. Chile creates new marine reserves
10. Mammal species outlived the dinosaurs
11. UN battle looms over climate costs
12. Supernova 'stream' in lab's sights
13. Nasa photo archive posted online
14. Ceres' spots remain mysterious
15. Additive promises crash-safe fuel
16. Charon moon seen in super detail
17. Africa's farming 'needs young blood'
18. VIDEO: Air pollution - the 'invisible hazard'
```

Type one of the numbers and you should be taken straight to the news story in your browser.

Using HTTP with Google Spreadsheets

Because of its simplicity and its platform independence, exposing data by HTTP and XML is one of the most popular ways to expose data publicly across the Internet. You can access a surprising amount of data using only HTTP and some JSON or XML processing. A useful application of this is accessing Google Spreadsheets published by their owners. You can see how to access Google Spreadsheets in Listing 10-2.

■ **Note**   The spreadsheet you'll access comes from the Guardian Data Store, which publishes many UK and world statics via Google Spreadsheets. You can find this extremely useful resource at `www.guardian.co.uk/data`.

Listing 10-2. Using HTTP to Access Google Spreadsheets

```
#if INTERACTIVE
#r "System.Xml.dll"
#else
module GoogleSheets
#endif

open System
open System.IO
open System.Net
open System.Xml
open System.Xml.XPath
```

```
// some namespace information for the XML
let namespaces =
    [ "at", "http://www.w3.org/2005/Atom";
      "openSearch", "http://a9.com/-/spec/opensearchrss/1.0/";
      "gsx", "http://schemas.google.com/spreadsheets/2006/extended" ]

// read the XML and process it into a matrix of strings
let queryGoogleSpreadSheet (xdoc: XmlDocument) xpath columnNames =
    let nav = xdoc.CreateNavigator()
    let mngr = new XmlNamespaceManager(new NameTable())
    do List.iter (fun (prefix, url) ->
                     mngr.AddNamespace(prefix, url)) namespaces
    let xpath = nav.Compile(xpath)
    do xpath.SetContext(mngr)
    let iter = nav.Select(xpath)
    seq { for x in iter ->
            let x  = x :?> XPathNavigator
            let getValue nodename =
                let node = x.SelectSingleNode(nodename, mngr)
                node.Value
            Seq.map getValue columnNames }

// read the spreadsheet from its web address
let getGoogleSpreadSheet (url: string) columnNames =
    let req = WebRequest.Create(url)
    use resp = req.GetResponse()
    use stream = resp.GetResponseStream()
    let xdoc = new XmlDocument()
    xdoc.Load(stream)
    queryGoogleSpreadSheet xdoc "/at:feed/at:entry" columnNames

// a location to hold the information we're interested in
type Location =
    { Country: string;
      NameValuesList: seq<string * option<float>> }

// creates a location from the row names
let createLocation names row  =
    let country = Seq.head row
    let row = Seq.skip 1 row
    let tryParse s =
        let success,res = Double.TryParse s
        if success then Some res else None
    let values = Seq.map tryParse row
    { Country = country;
      NameValuesList = Seq.zip names values }
// get the data and process it into records
let getDataAndProcess url colNames =
    // get the names of the columns we want
    let cols = Seq.map fst colNames
    // get the data
    let data = getGoogleSpreadSheet url cols
```

227

```
    // get the readable names of the columns
    let names = Seq.skip 1 (Seq.map snd colNames)
    // create strongly typed records from the data
    Seq.map (createLocation names) data

// function to create a spreadsheets URL from its key
let makeUrl = sprintf "http://spreadsheets.google.com/feeds/list/%s/od6/public/values"

let main() =
    // the key of the spreadsheet we're interested in
    let sheetKey = "phNtm3LmDZEP61UU2eSN1YA"
    // list of column names we're interested in
    let cols =
        [ "gsx:location", "";
          "gsx:hospitalbedsper10000population",
            "Hospital beds per 1000";
          "gsx:nursingandmidwiferypersonneldensityper10000population",
            "Nursing and Midwifery Personnel per 1000" ];
    // get the data
    let data = getDataAndProcess (makeUrl sheetKey) cols
    // print the data
    Seq.iter (printfn "%A") data

do main()
```

When you run the code from Listing 10-2, which you can do from F# Interactive, you get the following results:

```
...
{Country = "Sweden";
 NameValuesList =
  seq
    [("Hospital beds per 1000", null);
     ("Nursing and Midwifery Personnel per 1000", Some 109.0)];}
{Country = "Switzerland";
 NameValuesList =
  seq
    [("Hospital beds per 1000", Some 57.0);
     ("Nursing and Midwifery Personnel per 1000", Some 110.0)];}
...
```

The important thing to notice about this example is that the method you use to retrieve the data changes little; at the core of the example, you find the same few lines of code for making the HTTP request and retrieving an XML document from it:

```
let req = WebRequest.Create(url)
use resp = req.GetResponse()
use stream = resp.GetResponseStream()
let xdoc = new XmlDocument() '
xdoc.Load(stream)
```

Most of the rest of the example treats the XML data that's returned.

Using Suave.io

Now that you understand the basics of WebRequest, let's look at the other end of the pipeline: what to do if you want to write a service that responds to web requests and serves out responses. Traditionally in .NET we've used products such as ASP.NET and WCF to provide frameworks and templates for writing such services. Those are still great options if you are comfortable with at least some of the layers of your application being written in C#, and if you require the huge range of features (various security options, rich UIs, and so forth) that they offer. But the downside of these options is that they are quite heavyweight. Even a new "empty" project contains a great deal of code and many library dependencies. A great alternative, if you want to write a lightweight, all-F# solution, is an open source framework called Suave.io.

Let's use Suave.io to write a URL shortening service similar to tinyurl.com. The basic principle is that users can paste a long URL into the service and receive a much shorter URL in return. The shorter URL is much more email- and messaging-friendly. When someone else follows the URL, the shortening service resolves it back into the original URL and redirects them to the original location. You can write a URL-shortening service in a few lines of code using Suave.io, provided you accept some limitations:

- Your service won't be persistent. When the service is restarted, the mapping from shortened to full URLs will be lost. (You might find it an interesting exercise to add a persistence layer yourself.)

- Your service won't allow the user to specify her own text for the shortened URL. It'll always be a random string.

- Your service will only run on localhost. This is really just a matter of what host name is prepended to the shortened URL and could easily be generalized.

Start by creating a new F# console project, and use NuGet (or your favorite package manager) to add the package Suave.io:

```
PM> Install-Package Suave
```

Copy the code from Listing 10-3 into Program.fs, replacing its existing contents.

Listing 10-3. A URL Shortener

```
open System
open System.Collections.Concurrent
open Suave
open Suave.Http
open Suave.Web
open Suave.Filters
open Suave.Operators

// Initialize a .NET random number generator:
let random = Random()

// Generate a random string of lower-case letters
// of a specified length.  WARNING: this has the
// potential to generate rude words!
let randomString len =
    Array.init len (fun _ -> random.Next(26) + 97 |> char)
    |> String
```

```
// A dictionary of mappings from the long to the shortened URLs:
let longToShort = ConcurrentDictionary<string, string>()
// A dictionary of mappings from the shortened to the long URLs:
let shortToLong = ConcurrentDictionary<string, string>()

// Shorten a URL, and as a side-effect store the short->long
// and long->short mappings:
let shorten (long : string) =
    longToShort.GetOrAdd(long, fun _ ->
        let short = randomString 5
        shortToLong.[short] <- long
        short)

// Try resolve a shortened URL to the long version:
let tryResolve (short : string) =
    match shortToLong.TryGetValue short with
    | true, long -> Some long
    | false, _-> None

// Create a Suave app which can add and resolve URLs:
let app =
    choose
        [
            POST >=> choose
                [ path "/add" >=> request (fun req ->
                    match (req.formData "url") with
                    | Choice1Of2 long ->
                        let short = shorten long
                        // You may need to amend the port number:
                        let url = sprintf "localhost:8083/go/%s" short
                        Successful.CREATED url
                    | _ ->
                        RequestErrors.BAD_REQUEST "Url not supplied")
                ]
            GET >=> choose
                [ pathScan "/go/%s" (fun short ->
                    match tryResolve short with
                    | Some long ->
                        Redirection.MOVED_PERMANENTLY (sprintf "http://%s" long)
                    | None ->
                        RequestErrors.NOT_FOUND "Url not found")
                ]
        ]

[<EntryPoint>]
let main args =
    // Start the service:
    startWebServer defaultConfig app
    0
```

Before we analyze the code, try it out so that you are clear on what the code is trying to achieve. Start by running the project. You should see a console window with text something like this:

```
[I] 2015-10-21T08:12:26.6241031Z: listener started in 49.036 ms with binding 127.0.0.1:8083
[Suave.Tcp.tcpIpServer]
```

Take a moment to check that the port number shown (in this case 8083) is the same as the one you have in this line of code:

```
let url = sprintf "localhost:8083/go/%s" short
```

If it isn't, stop the project, edit the code to match what was shown in the console window, and run it again.

Next, you are going to need a means of sending a POST message to your new server, containing a URL that you want to be shortened. There are a number of tools to achieve this; a common one on Windows .NET is Fiddler, which you can download free from www.telerik.com/fiddler. Linux users often use a tool called Curl (go to http://curl.haxx.se/download.html). Run Fiddler (or the tool of your choice) and set it up to send a POST to localhost:8083/add, with a request body that specifies a value of www.bbc.co.uk (or whatever URL you prefer) for a variable called url. Figure 10-1 shows what the Compose tab in Fiddler should look like once you've done this.

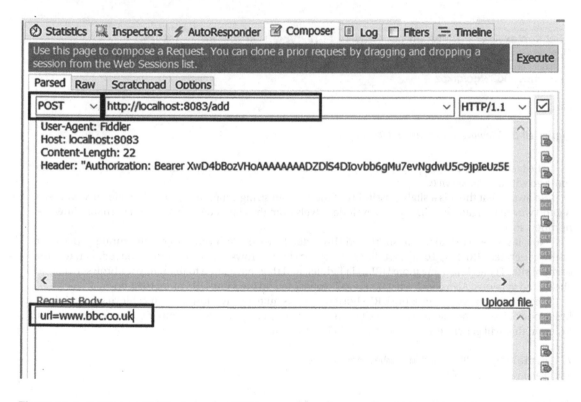

Figure 10-1. *Setting up Fiddler to send a POST*

Once again, you may have to adjust the port number to match the one shown in the console window for your running service. When you've got these values entered, press "Execute." This will post the request body `url=www.bbc.co.uk` to your service, and your service will then generate a shortened version, store it away, and return the shortened version back to the client. How can you see the shortened version? You need to look through the Fiddler history list (the left-hand window in the default layout) to find an entry that looks like the one highlighted in Figure 10-2.

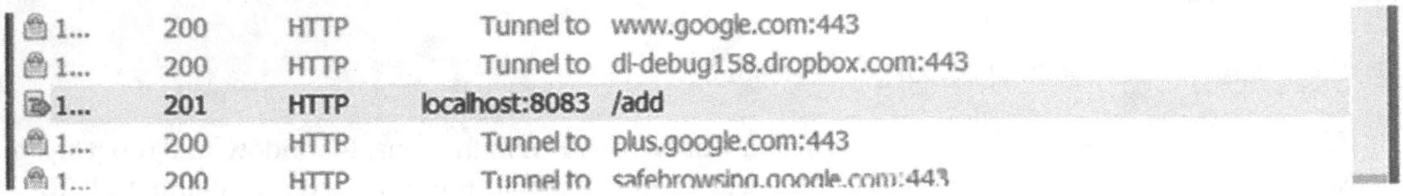

🔒 1...	200	HTTP		Tunnel to	www.google.com:443
🔒 1...	200	HTTP		Tunnel to	dl-debug158.dropbox.com:443
📄 1...	201	HTTP	localhost:8083	/add	
🔒 1...	200	HTTP		Tunnel to	plus.google.com:443
🔒 1...	200	HTTP		Tunnel to	safebrowsing.google.com:443

Figure 10-2. *Finding a response in Fiddler*

Double-click the entry and locate the TextView tab. Here you should see the shortened version that your service returned (Figure 10-3). Note that it may not actually be shorter, depending on the length of the URL you originally sent.

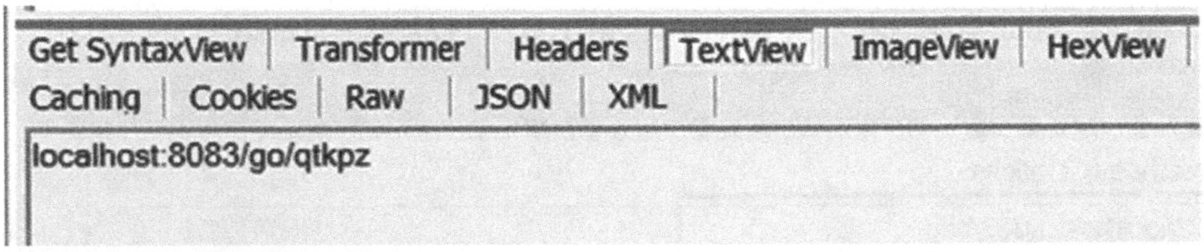

| Get SyntaxView | Transformer | Headers | TextView | ImageView | HexView |
| Caching | Cookies | Raw | JSON | XML | |

localhost:8083/go/qtkpz

Figure 10-3. *Viewing a response in Fiddler*

The last few characters (`qtkpz`) are the random short URL; the rest is just the server and port, and the route go within your service.

Be aware that there is a slight possibility of the random string generator generating offensive words. A good way to mitigate this simply is to exclude vowels from the character set used, and perhaps allow numbers instead.

Now it's time to test that your shortened URL actually works. With your project still running, paste the entire generated URL (e.g. `localhost:8083/go/qtkpz`) into a browser, and you should be redirected to the original site. Try adding a few more URLs via Fiddler, and then navigating to them in your browser via the shortened versions. Also check what happens if you try to add the same URL more than once.

As you can see, your miniature URL shortener works quite nicely. How did you achieve so much with so little code? First, there is some simple utility code: you bind a .NET random number generator and use it in a function that will generate a random string of a fixed length:

```
// Initialize a .NET random number generator:
let random = Random()

// Generate a random string of lower-case letters
// of a specified length.  WARNING: this has the
// potential to generate rude words!
let randomString len =
    Array.init len (fun _ -> random.Next(26) + 97 |> char)
    |> String
```

Next, you declare a couple of ConcurrentDictionary instances:

```
// A dictionary of mappings from the long to the shortened URLs:
let longToShort = ConcurrentDictionary<string, string>()
// A dictionary of mappings from the shortened to the long URLs:
let shortToLong = ConcurrentDictionary<string, string>()
```

These instances are how you store a bidirectional mapping between the original and shortened version of each URL. You need two dictionaries to ensure that the program can look up rapidly in both directions. (This is quite a useful coding pattern when you need bidirectional access.) You use concurrent dictionaries because requests to your server may overlap; the plain .NET Dictionary is not thread safe and would cause exceptions as soon as the load on your service got heavy.

Now we get to the real heart of your service:

```
// Shorten a URL, and as a side-effect store the short->long
// and long->short mappings:
let shorten (long : string) =
    longToShort.GetOrAdd(long, fun _ ->
        let short = randomString 5
        shortToLong.[short] <- long
        short)
```

This is the code that takes the original long URL, creates a shorter alias for it, stores the original and shortened versions in your two dictionaries, and returns the shortened version to the caller. It's quite a dense piece of code so we are going to walk though it very carefully. You start by calling longToShort.GetOrAdd, which is a method of the ConcurrentDictionary class, one which may seem very strange if you are only familiar with classic dictionaries. The reason it's a little convoluted is that ConcurrentDictionary wants to make sure that it has control of the entire process of checking whether a value is already a dictionary, and adding it if it is not. If it did not have this level of control, there would be a chance of another thread coming in and doing something to the dictionary contents between the already-exists check and the adding of the value. GetOrAdd takes two arguments. The first is the dictionary key that you want to add to the dictionary (if it is not already there). The second is a function whose job is to provide a value that corresponds to the key. This function will only be called by ConcurrentDictionary if the key from the first argument isn't already in the dictionary.

You specify a body for the value-generating function using a classic F# lambda expression (fun _ ->). Note that the function takes an argument that can be the input key, but as you already know the value of that in this context, you ignore that parameter using an underscore (_).

Now let's look at the body of your lambda function. Remember, the aim here is to provide a value that corresponds to the given key: the value returned from this function will be added to the dictionary along with the key–but only if the key does not already exist. You achieve this by calling your randomString function and binding the result as short:

```
let short = randomString 5
```

At this point, your random string has no inherent association with the long version; it's just a random string. You make the association from short to long by adding it to the shortToLong dictionary:

```
shortToLong.[short] <- long
```

How do you make the association in the other direction? You do so by simply returning the value short from the lambda function. This works because the whole purpose of this lambda function is to generate a value to be associated with long when called by the longToShort dictionary's GetOrAdd method.

Incidentally, there is a weakness in this code: because you don't check if a given random string has been used before, there is a non-zero chance that you could end up trying to use the same shortened URL for two different long URLs. The later entry would overwrite the earlier one. The chance of this is very low for the second entry you add, but increases each time as existing values accumulate. This might not be acceptable in production! You could mitigate it somewhat by extending the character set used in the random string, using a longer random string, or, ideally, by checking if the random string already exists. We have not done this here because to do so in a fully thread-safe way would make the example rather long.

Now you have the function to create a mapping, so you need one to go the other way: to take a shortened URL and return the original long URL supplied by the caller. As you have no control over what input is sent (it might not be a valid shortened URL) you will do this using the try... idiom, where you either return Some(value) on success or None on failure. Here is the code:

```
// Try to resolve a shortened URL to the long version:
let tryResolve (short : string) =
  match shortToLong.TryGetValue short with
  | true, long -> Some long
  | false, _ -> None
```

Here you are making a call to the shortToLong dictionary's TryGetValue method, which will look up the value short in the dictionary and return a tuple of true and the value if it exists, or false and null if it does not. (In C#, TryGetValue places the value, if found, in a by-reference argument and returns a Boolean; the F# compiler uses some magic to transform the call so that the success-Boolean and the by-reference argument are instead returned as a tuple.) You can then pattern match on the returned tuple to translate it into Some(value) or None.

That's all the business logic you need; the rest is just a matter of binding that logic to the HTTP handling that is needed to make the application work as a web service. This where you need to make use of Suave.io. Suave.io apps consist of nested sets of calls to the Suave.io function choose. The choose function takes a single argument: a list of WebPart instances (a WebPart being a function that can map from an HTTP context to another HTTP context). Each of these WebPart instances may or may not match the incoming value; the first one that actually does match is returned. This continues in a recursive way until the app can return a response. A custom operator (>=>) is defined to help you bind pairs of async workflows together.

So at the outer level here,

```
choose
  [
    POST >=> choose
  ...
    GET >=> choose
  ]
  ...
```

you are effectively saying "if the incoming request uses the HTTP verb POST, go down the first branch, and if the incoming request uses the HTTP verb GET, go down the second branch." Zooming in on the first branch here,

```
... choose
[ path "/add" >=> request (fun req ->
  match (req.formData "url") with
  | Choice1Of2 long ->
```

```
      let short = shorten long
      // You may need to amend the port number:
      let url = sprintf "localhost:8083/go/%s" short
      Successful.CREATED url
  | _ ->
      RequestErrors.BAD_REQUEST "Url not supplied")
]
```

you are saying "if the path of the request is /add, check that there is a value labelled url in the posted form data, and if there is, attempt to shorten it using the business logic defined above." If the shortening succeeds, you return the HTTP response CREATED (201) together with the shortened URL.

In the second branch here,

```
... choose
[ pathScan "/go/%s" (fun short ->
    match tryResolve short with
    | Some long ->
      Redirection.MOVED_PERMANENTLY (sprintf "http://%s" long)
    | None ->
      RequestErrors.NOT_FOUND "Url not found")
]
```

you are trying to resolve a shortened URL, and if successful, you return a MOVED PERMANENTLY (301) message, which will cause the requesting browser to move on to the lengthened URL.

Suave.io's choose idiom can be more than a little bewildering at first, but you can normally get things working by editing examples, such as the one above, to fit your requirements, until you get more of a handle on the underlying concepts. Suave.io pays off handsomely in situations where you want to put together a simple, non-blocking web service from scratch with the minimum of code. For example, it is extremely useful in cases where you need to embed web-serving features into a product that is not essentially web-based. It is also very useful when you want to write simple fake servers to form part of an automated testing infrastructure.

Creating Web Services

Suave.io is a great, F#-friendly way of creating an HTML-based service. But what if you want to create a more conventional web service based on Microsoft's .NET Web API framework? (The following section is necessarily Microsoft .NET-specific because of the Visual Studio template that it uses.)

Let's say you want the same URL shortener that you created above, but this time in the form of an ASP.NET Web API 2.0 project. Microsoft does not currently supply Visual Studio templates for creating ASP.NET MVC web sites or services in F#; but fortunately the open source community has stepped in to fill the breach. To benefit from their efforts, start by going the Visual Studio gallery web site (https://visualstudiogallery.msdn.microsoft.com) and searching for "F# MVC." In the results you should find a package called "F# Web Application templates (MVC 5 and Web API 2.2)" by Ryan Riley and Daniel Mohl. Download and run the .vsix file.

Run Visual Studio and create a new Project. Under Installed ➤ Templates ➤ Visual F# ➤ ASPNET you should find a template called "F# ASP.NET MVC 5 and Web API 2" (Figure 10-4).

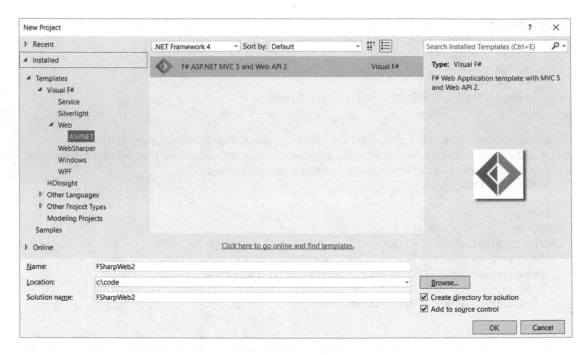

Figure 10-4. *Selecting the "F# ASP.NET MVC 5/Web API 2" template*

Select this, and in the same dialog give your project a name. Click OK. You will be presented with a dialog that allows you to choose from a number of related project types (Figure 10-5).

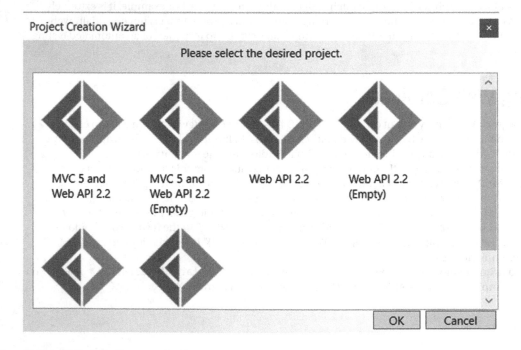

Figure 10-5. *Selecting a project type*

For this exercise, select "Web API 2.2". Note that there are also options to create MVC web sites that also contain Web API services. You may find these useful for more ambitious projects.

Click OK, and you should see a fully working, but almost content-free, project. Before you change anything, check that the project compiles and runs, by simply clicking Visual Studio's Run button. A short list of cars should appear in your browser. This has been rendered by a simple JavaScript program (main.js) that calls the service that your project provides. Try getting "under the hood" by going to your browser and editing the URL so that the API endpoint's URL is called directly. The URL should look something like this, although the port number is likely to differ:

```
http://localhost:48213/api/cars
```

You should see the same content–a very short list of cars–but this time rendered in an unformatted form. Depending on your browser, you may see the car list in XML or in JSON.

Now you need to change the project to transform it into a Web API-based version of your URL shortener. Start by adding a new F# library project to the solution. Call the new project Shorten. Once you've added it, right-click it in Solution Explorer, select Properties, and change the Target Framework value to .NET 4.5.1 and ensure that the F# Target Runtime value is set to F# 4.0. Then select the web project, and change these same two properties for that project to the same values: .NET 4.5.1 and F# 4.0.

Now rename the Library1.fs file in that project to Shortener.fs and add code from Listing 10-4, replacing the existing content.

Listing 10-4. A URL Shortener

```
module Shortener

open System
open System.Collections.Concurrent

// Initialize a .NET random number generator:
let private random = Random()

// Generate a random string of lower-case letters
// of a specified length.  WARNING: this has the
// potential to generate rude words!
let private randomString len =
    Array.init len (fun _ -> random.Next(26) + 97 |> char)
    |> String

// A dictionary of mappings from the long to the shortened URLs:
let private longToShort = ConcurrentDictionary<string, string>()
// A dictionary of mappings from the shortened to the long URLs:
let private shortToLong = ConcurrentDictionary<string, string>()

// Shorten a URL, and as a side-effect store the short->long
// and long->short mappings:
let Shorten (long : string) =
    longToShort.GetOrAdd(long, fun _ ->
        let short = randomString 5
        shortToLong.[short] <- long
        short)
```

```
// Try to resolve a shortened URL to the long version:
let TryResolve (short : string) =
    match shortToLong.TryGetValue short with
    | true, long -> Some long
    | false, _ -> None
```

You'll notice that this code is pretty much identical to the code you used in the previous, Suave-based example.

Now you need to integrate your URL-shortening library with the web service code created by the template. Start by adding a reference to your new Shorten library in the original Web project: in Solution Explorer, right-click the References node of the web project and select Add Reference. Find and tick the Shorten item in the Solution tab. Now find the file called CarsController.fs in the web project, and rename it ShortenerController.fs. In this file, remove everything except the initial "open" statements, and then add your own controller code from Listing 10-5.

Listing 10-5. Controller for the URL Shortener

```
[<RoutePrefix("api")>]
type ShortenerValuesController() =
    inherit ApiController()

    [<Route("add")>]
    [<HttpPost>]
    member x.Add(long : string) : IHttpActionResult =
        let short = Shortener.Shorten(long)
        // You may need to update the port number:
        let url = sprintf "localhost:48213/api/go/%s" short
        x.Ok(url) :> _
```

As before, you may need to change the port number. Here you are creating your own ASP.NET Web API controller. Let's go through the code line by line.

You start by defining a controller:

```
[<RoutePrefix("api")>]
type ShortenerController() =
    inherit ApiController()
```

This inherits from ApiController, which is a standard ASP.NET class that provides various methods useful in the construction of Web APIs. The RoutePrefix attribute means that any handlers within this controller can be reached using a URL that starts with api (after the hostname section, obviously).

Here you define a handler for a route called add:

```
[<Route("add")>]
[<HttpPost>]
member x.Add(long : string) : IHttpActionResult =
```

The handler will only respond to the HTTP method POST, and accepts one argument called long, which the caller will use to send in the long version of the URL they want to be shortened. The hander returns an IHttpActionResult, which enables you to return an HTTP response message that contains a response code (e.g. 200 OK) and a message (such as an error description if there is a problem).

```
let short = Shortener.Shorten(long)
// You may need to update the port number:
let url = sprintf "localhost:48213/api/go/%s" short
```

These lines call your shortening service, and embed the shortened version in a URL which the caller can later use to resolve the shortened version and navigate to the original site.

The last line is a little obscure:

```
x.Ok(url) :> _
```

The first part, x.Ok(url), is where you return the shortened URL to the caller, along with an OK (200) return code that tells the caller that the transaction went successfully. The final part, :> _, results from F#'s requirement that types are cast explicitly to interfaces when an interface type is expected. The Ok method of ApiController returns something that implements IHttpActionResult, but it isn't of itself an IHttpActionResult, so you must cast it using the :> operator. The good news is that F# has enough information (from the defined return type of the Add method) to infer that what you need to cast to is indeed an IHttpActionResult, so that you can use the _ symbol instead of the whole interface name.

Now you need to add a route that will let the caller resolve a previously shortened URL. See Listing 10-6 for the code.

Listing 10-6. Adding a Go Route for the URL Shortener

```
[<Route("go/{short}")>]
[<HttpGet>]
member x.Go(short : string) : IHttpActionResult =
   match Shortener.TryResolve short with
   | Some long ->
       let url = sprintf "http://%s" long
       x.Redirect(url) :> _
   | None ->
       x.NotFound() :> _
```

Here you use the Route attribute to say that this handler will respond to the route go followed by a value called short, which will be the shortened URL that the caller wants to resolve. This handler will only respond to GET verbs. In the body of the handler, you call your TryResolve method, and if it succeeds, you return a redirect response (code 302), sending the caller to the full version of the URL. If the shortened URL couldn't be resolved, you return a "not found" response, code 404. On both the return branches you again have to cast the returned value to IHttpActionResult using :> _.

It's time to try out your Web API-based URL shortener. Make sure your Web API project is set as the startup project and run it. You should get a more or less empty page in your browser. Fire up Fiddler or your favorite web debugging tool and use it to send a post to the api/add route, as shown in Figure 10-6.

Figure 10-6. Using Fiddler to send a post with a query string

You should get the shortened URL in your response, similar to Figure 10-7.

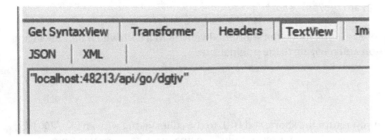

Figure 10-7. *Viewing a response in Fiddler*

Copy this path back into your browser address bar and hit Enter. Voila! You're redirected to the original site.

Summary

This chapter covered some useful, F#-friendly options for creating distributed applications. You looked at System.Net.WebRequest, which allows you to request data using HTTP, and you used this to access data in published Google spreadsheets. You saw how to serve HTTP requests in two different ways: using Suave.io, which allows a highly idiomatic and concise approach, and using Web API via an open source Visual Studio template, which developers coming from an ASP .NET MVC background may find more familiar. What you saw here only scratches the surface of what is possible using F# and the Internet, so we encourage you to go out and explore F#'s rich, largely open source network ecosystem.

■ ■ ■

CHAPTER 11

Language-Oriented Programming

In this chapter, you will begin by taking a look at what I mean by *language-oriented programming*, a term that has been used by many people to mean different things. I'll also briefly discuss its advantages and disadvantages. Next, you'll look at several different approaches to language-oriented programming in F#. These techniques include using F# literals to create *little languages* and using F# `quotations`. You'll spend the bulk of this chapter looking at examples where you create a language and then create an interpreter to execute that language. Finally, you'll take a more detailed look at how languages are executed, including a performance comparison of interpreted or compiled execution techniques.

What Is Language-Oriented Programming?

People use the term *language-oriented programming* to describe many different programming techniques, but the techniques they refer to tend to share a common theme. It's quite common for programmers to have to implement a predefined language; often this is because you need to extract structured data from information stored or received as string or XML that conforms to this predefined language. The techniques introduced in this chapter will help you do this more reliably. Related to this is the idea of little languages, or *domain-specific languages* (DSLs); you might want to create a DSL when the best way to solve a problem is to create a custom language to describe the problem and then use this language to solve that problem. Note that you don't have to create an entire, compilable programming language to implement a DSL. A DSL is simply a set of labels, data structures, and functions that you can use in a language-like way from your "normal" code. Functional programming has always had a strong relationship with language-oriented programming because functional programming languages generally have features that are well suited to creating parsers and compilers.

Data Structures as Little Languages

Taking advantage of language-oriented development doesn't necessarily mean writing your own parser or compiler. You can accomplish a lot by creating data structures that describe *what* you want to do and then creating functions or modules that define *how* the structure should be interpreted. You can create data structures that represent a program in just about any language, but F# lends itself well to this approach. F#'s literal lists and arrays are easy to define and require no bulky type annotations. Its discriminated union types allow you to create structures that express concepts that are related, but which do not necessarily contain the same types of data. You can take advantage of this to build tree-like structures, which prove useful when creating languages. Finally, you can treat functions as values, so you can easily embed functions within data structures. This means F# expressions can become part of your language, usually as an action in response to some particular condition of the language.

© Robert Pickering and Kit Eason 2016

R. Pickering and K. Eason, *Beginning F# 4.0*, DOI 10.1007/978-1-4842-1374-2_11

Let's start by taking a look at a beautiful and very practical library that lets you write your own tiny DSL for parsing command line arguments. It's called Argu (formerly UnionArgParser) and you can install it using NuGet or your favorite package manager. Let's imagine that you want to create a command line application that can list the contents of a folder in CSV format, allowing the user to specify (using command line parameters) which information about each file to display, and what separator to use (comma, tab, and so forth). Even for this relatively simple requirement, parsing the command line into flags you can use to control the behavior of your program would be a pain. But solving the problem by thinking of the arguments as a DSL makes it super simple.

Start by creating an F# command line application called DirList and install Argu. At the beginning of Program.fs, replace everything before the main function and its EntryPoint attribute with the code from Listing 11-1.

Listing 11-1. A DSL as a Discriminated Union

```
open Argu

type Arguments =
| Dir of string
| Sep of string
| Date of bool
| Size of bool
with
    interface IArgParserTemplate with
        member s.Usage =
            match s with
            | Dir _ -> "specify a directory to list."
            | Sep _ -> "specify a separator."
            | Date _ -> "specify whether to include the date."
            | Size _ -> "specify whether to include the size."
```

This is a classic way of getting started with a DSL: defining a discriminated union that indicates the main keywords of the language and the argument types they take. In this case, you are saying "the arguments can contain a directory name that is a string; a CSV separator that is a string; a date flag that is a bool;" and so forth. When getting started in this way, you firmly avoid thinking about *how* you are going to implement the DSL; you just declare its shape.

In the latter part of Listing 11-1, you also implement an interface called IArgParserTemplate, whose Usage member will come in handy when telling the user what arguments are available. Binding the DSL keywords directly with their documentation is where you start getting the benefits of the Argu library.

Now let's think about how you are going to implement the actual listing of the files. Listing 11-2 shows a simple function that, given the appropriate arguments, will list the files in the specified way.

Listing 11-2. A Function to List Files in a CSV-Friendly Style

```
open System.IO

let ListFiles
    (directory : string) (sep : string)
    (includeDate : bool) (includeSize : bool) =
    directory
    |> Directory.EnumerateFiles
    // If you are limited to F# 3.x you will have to replace the following line with
    // |> Seq.map (fun name -> FileInfo name)
    |> Seq.map FileInfo
    |> Seq.iter (fun info ->
```

```
        printfn "%s%s%s"
            info.Name
            (if includeDate then
                sprintf "%s%s" sep (info.LastWriteTime.ToString())
             else
                "")
            (if includeSize then
                sprintf "%s%s" sep (info.Length.ToString())
             else
                "")
    )
```

This code performs a Directory.EnumerateFiles to list the names of files; maps those names into FileInfo instances using Seq.map; then iterates over the results, printing out the required columns, separated by the required separators.

You haven't joined this function onto the parsed arguments yet, but you can still send the function to F# Interactive and execute it manually as a simple exploratory test.

```
>

val ListFiles :
  directory:string ->
    sep:string -> includeDate:bool -> includeSize:bool -> unit

> ListFiles @"c:\temp" "," true true;;
akkaissue.png,01/06/2015 09:03:26,24917
animals.xml,08/09/2015 07:00:03,81
archie.png,19/10/2015 12:02:49,41092
asyncdemo.txt,27/01/2015 09:09:04,41
bike.jpg,28/02/2015 21:17:17,20953
bootstrap.sh,26/10/2015 15:36:21,47
bootstrap3.sh,10/11/2015 09:18:30,167
cluster.txt,08/12/2015 11:38:14,17
createuat.sql,24/09/2015 08:33:31,2341
CreatingAnArray.fs,18/04/2014 19:23:38,1269
```

At this point, you've got both ends of the pipeline defined. Next, you need to do the bit in the middle: mapping from the command line arguments the user typed to the parameters the ListFiles function requires. Here's where you need Argu magic! Place the contents of Listing 11-3 into Program.fs, replacing the existing main function.

Listing 11-3. Linking Your Arguments DSL with the ListFiles Function

```
[<EntryPoint>]
let main argv =
    let parser = ArgumentParser.Create<Arguments>()
    let args =
        try
            parser.Parse argv |> Some
        with
        | _ ->
```

```
            printfn "Usage: %s" (parser.Usage())
            None
    match args with
    | Some a ->
        let dir = a.GetResult(<@ Dir @>, defaultValue = ".")
        let incDate = a.GetResult(<@ Date @>, defaultValue = false)
        let incSize = a.GetResult(<@ Size @>, defaultValue = false)
        let sep = a.GetResult(<@ Sep @>, defaultValue = ",")
        ListFiles dir sep incDate incSize
        0
    | None -> 1
```

Here you create a parser using ArgumentParser.Create and, crucially, you provide the Arguments discriminated union as a type argument. You are telling Argu the definition of your tiny DSL, so it knows what elements it is expected to parse from the argument string you will give it later.

Next (and in a try block in case of invalid arguments) you call parser.Parse, providing the contents of argv. In case you didn't know, argv is a parameter that is automatically populated for you by the runtime environment, with an array of strings representing the arguments that the user typed in the command line. The command line string is just split up on spaces; there is no intelligence at this stage regarding which items are flag names (e.g. –date) and which are values (e.g. true).

Because it's possible that the arguments couldn't be parsed, you handle the resulting exception by returning a None. This means that on success you must pass the output of parser.Parse to Some.

If the arguments were successfully parsed, you can start to access the parameter values. Argu lets you do that using the F# Quotation mechanism, which you first explored in Chapter 6. All you have to do is pass in the discriminated union case (in this example, Dir), which represents the argument whose value you want to get:

```
let dir = a.GetResult(<@ Dir @>, defaultValue = ".")
```

See how you can also specify a default value. This will be used if the relevant argument doesn't appear in the command line.

Now that you have all of the argument values, you can finally call your ListFiles function. You return 0 for success or 1 for failure, in case your program is being used a part of a larger pipeline that needs to know if the file listing succeeded.

On Windows, you can try your file list out by compiling it, opening a command line window, and navigating to the directory where your compiler outputs its executable. Then type something like this, substituting in whatever directory path is appropriate in your environment):

```
dirlist --dir c:\temp
```

```
C:\DirList\bin>dirlist --dir c:\temp
akkaissue.png
animals.xml
archie.png
asyncdemo.txt
bike.jpg
bootstrap.sh
bootstrap3.sh
cluster.txt
createuat.sql
CreatingAnArray.fs
```

On Linux and OS X, you need to run a console window and then execute the following commands, varying the path in the cd command to suit where you created the project:

```
cd ~/Code/DirList/DirList/bin/Debug
chmod 744  DirList.exe
./DirList.exe --dir ~
```

This should show you a list of the files in your home directory.

Now experiment with the parameters (if you can't remember then, type dirlist -help). For example,

```
dirlist --dir c:\temp --date true --size true
```

On Linux and OS X this would be

```
./DirList.exe --dir ~ --date true --size true
```

Also, see what happens when you type incorrect arguments, such as:

```
dirlist --foo bar
```

I am particularly fond of this kind of DSL because I think it makes it clear what arguments the program is expecting and what processing should take place if that argument is received. The fact that the help text is bound more or less directly to the union cases serves a double purpose; it allows the function processing the command line arguments to print out help text automatically if anything goes wrong, and it also reminds you what the argument is in case you forget. I also like this method of creating a command line interpreter because I have written several command line interpreters in imperative languages, and it is not a satisfying experience—you end up having to write lots of code to detail how your command line should be broken up. If you write that code in a traditional imperative way, then you usually spend way too much time calling the string type's IndexOf and Substring methods.

A Data Structure–Based Language Implementation

Creating any DSL should start with defining what problem you need to solve; in this case, let's imagine that you need to define a DSL library (sometimes called a *combinators library*) for drawing 2D images. This is something of an obvious choice. This example demonstrates how you can build up complicated structures out a number of simple primitives. An image on a computer screen is essentially just a collection of lines and polygons, although the image displayed might be extremely intricate. You begin by walking through the main points of the design process and conclude by looking at the full listings.

■ **Note** This example was largely inspired by work done on a similar but much larger system by Chance Coble and Roger Castillo.

You start by designing a set of types that that will describe your picture; these types form the primitives of your image:

```
// represents the basic shapes that will make up the scene
type Shape =
    | Line of Position * Position
    | Polygon of List<Position>
    | CompositeShape of List<Shape>
```

This type is recursive, and the CompositeShape union case contains a list of shapes that it will use to form a tree-like structure. In compiler development, this tree-like structure is referred to as the *abstract syntax tree* (AST). You'll see another example of using an AST to represent a program at the end of the chapter.

So far, you have created your picture using three basic elements: lines, polygons, and shapes. The fact that your type is made up of just three simple elements is an important design decision; making your primitives simple makes implementing the engine that will render the image much simpler. The fact that your primitives are so simple means you don't expect your user to spend time interacting with them directly; instead you'll provide a set of higher-level wrapper functions that return values of type shape. These are your *combinators*. The CompositeShape case in your union is an important example of this; it allows you to build up more complicated shapes out of simpler elements. You expose this through the compose function:

```
// allows us to compose a list of elements into a
// single shape
let compose shapes = CompositeShape shapes
```

You use this function to implement a number of higher-level functions. For example, the lines function, which takes a list of positions and returns a shape that is a path through those positions, takes advantage of the compose function to combine a number of individual lines into a single line:

```
// a line composed of two or more points
let lines posList =
    // grab first value in the list
    let initVal =
        match posList with
        | first :: _ -> first
        | _ -> failwith "must give more than one point"
    // creates a new link in the line
    let createList (prevVal, acc) item =
        let newVal = Line(prevVal, item)
        item, newVal :: acc
    // folds over the list accumlating all points into a
    // list of line shapes
    let _, lines = List.fold createList (initVal, []) posList
    // compose the list of lines into a single shape
    compose lines
```

Next, you use this `lines` function in the implementation of several high-level shapes, such as the `square` function:

```
let square filled (top, right) size =
    let pos1, pos2 = (top, right), (top, right + size)
    let pos3, pos4 = (top + size, right + size), (top + size, right)
    if filled then
        polygon [ pos1; pos2; pos3; pos4; pos1 ]
    else
        lines [ pos1; pos2; pos3; pos4; pos1 ]
```

The `square` function uses the `lines` function to plot the outline of a `square` with the calculated points. You can see the full module in Listing 11-4, although a more realistic implementation would probably contain more basic shapes for the users of the library to choose from.

To get this code working, start by creating a new F# Console Application. Add references to `System.Drawing` and `System.Windows.Forms`. Add new source files called `Combinators.fs` and `Form.fs`, and ensure that the three source files appear in the project in the order `Combinators.fs`, `Form.fs`, and then `Program.fs`. (In Visual Studio, you can reorder in Solution Explorer by right-clicking a source file and choosing "Move Up" or "Move Down." In Xamarin Studio and MonoDevelop, it's even easier: just drag source files into the required order in Solution Explorer.) Listing 11-4 goes in `Combinators.fs`, Listing 11-5 goes in `Form.fs`, and Listing 11-6 goes in `Program.fs`.

Listing 11-4. A Combinator Library for Creating Images

```
namespace Strangelights.GraphicDSL
open System.Drawing

// represents a point within the scene
type Position = int * int

// represents the basic shapes that will make up the scene
type Shape =
    | Line of Position * Position
    | Polygon of List<Position>
    | CompositeShape of List<Shape>

// allows us to give a color to a shape
type Element = Shape * Color

module Combinators =
    // allows us to compose a list of elements into a
    // single shape
    let compose shapes = CompositeShape shapes

    // a simple line made from two points
    let line pos1 pos2 = Line (pos1, pos2)

    // a line composed of two or more points
    let lines posList =
        // grab first value in the list
        let initVal =
            match posList with
```

```
        | first :: _ -> first
        | _ -> failwith "must give more than one point"
    // creates a new link in the line
    let createList (prevVal, acc) item =
        let newVal = Line(prevVal, item)
        item, newVal :: acc
    // folds over the list accumlating all points into a
    // list of line shapes
    let _, lines = List.fold createList (initVal, []) posList
    // compose the list of lines into a single shape
    compose lines

// a polygon defined by a set of points
let polygon posList = Polygon posList

// a triangle that can be either hollow or filled
let triangle filled pos1 pos2 pos3 =
    if filled then
        polygon [ pos1; pos2; pos3; pos1 ]
    else
        lines [ pos1; pos2; pos3; pos1 ]

// a square that can either be hollow or filled
let square filled (top, right) size =
    let pos1, pos2 = (top, right), (top, right + size)
    let pos3, pos4 = (top + size, right + size), (top + size, right)
    if filled then
        polygon [ pos1; pos2; pos3; pos4; pos1 ]
    else
        lines [ pos1; pos2; pos3; pos4; pos1 ]
```

You now have the basic elements of your language; next you need to implement an interpreter to display the image. The interpreter described in this chapter is a WinForm. The advantage to this approach is that you might also implement an interpreter in WPF or some other graphics environment, which means that it is quite portable between GUI libraries and platforms. Implementing the interpreter is straightforward. You just need to implement each of your union cases. In the case of Line and Polygon, you draw these shapes using the GDI+ objects that WinForms are based on. Fortunately, GDI+ makes it straightforward to draw a line or polygon. The third CompositeShape case is also straightforward; you simply call your drawing function recursively. You can see the full source code for this in Listing 11-5.

Listing 11-5. An Interpreter to Render Images from Your Combinator Library

```
namespace Strangelights.GraphicDSL

open System.Drawing
open System.Windows.Forms

// a form that can be used to display the scene
type EvalForm(items: List<Element>) as x =
    inherit Form()
    // handle the paint event to draw the scene
    do x.Paint.Add(fun ea ->
```

```
    let rec drawShape (shape, (color: Color)) =
        match shape with
        | Line ((x1, y1), (x2, y2)) ->
            // draw a line
            let pen = new Pen(color)
            ea.Graphics.DrawLine(pen, x1, y1, x2, y2)
        | Polygon points ->
            // draw a polygon
            let points =
                points
                |> List.map (fun (x,y) -> new Point(x, y))
                |> Array.ofList
            let brush = new SolidBrush(color)
            ea.Graphics.FillPolygon(brush, points)
        | CompositeShape shapes ->
            // recursively draw the other contained elements
            List.iter (fun shape -> drawShape(shape, color)) shapes
    // draw all the items we have been passed
    items |> List.iter drawShape)
```

Putting together a simple image composed of two squares and a triangle now becomes straightforward. You simply call the appropriate functions from your combinator library and then combine them with a color to make a full description of the scene. Listing 11-6 shows how to do this; you can see the resulting image in Figure 11-1.

Listing 11-6. Calling Your Combinator Library

```
open System.Drawing
open System.Windows.Forms
open Strangelights.GraphicDSL

// two test squares
let square1 = Combinators.square true (100, 50) 50
let square2 = Combinators.square false (50, 100) 50

// a test triangle
let triangle1 =
    Combinators.triangle false
        (150, 200) (150, 150) (250, 200)

// compose the basic elements into a picture
let scence = Combinators.compose [square1; square2; triangle1]

// create the display form
let form = new EvalForm([scence, Color.Red])

[<EntryPoint>]
let main argv =
    // show the form
    Application.Run form
    0
```

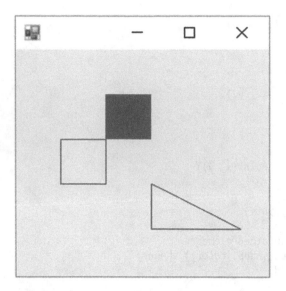

Figure 11-1. *A scene rendered by your combinator library*

The simple example given in Listing 11-6 probably doesn't represent how you would create images using the combinator library. You'll take look at a more realistic scenario in Listing 11-7. The best approach to using the combinator library would probably be to carry on programming in the style you wrote the original combinator library in; that is, you would build up simple elements that you can reuse in your image. Next, you'll look at how to create a scene composed of seven stars. The obvious place to start is with the creation of the star; you can see how to create the star function defined in Listing 11-7. This function creates triangles that are mirror images and combines them with a slight offset to form a six-sided star. This example might give you some idea of how to build up more complex shapes out of simpler ones. Once you have the definition of your star, you simply need a list of positions that tell where to print the stars. You can see this list of points in Listing 11-7. Once you have these two elements, you can combine them using the List.map function and the compose function to create your scene. Next, you can display your scene the same way you did in the previous listing.

Listing 11-7. Creating a More Complex Image Using Your Combinator Library

```
open System.Drawing
open System.Windows.Forms
open Strangelights.GraphicDSL

// define a function that can draw a 6 sided star
let star (x, y) size =
    let offset = size / 2
    // calculate the first triangle
    let t1 =
        Combinators.triangle false
            (x, y - size - offset)
            (x - size, y + size - offset)
            (x + size, y + size - offset)
```

```
    // calculate another inverted triangle
    let t2 =
        Combinators.triangle false
            (x, y + size + offset)
            (x + size, y - size + offset)
            (x - size, y - size + offset)
    // compose the triangles
    Combinators.compose [ t1; t2 ]

// the points where stars should be plotted
let points = [ (10, 20); (200, 10);
               (30, 160); (100, 150); (190, 150);
               (20, 300); (200, 300);  ]

// compose the stars into a single scene
let scence =
    Combinators.compose
        (List.map (fun pos -> star pos 5) points)

// show the scene in red on the EvalForm
let form = new EvalForm([scence, Color.Red],
                        Width = 260, Height = 350)

[<EntryPoint>]
let main argv =
    // show the form
    Application.Run form
    0
```

Replace the contents of Program.fs with Listing 11-7 and run your project. Figure 11-2 shows the resulting image.

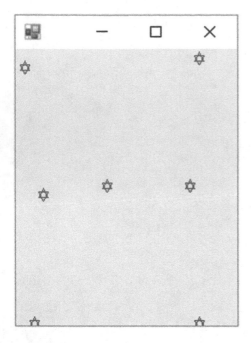

Figure 11-2. *Another scene rendered by your combinator library*

You've now seen two approaches for creating combinator libraries (libraries that create little languages though data structures). At this point, you're probably beginning to see how you can break a problem down into an abstract description of the problem based on a small set of primitives, possibly with aid of other libraries that you build on these primitives.

■ **Note**   If you're looking for a more in-depth view of a combinator library, take a look at the paper by Simon Peyton Jones, Jean-Marc Eber, and Julian Seward called "Composing contracts: an adventure in financial engineering." The paper gives an in-depth, yet understandable, study of a combinator library for describing derivatives contracts. The examples in the paper are in Haskell rather than F#, but you could translate them to F# with some effort. You can read this paper at `http://research.microsoft.com/en-us/um/people/simonpj/papers/financial-contracts/contracts-icfp.htm`.

Metaprogramming with Quotations

In Chapter 6, you used quotations; these are quoted sections of F# code where the quote operator instructs the compiler to generate data structures representing the code, rather than IL representing the code. This means you have a data structure that represents the code that was coded, rather than code you can execute, and you're free to do what you want with it. You can either interpret it, performing the actions you require as you go along, or you can compile it into another language. Or you can simply ignore it if you want. You could, for example, take a section of quoted code and compile it for another runtime, such as the Java Virtual Machine (JVM).

In the next example, you'll write an interpreter for integer-based arithmetic expressions in F#. This might be useful for learning how stack-based calculations work. Here, your language is already designed for you; it is the syntax available in F#. You'll work exclusively with arithmetic expressions of the form <@ (2 * (2 - 1)) / 2 @>. This means you need to generate an error whenever you come across syntax that is neither an integer nor an operation. Quotations are based on discriminated union types. When working with quotations, you have to query the expression that you receive using F#'s pattern matching and active patterns. For example, here you query an expression using an active pattern and a when guard to see whether it is an integer; if it is, you push it onto the stack:

```
| Value (x,ty) when ty = typeof<int> ->
                            let i = x :?> int
                            printfn "Push %i" i
                            operandsStack.Push(x :?> int)
```

If it isn't an integer, you could go on to check whether it is one of several other types. There also several parameterized active patterns that you might find useful. For example, SpecificCall accepts a quotation that is a function expression and allows you to query whether the quotation being matched over is a call to that function. You use this to determine whether a call to an operator is made. For example, the following example checks whether a call to the plus operator is made:

```
| SpecificCall <@ (+) @> (_,_, [l;r])  -> interpretInner l
                            interpretInner r
                            preformOp (+) "Add"
```

You can see the full code in Listing 11-8.

Listing 11-8. Stack-Based Evaluation of F# Quoted Arithmetic Expressions

```
open System.Collections.Generic
open Microsoft.FSharp.Quotations
open Microsoft.FSharp.Quotations.Patterns
open Microsoft.FSharp.Quotations.DerivedPatterns

let interpret exp =
    let operandsStack = new Stack<int>()
    let preformOp f name =
        let x, y = operandsStack.Pop(), operandsStack.Pop()
        printfn "%s %i, %i" name x y
        let result = f x y
        operandsStack.Push(result)
    let rec interpretInner exp =
        match exp with
        | SpecificCall <@ (*) @> (_,_, [l;r])  -> interpretInner l
                            interpretInner r
                            preformOp (*) "Mult"
        | SpecificCall <@ (+) @> (_,_, [l;r])  -> interpretInner l
                            interpretInner r
                            preformOp (+) "Add"
        | SpecificCall <@ (-) @> (_,_, [l;r])  -> interpretInner l
                            interpretInner r
                            preformOp (-) "Sub"
```

```
        | SpecificCall <@ (/) @> (_,_, [l;r])  -> interpretInner l
                                                  interpretInner r
                                                  preformOp (/) "Div"
        | Value (x,ty) when ty = typeof<int>    ->
                                                  let i = x :?> int
                                                  printfn "Push: %i" i
                                                  operandsStack.Push(x :?> int)

        | _ -> failwith "not a valid op"
    interpretInner exp
    printfn "Result: %i" (operandsStack.Pop())

interpret <@ (2 * (2 - 1)) / 2 @>
```

You can run this code in F# Interactive, producing the following results:

```
Push: 2
Push: 2
Push: 1
Sub 1, 2
Multi 1, 2
Push: 2
Div 2, 2
Result: 1
```

You are always working with F# syntax when you use quotations, which is both an advantage and a disadvantage. The advantage is that you can produce powerful libraries based on this technique that integrate well with F# code, but without having to create a parser. The disadvantage is that it is difficult to produce tools suitable for end users based on this technique. However, libraries that consume or transform F# quotations can still be used from other .NET languages because the F# libraries include functions and samples to convert between F# quotations and other common metaprogramming formats, such as LINQ quotations. For some interesting uses of quotations as little languages, you can see the F# DSL in Microsoft Solver Foundation at https://msdn.microsoft.com/en-us/library/ff524501(v=vs.93).aspx. You can also see my discussion of it on my blog at http://strangelights.com/blog/archive/2008/09/21/1628.aspx.

This concludes your examination of DSLs; the rest of the chapter will dig a bit deeper into the implementation of an interpreter or compiler for your language.

Implementing a Compiler and an Interpreter for an Arithmetic Language

So far, we've focused more on the design of the languages themselves, the *front end*, rather than the implementation of the compiler or interpreter for the language, the *back end*. In this section, you'll focus on the implementation of a back end for a simple arithmetic language defined by an AST. The AST syntax tree shown in the first section is based on a union type.

To build a front end for this little language, in other words a parser that translates text input in the language, is beyond the scope of this book. If you want to take the example further, look at the NuGet package named fparsec (www.quanttec.com/fparsec/).

You have two distinct modes of acting on the results of the parser: compiling the results and interpreting them. Compiling refers to changing the AST into some other format that is faster or easier for a machine to execute. Originally, this nearly always meant native code; these days, it's more likely to refer to something a little more abstract, such as IL, F#, or even C#. Interpreting the results means acting on the results straightaway, without any transformation of the AST. You'll look briefly at both of these topics in the "Interpreting the AST" and "Compiling the AST" sections; then you'll compare the two approaches to get some idea of when to use each in the "Compilation vs. Interpretation" section.

The Abstract Syntax Tree

An AST is a representation of the construct that makes up the program; it's intended to be easy for the programmer to use. One reason that F# is good for this kind of development is its union type. This type is great for representing languages because you can use it to represent items that are related yet do not share the same structure. The following example shows how to use an AST:

```
type Ast =
    | Ident of string
    | Val of System.Double
    | Multi of Ast * Ast
    | Div of Ast * Ast
    | Plus of Ast * Ast
    | Minus of Ast * Ast
```

The tree consists of only one type because it is quite simple. A complicated tree would contain many more types, but it would still follow this basic pattern. Here you can see that the tree, which is of the type Ast, will consist of either identifiers (the Ident type); the names of the identifiers represented by a string; or values (the Val type), which will be values represented by a System.Double. The type also includes four more types (Multi, Div, Plus, and Minus) that represent the arithmetic operations. They use recursion, allowing them to be composed of other expressions.

Interpreting the AST

Once you create your AST, you have two choices: you can either interpret it or compile it. Interpreting it simply means walking the tree and performing actions as you go. Compiling it means changing it into some other form that is easier, or more typically, faster, for the machine to execute. This section will examine how to interpret the results; the next section will look at the options for compiling them; and finally, you will look at when you should use interpretation and when you should use compilation.

The following example shows a short interpreter for your program. The main work of interpreting the AST is done by the function interpret, which walks the tree, performing the necessary actions as it goes. The logic is quite simple. If you find a literal value or an identifier, you return the appropriate value:

```
| Ident (s) -> variableDict.[s]
| Val (v) -> v
```

If you find an operand, you recursively evaluate the expressions it contains to obtain its values and then perform the operation:

```
| Multi (e1, e2) -> (interpretInner e1) * (interpretInner e2)
```

You can see the complete interpreter in Listing 11-9.

Listing 11-9. Interpreting an AST Generated from Command-Line Input

```
open System

type Ast =
    | Ident of string
    | Val of System.Double
    | Multi of Ast * Ast
    | Div of Ast * Ast
    | Plus of Ast * Ast
    | Minus of Ast * Ast

// requesting a value for variable from the user
let getVariableValues e =
    let rec getVariableValuesInner input (variables : Map<string, float>) =
        match input with
        | Ident (s) ->
            match variables.TryFind(s) with
            | Some _ -> variables
            | None ->
                printfn "%s: " s
                let v = float(Console.ReadLine())
                variables.Add(s,v)
        | Multi (e1, e2) ->
            variables
            |> getVariableValuesInner e1
            |> getVariableValuesInner e2
        | Div (e1, e2) ->
            variables
            |> getVariableValuesInner e1
            |> getVariableValuesInner e2
        | Plus (e1, e2) ->
            variables
            |> getVariableValuesInner e1
            |> getVariableValuesInner e2
        | Minus (e1, e2) ->
            variables
            |> getVariableValuesInner e1
            |> getVariableValuesInner e2
        | _ -> variables
    getVariableValuesInner e (Map.empty)

// function to handle the interpretation
let interpret input (variableDict : Map<string,float>) =
    let rec interpretInner input =
        match input with
        | Ident (s) -> variableDict.[s]
        | Val (v) -> v
```

```
        | Multi (e1, e2) -> (interpretInner e1) * (interpretInner e2)
        | Div (e1, e2) -> (interpretInner e1) / (interpretInner e2)
        | Plus (e1, e2) -> (interpretInner e1) + (interpretInner e2)
        | Minus (e1, e2) -> (interpretInner e1) - (interpretInner e2)
    interpretInner input

// the expression to be interpreted
let e = Multi(Val 2., Plus(Val 2., Ident "a"))

// collect the arguments from the user
let args = getVariableValues e

// interpret the expression
let v = interpret e args

// print the results
printf "result: %f" v
```

Executing this code in F# Interactive produces the following results:

```
[a]: 12
result: 28.000000
```

Compiling the AST

To many developers, compilation means generating native code, so it has a reputation for being difficult. But it doesn't have to mean generating native code. For a DSL, you typically generate another, more general-purpose programming language. The .NET Framework provides several features for compiling an AST into a program.

Your choice of technology depends on several factors. For example, if you want to target your language at developers, it might be enough to generate a text file containing F#, some other language, or a compiled assembly that can then used within an application. However, if you want to target end users, you will almost certainly have to compile and then execute it on the fly. Table 11-1 summarizes the various options available.

You use the System.Reflection.Emit.DynamicMethod class, not because you need the flexibility of IL, but because IL includes built-in instructions for floating-point arithmetic, which makes it well-suited for implementing a little language. The DynamicMethod class also provides a fast and easy way to let you call into the resulting program.

Table 11-1. *.NET Code-Generation Technologies*

Technology	Description
Microsoft.CSharp.CSharpCodeProvider	This class supports compilation of a C# file that has been created on the fly, either by using simple string concatenation or by using the System.CodeDom namespace. Once the code has been compiled into an assembly, it can be loaded dynamically into memory and executed via reflection. This operation is relatively expensive because it requires writing to the disk and using reflection to execute methods.
System.CodeDom	This is a set of classes aimed at abstracting between operations available in different languages. The idea is to describe your operations using the classes available in this namespace, and then use a provider to compile them into the language of your choice. Providers are available for C# and Roslyn.
FSharp.Compiler.CodeDom	This is a CodeDom provider that can be used to compile F# on the fly in a similar way to the C# CodeDom provider. It can be downloaded from GitHub at http://github.com/fsprojects/FSharp.Compiler.CodeDom.
System.Reflection.Emit	This namespace allows you to build up assemblies using IL. IL offers more features than either F#, C#, or System.CodeDom, so it provides more flexibility; however, it is lower level so it also requires more patience and will probably take more time to get right.
FSharp.Compiler.Service	F# Compiler Services is a component derived from the F# compiler source code that exposes additional functionality for implementing F# language bindings, additional tools based on the compiler, or refactoring tools. The package also includes the F# Interactive service that can be used for embedding F# scripting into your applications.
Mono.Cecil	This is a library extensively used in the Mono framework for both parsing assemblies and dynamically creating them.

The method `createDynamicMethod` compiles the AST by walking the AST and generating code. It begins by creating an instance of the `DynamicMethod` class to hold the IL you define to represent the method:

```
let temp = new DynamicMethod("", (type float), paramsTypes, meth.Module)
```

Next, `createDynamicMethod` starts walking the tree. When you encounter an identifier, you emit some code to load an argument of your dynamic method:

```
| Ident name ->
    il.Emit(OpCodes.Ldarg, paramNames.IndexOf(name))
```

When you encounter a literal, you emit the IL code to load the literal value:

```
| Val x -> il.Emit(OpCodes.Ldc_R8, x)
```

When you encounter an operation, you must recursively evaluate both expressions and then emit the instruction that represents the required operation:

```
| Multi (e1 , e2) ->
    generateIlInner e1
    generateIlInner e2
    il.Emit(OpCodes.Mul)
```

Note how the operation is emitted last, after both expressions have been recursively evaluated. You do it this way because IL is stack-based, so data from the other operations must be pushed onto the stack before you evaluate the operator.

You can see the complete compiler in Listing 11-10.

Listing 11-10. Compiling an AST Generated from Command Line Input

```
open System
open System.Reflection
open System.Reflection.Emit

type Ast =
    | Ident of string
    | Val of System.Double
    | Multi of Ast * Ast
    | Div of Ast * Ast
    | Plus of Ast * Ast
    | Minus of Ast * Ast

// get a list of all the parameter names
let rec getParamList e =
    let rec getParamListInner e names =
        match e with
        | Ident name ->
            if not (List.exists (fun s -> s = name) names) then
                name :: names
            else
                names
        | Multi (e1 , e2) ->
            names
            |> getParamListInner e1
            |> getParamListInner e2
        | Div (e1 , e2) ->
            names
            |> getParamListInner e1
            |> getParamListInner e2
        | Plus (e1 , e2) ->
            names
            |> getParamListInner e1
            |> getParamListInner e2
        | Minus (e1 , e2) ->
```

```
            names
            |> getParamListInner e1
            |> getParamListInner e2
        | _ -> names
    getParamListInner e []

// create the dynamic method
let createDynamicMethod e (paramNames: string list) =
    let generateIl e (il : ILGenerator) =
        let rec generateIlInner e  =
            match e with
            | Ident name ->
                let index = List.findIndex (fun s -> s = name) paramNames
                il.Emit(OpCodes.Ldarg, index)
            | Val x -> il.Emit(OpCodes.Ldc_R8, x)
            | Multi (e1 , e2) ->
                generateIlInner e1
                generateIlInner e2
                il.Emit(OpCodes.Mul)
            | Div (e1 , e2) ->
                generateIlInner e1
                generateIlInner e2
                il.Emit(OpCodes.Div)
            | Plus (e1 , e2) ->
                generateIlInner e1
                generateIlInner e2
                il.Emit(OpCodes.Add)
            | Minus (e1 , e2) ->
                generateIlInner e1
                generateIlInner e2
                il.Emit(OpCodes.Sub)
        generateIlInner e
        il.Emit(OpCodes.Ret)

    let paramsTypes = Array.create paramNames.Length (typeof<float>)
    let meth = MethodInfo.GetCurrentMethod()
    let temp = new DynamicMethod("", (typeof<float>), paramsTypes, meth.Module)
    let il = temp.GetILGenerator()
    generateIl e il
    temp

// function to read the arguments from the command line
let collectArgs (paramNames : string list) =
    paramNames
    |> Seq.map
        (fun n ->
            printf "%s: " n
            box (float(Console.ReadLine())))
    |> Array.ofSeq
```

```
// the expression to be interpreted
let e = Multi(Val 2., Plus(Val 2., Ident "a"))

// get a list of all the parameters from the expression
let paramNames = getParamList e

// compile the tree to a dynamic method
let dm = createDynamicMethod e paramNames

// print collect arguments from the user
let args = collectArgs paramNames

// execute and print out the final result
printfn "result: %O" (dm.Invoke(null, args))
```

Running the code in Listing 11-10 produces the following results:

```
a: 14
result: 32
```

Compilation vs. Interpretation

So when should you use compilation and when should you use interpretation? The final result is basically the same, so the answer generally comes down to the raw speed of the final generated code, though memory usage and start-up times can also play a role in the decision. If you need your code to execute more quickly, then compilation will generally give you better results.

The test harness in Listing 11-11 enables you to execute the interpret function results of createDynamicMethod repeatedly and time how long this takes. It also tests an important variation on dynamic methods; that is where you also generate a new .NET delegate value to act as the handle by which you invoke the generated code. As you can see, it turns out that this is by far the fastest technique. Remember, you're timing how long it takes to evaluate the AST either directly or in a compiled form; you're not measuring the parse time or compilation time.

Listing 11-11. A Test Harness for Comparing Performance

```
open System
open System.Diagnostics
open Strangelights.Expression

// expression to process
let e = Multi(Val 2., Plus(Val 2., Val 2.))

// collect the inputs
printf "Interpret/Compile/Compile Through Delegate [i/c/cd]: "
let interpertFlag = Console.ReadLine()
printf "reps: "
let reps = int(Console.ReadLine())
```

```
type Df0 = delegate of unit -> float
type Df1 = delegate of float -> float
type Df2 = delegate of float * float -> float
type Df3 = delegate of float * float * float -> float
type Df4 = delegate of float * float * float * float -> float


// run the tests
match interpertFlag with
| "i" ->
    let args = Interpret.getVariableValues e
    let clock = new Stopwatch()
    clock.Start()
    for i = 1 to reps do
        Interpret.interpret e args |> ignore
    clock.Stop()
    printf "%i" clock.ElapsedTicks
| "c" ->
    let paramNames = Compile.getParamList e
    let dm = Compile.createDynamicMethod e paramNames
    let args = Compile.collectArgs paramNames
    let clock = new Stopwatch()
    clock.Start()
    for i = 1 to reps do
        dm.Invoke(null, args) |> ignore
    clock.Stop()
    printf "%i" clock.ElapsedTicks
| "cd" ->
    let paramNames = Compile.getParamList e
    let dm = Compile.createDynamicMethod e paramNames
    let args = Compile.collectArgs paramNames
    let args = args |> Array.map (fun f -> f :?> float)
    let d =
        match args.Length with
        | 0 -> dm.CreateDelegate(typeof<Df0>)
        | 1 -> dm.CreateDelegate(typeof<Df1>)
        | 2 -> dm.CreateDelegate(typeof<Df2>)
        | 3 -> dm.CreateDelegate(typeof<Df3>)
        | 4 -> dm.CreateDelegate(typeof<Df4>)
        | _ -> failwith "too many parameters"
    let clock = new Stopwatch()
    clock.Start()
    for i = 1 to reps do
        match d with
        | :? Df0 as d -> d.Invoke() |> ignore
        | :? Df1 as d -> d.Invoke(args.[0]) |> ignore
        | :? Df2 as d -> d.Invoke(args.[0], args.[1]) |> ignore
        | :? Df3 as d -> d.Invoke(args.[0], args.[1], args.[2]) |> ignore
        | :? Df4 as d -> d.Invoke(args.[0], args.[1], args.[2], args.[4]) |> ignore
        | _ -> failwith "too many parameters"
    clock.Stop()
    printf "%i" clock.ElapsedTicks
| _ -> failwith "not an option"
```

Table 11-2 summarizes the results of executing this program against this expression: Multi(Val 2., Plus(Val 2., Val 2.)).

Table 11-2. *Summary of Processing the Expression Multi(Val 2., Plus(Val 2., Val 2 for Various Numbers of Repetitions (times in milliseconds)*

Repetitions	1	10	100	1,000	10,000	100,000	1,000,000
Interpreted	6,890	6,979	6,932	7,608	14,835	84,823	799,788
Compiled via delegate	865	856	854	1,007	2,369	15,871	151,602
Compiled	1,112	1,409	2,463	16,895	151,135	1,500,437	14,869,692

Table 11-2 and Figure 11-3 indicate that *Compiled* and *Compiled via delegate* are much faster over a small number of repetitions. But notice that over 1, 10, and 100 repetitions, the amount of time required grows negligibly. This is because over these small numbers of repetitions, the time taken for each repetition is insignificant. It is only the time that the JIT compiler takes to compile the IL code into native code that is significant. This is why the *Compiled* and *Compiled via delegate* times are so close. They both have a similar amount of code to JIT compile. The *Interpreted* time takes longer because you must JIT compile more code, specifically the interpreter. But JIT is a one-off cost because you need to JIT each method only once; therefore, as the number of repetitions goes up, this one-off cost is paid for, and you begin to see a truer picture of the relative performance cost.

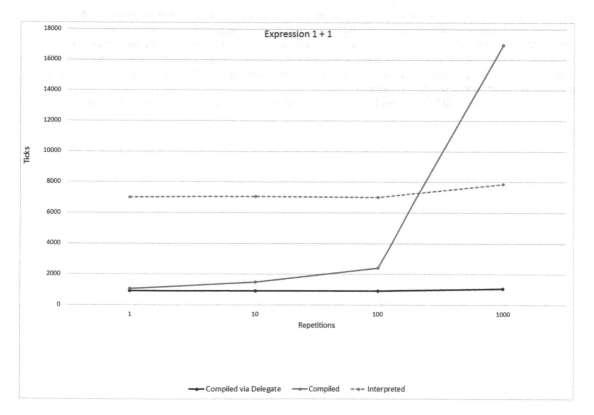

Figure 11-3. *The evaluation time in machine ticks of the expression 1 + 1 against the number of evaluations of the express*

You can see clearly from Figure 11-3 that, as the number of repetitions goes up, the cost of *Compiled* goes up steeply. This is because accessing the compiled DynamicMethod through its Invoke method is expensive, and you incur this cost on every repetition. This means that the time taken for a *Compiled* method increases at the same rate as the number of repetitions. However, the problem lies not with compilation, but with how you invoke the compiled code. It turns out that calling a DynamicMethod through a delegate rather than the Invoke member on the dynamic delegate allows you to pay only once for the cost of binding to the method, so executing a DynamicMethod this way is much more efficient if you intend to evaluate the expression multiple times. Based on these results, compilation with invocation via a delegate provides the best option in terms of speed.

This analysis shows the importance of measurement: don't assume that compilation has given you the expected performance gains until you actually see the benefits on realistic data sets and have used all the available techniques to ensure no unnecessary overhead is lurking in your code. However, many other factors can affect your performance in the real world. For example, if your expressions change often, your interpreter will need to be JIT compiled only once, but each compiled expression will need to be JIT compiled, which means you'll need to run your compiled code many times if you want to see any performance gains. Given that interpreted code is usually easier to implement, and that compiled code provides significant performance gains only in certain situations, interpreted code is often your best choice.

When dealing with situations that require code to perform as quickly as possible, it's generally best to try a few different approaches and then profile your application to see which approach gives the best results.

Summary

In this chapter, you looked at the main features and techniques for language-oriented programming in F#. You saw various techniques; some use data structures as little languages or work with quotations, which involve working with the existing F# syntax to change or extend it. Others, such as implementing a parser, enable you to work with just about any language that is text-based, whether this language is of your own design (or perhaps more commonly) a preexisting language. All these techniques can lead to big productivity gains if you use them correctly.

The next chapter will look at how F# interacts with other existing languages, such as C# and C++.

■ ■ ■

CHAPTER 12

Compatibility and Advanced Interoperation

In this chapter, you will look at everything you need to make F# interoperate well with other languages, not just within the .NET Framework but also using unmanaged code from F# and using F# from unmanaged code.

■ **Caution**   Throughout this book, I have made every effort to make sure the only language you need to understand is F#. However, in this chapter, it will help if you know a little C#, C++, or .NET Common IL, although I've kept the code in these languages to the minimum necessary.

Calling F# Libraries from C#

You can create two kinds of libraries in F#: libraries that are just designed to be used from F# only and libraries that are designed to be used from any .NET language. This is because F# utilizes the .NET type system in a rich and powerful way, so some types can look a little unusual to other .NET languages. However, these types will always look like they should when viewed from F#.

Although you can use any library written in F# from any .NET language, you need to follow a few rules if you want to make the library as friendly as possible. Here is how I summarize these rules:

- Avoid public functions that return tuples.

- If you want to expose a function that takes another function as a value, expose the value as a delegate.

- Avoid using union types in the API, but if you absolutely must use these types, consider adding members to make them easier to use.

- Avoid returning F# lists, and use the array `System.Collections.Generic.IEnumerable` or better yet `Collection` or `ReadOnlyCollection` from the `System.Collections.ObjectModel` namespace instead.

- When possible, place type definitions in a namespace, and place only value definitions within a module.

- Be careful with the signatures you define on classes and interfaces; a small change in the syntax can make a big difference.

- You may also want to consider adding a signature .fsi file or the private and internal keywords to hide implementation details and document the API expected by clients.

I will illustrate these points with examples in the following sections.

Returning Tuples

First, I'll talk about why you should avoid tuples. If you return a tuple from your function, you will force the user to reference FSharp.Core.dll. Also, the code needed to use the tuple just doesn't look that great from C#. Consider the following example where you define the function hourAndMinute that returns the hour and minute from a DateTime structure:

```
module Strangelights.DemoModule
open System

// returns the hour and minute from the given date as a tuple
let hourAndMinute (time: DateTime) = time.Hour, time.Minute

// returns the hour from the given date
let hour (time: DateTime) = time.Hour
// returns the minutes from the given date
let minute (time: DateTime) = time.Minute
```

To call this from C#, you need to follow the next example. You need to create a C# project alongside your F# solution. To do this, choose File ➤ Add ➤ New Project, and then choose a C# console project.

Next, you need to add a project reference from the C# project to the F# project. Then add the following C# class to the newly created project:

```
// !!! C# Source !!!
using System;
using Strangelights;
using FSharp.Core;

static class PrintClass {
        internal static void HourMinute() {
                // call the "hourAndMinute" function and collect the
                // tuple that's returned
                Tuple<int, int> t = DemoModule.hourAndMinute(DateTime.Now);
                // print the tuple's contents
                Console.WriteLine("Hour {0} Minute {1}", t.Item1, t.Item2);
        }
}
```

This example, when executed, returns the following:

```
Hour 16 Minute 1
```

Although the C# in this example isn't too ugly, it would be better if the function had been split in two, one to return the hour and one to return the minute.

Exposing Functions That Take Functions As Parameters

If you want to expose functions that take other functions as parameters, the best way to do this is using delegates. Consider the following example that defines one function that exposes a function, and another that exposes a function as a delegate:

```
module Strangelights.DemoModule
open System

/// a function that provides filtering
let filterStringList f ra =
    ra |> Seq.filter f

// another function that provides filtering
let filterStringListDelegate (pred: Predicate<string>) ra =
        let f x = pred.Invoke(x)
        new ResizeArray<string>(ra |> Seq.filter f)
```

Although the filterStringList is considerably shorter than filterStringListDelegate, the users of your library will appreciate the extra effort you've put in to expose the function as a delegate. When you look at using the functions from C#, it's pretty clear why. The following example demonstrates calling filterStringList. To call your function, you need to create a delegate and then use the FuncConvert class to convert it into a FastFunc, which is the type F# uses to represent function values. As well as being pretty annoying for the user of your library, this also requires a dependency on FSharp.Core.dll that the user probably doesn't want.

```
// !!! C# Source !!!
using System;
using System.Collections.Generic;
using Strangelights;
using FSharp.Core;

class MapOneClass {
        public static void MapOne() {
                // define a list of names
                List<string> names = new List<string>(
                        new string[] { "Stefany", "Oussama",
        "Sebastien", "Frederik" });

                // define a predicate delegate/function
                Converter<string, bool> pred =
                        delegate(string s) { return s.StartsWith("S"); };

                // convert to a FastFunc
                FastFunc<string, bool> ff =
                        FuncConvert.ToFastFunc<string, bool>(pred);
```

```
                    // call the F# demo function
                    IEnumerable<string> results =
                            DemoModule.filterStringList(ff, names);

                    // write the results to the console
                    foreach (var name in results) {
                            Console.WriteLine(name);
                    }
            }
    }
}
```

This example, when executed, returns the following:

```
Stefany
Sebastien
```

Now, compare and contrast this to calling the filterStringListDelegate function, shown in the following example. Because you used a delegate, you can use the C# anonymous delegate feature and embed the delegate directly into the function call, reducing the amount of work the library user has to do and removing the compile-time dependency on FSharp.Core.dll.

```
// !!! C# Source !!!
using System;
using System.Collections.Generic;
using Strangelights;

class MapTwoClass {
        public static void MapTwo() {
                // define a list of names
                List<string> names = new List<string>(
                        new string[] { "Aurelie", "Fabrice",
            "Ibrahima", "Lionel" });

                // call the F# demo function passing in an
                // anonymous delegate
                List<string> results =
                        DemoModule.filterStringListDelegate(
                                delegate(string s) { return s.StartsWith("A"); }, names);

                // write the results to the console
                foreach (var s in results) {
                        Console.WriteLine(s);
                }
        }
}
```

This example, when executed, returns the following:

```
Aurelie
```

Using Union Types

You can use union types from C#, but because C# has no real concept of a union type, they do not look very pretty when used in C# code. In this section, you will examine how you can use them in C# and how you as a library designer can decide whether and how your library will expose them. Personally I recommend avoiding exposing them in cross-language scenarios.

For the first example, you define the simple union type Quantity, which consists of two constructors, one containing an integer and the other a floating-point number. You also provide the function getRandomQuantity() to initialize a new instance of Quantity.

```
module Strangelights.DemoModule
open System

// type that can represent a discrete or continuous quantity
type Quantity =
| Discrete of int
| Continuous of float

// initalize random number generator
let rand = new Random()
// create a random quantity
let getRandomQuantity() =
    match rand.Next(1) with
    | 0 -> Quantity.Discrete (rand.Next())
    | _ ->
        Quantity.Continuous
            (rand.NextDouble() * float (rand.Next()))
```

Although you provide getRandomQuantity() to create a new version of the Quantity type, the type itself provides static methods for creating new instances of the different constructors that make up the type. These static methods are available on all union types that are exposed by the assembly by default; you do not have to do anything special to get the compiler to create them. They are named after the DU case, prefixed with the word "New." The following example shows how to use these methods from C#:

```
using System;
using Strangelights;

static class GetQuantityZeroClass {
        public static void GetQuantityZero() {
                // initialize both a Discrete and Continuous quantity
                DemoModule.Quantity d = DemoModule.Quantity.NewDiscrete(12);
                DemoModule.Quantity c = DemoModule.Quantity.NewContinuous(12.0);
        }
}
```

Now you know how to create union types from C#, so the next most important task is being able to determine the case to which a particular Quantity value belongs. You can do this in three ways: using the Tag property, using the IsCase methods, or providing explicit functionality within your F# code.

The first option is that you can switch on the value's Tag property. This property is just an integer, but the compiled version of the union type provides constants, contained in an inner class called Tags, to help you decode the meaning of the integer. If you want to use the Tag property to find out what kind of Quantity you have, you usually write a switch statement, as shown in the following example. Notice also how you have to cast q to the appropriate DU case in order to access its value in the Item property.

```
// !!! C# Source !!!
using System;
using Strangelights;

static class GetQuantityOneClass
{
    public static void GetQuantityOne()
    {
        // get a random quantity
        DemoModule.Quantity q = DemoModule.getRandomQuantity();

        // use the .Tags property to switch over the quatity
        switch (q.Tag)
        {
            case DemoModule.Quantity.Tags.Discrete:
                Console.WriteLine("Discrete value: {0}", (q as DemoModule.Quantity.
                Discrete).Item);
                break;
            case DemoModule.Quantity.Tags.Continuous:
                Console.WriteLine("Continuous value: {0}", (q as DemoModule.Quantity.
                Continuous).Item);
                break;
        }
    }
}
```

This example, when executed, returns the following:

```
Discrete value: 65676
```

If you prefer, the compiled form of the union type also offers a series of properties, all prefixed with Is. This allows you to check whether a value belongs to a particular case within the union type. For example, on the Quantity union type, two properties, IsDiscrete and IsContinuous, allow you to check whether the Quantity is Discrete or Continuous. The following example demonstrates how to use them:

```
// !!! C# Source !!!
using System;
using Strangelights;

static class GetQuantityTwoClass
{
    public static void GetQuantityTwo()
    {
        // get a random quantity
        DemoModule.Quantity q = DemoModule.getRandomQuantity();
```

```
        // use if … else chain to display value
        if (q.IsDiscrete)
        {
            Console.WriteLine("Discrete value: {0}", (q as DemoModule.Quantity.Discrete).Item);
        }
        else if (q.IsContinuous)
        {
            Console.WriteLine("Continuous value: {0}", (q as DemoModule.Quantity.
            Continuous).Item);
        }
    }
}
```

This example, when executed, returns the following:

```
Discrete value: 2058
```

Neither option is particularly pleasing because the code required to perform the pattern matching is quite bulky. There is also a risk that the user could get it wrong and write something like the following example where they check whether a value is Discrete and then mistakenly cast to the Continuous case. This would lead to an InvalidCastException being thrown.

```
DemoModule.EasyQuantity q = DemoModule.getRandomQuantity();
if (q.IsDiscrete) {
    Console.WriteLine("Discrete value: {0}", (q as DemoModule.Quantity.Continuous).Item);
}
```

To provide the users of your libraries some protection against this, it is a good idea where possible to add members to union types that perform the pattern matching for them. The following example revises the Quantity type to produce EasyQuantity, adding two members to transform the type into an integer or a floating-point number:

```
module Strangelights.ImprovedModule
open System

// type that can represent a discrete or continuous quantity
// with members to improve interoperability
type EasyQuantity =
| Discrete of int
| Continuous of float
    // convert quantity to a float
    member x.ToFloat() =
        match x with
        | Discrete x -> float x
        | Continuous x -> x
    // convert quantity to a integer
    member x.ToInt() =
        match x with
        | Discrete x -> x
        | Continuous x -> int x
```

```
// initalize random number generator
let rand = new Random()

// create a random quantity
let getRandomEasyQuantity() =
    match rand.Next(1) with
    | 0 -> EasyQuantity.Discrete (rand.Next())
    | _ ->
        EasyQuantity.Continuous
            (rand.NextDouble() * float (rand.Next()))
```

This will allow the user of the library to transform the value into either an integer or a floating-point without having to worry about pattern matching, as shown in the following example:

```
// !!! C# Source !!!
using System;
using Strangelights;

class GetQuantityThreeClass {
        public static void GetQuantityThree() {
                // get a random quantity
                ImprovedModule.EasyQuantity q = ImprovedModule.getRandomEasyQuantity();
                // convert quantity to a float and show it
                Console.WriteLine("Value as a float: {0}", q.ToFloat());
        }
}
```

Obviously the applicability of this approach varies, but there is often a sensible behavior that you can define for each case of your discriminated union for the benefit of C# callers.

Using F# Lists

It is entirely possible to use F# lists from C#, but I recommend avoiding this since a little work on your part will make things seem more natural for C# programmers. For example, it is simple to convert a list to an array using the List.toArray function; to a System.Collections.Generic.List using the new ResizeArray<_>() constructor; or to a System.Collections.Generic.IEnumerable using the List.toSeq function. These types are generally a bit easier for C# programmers to work with, especially System.Array and System.Collections.Generic.List, because they provide a lot more member methods. You can do the conversion directly before the list is returned to the calling client, making it entirely feasible to use the F# list type inside your F# code. MSDN recommends using the types Collection or ReadOnlyCollection from the System.Collections.ObjectModel namespace to expose collections. Both of these classes have a constructor that accepts an IEnumerable, and so can be constructed from an F# list.

If you need to return an F# list directly, you can do so as follows:

```
module Strangelights.DemoModule

// gets a preconstructed list
let getList() =
    [1; 2; 3]
```

To use this list in C#, you typically use a foreach loop:

```
using System;
using Strangelights;
using FSharp.Core;
using FSharp.Collections;

class Program {
        static void Main(string[] args) {
                // get the list of integers
                List<int> ints = DemoModule.getList();

                // foreach over the list printing it
                foreach (int i in ints) {
                        Console.WriteLine(i);
                }
        }
}
```

This example, when executed, returns the following:

```
1
2
3
```

Defining Types in a Namespace

If you are defining types that will be used from other .NET languages, then you should place them inside a namespace rather than inside a module. This is because modules are compiled into what C# and other .NET languages consider to be a class, and any types defined within the module become inner classes of that type. Although this does not present a huge problem to C# users, the C# client code does look cleaner if a namespace is used rather than a module. This is because in C# you can open namespaces but not modules using the using statement, so if a type is inside a module, it must always be prefixed with the module name when used from C#.

Let's take a look at an example of doing this. The following example defines TheClass, which is defined inside a namespace. You also want to provide some functions that go with this class. These can't be placed directly inside a namespace because values cannot be defined inside a namespace. In this case, you define a module with a related name, such as TheModule, to hold the function values.

```
namespace Strangelights
open System.Collections.Generic

// this is a counter class
type TheClass(i) =
    let mutable theField = i
    member x.TheField
        with get() = theField
    // increments the counter
    member x.Increment() =
        theField <- theField + 1
```

273

```
    // decrements the count
    member x.Decrement() =
        theField <- theField - 1

// this is a module for working with the TheClass
module TheModule = begin
    // increments a list of TheClass
    let incList (theClasses: List<TheClass>) =
        theClasses |> Seq.iter (fun c -> c.Increment())
    // decrements a list of TheClass
    let decList (theClasses: List<TheClass>) =
        theClasses |> Seq.iter (fun c -> c.Decrement())
end
```

Using the TheClass class in C# is now straightforward because you do not have to provide a prefix, and you can also get access to the related functions in TheModule easily:

```
// !!! C# Source !!!
using System;
using System.Collections.Generic;
using Strangelights;

class Program {
        static void UseTheClass() {
                // create a list of classes
                List<TheClass> theClasses = new List<TheClass>() {
                        new TheClass(5),
                        new TheClass(6),
                        new TheClass(7)};

                // increment the list
                TheModule.incList(theClasses);

                // write out each value in the list
                foreach (TheClass c in theClasses) {
                        Console.WriteLine(c.TheField);
                }
        }
        static void Main(string[] args) {
                UseTheClass();
        }
}
```

Defining Classes and Interfaces

In F# there are two ways you can define parameters for functions and members of classes: the "curried" style where members can be partially applied and the "tuple" style where all members must be given at once. Fortunately, from the point of view of C#, both such styles appear as tuple-style calls.

Consider the following example in which you define a class in F#. Here one member has been defined in the curried style, called CurriedStyle, and the other has been defined in the tuple style, called TupleStyle.

```
namespace Strangelights

type DemoClass(z: int) =
    // method in the curried style
    member this.CurriedStyle x y = x + y + z
    // method in the tuple style
    member this.TupleStyle (x, y) = x + y + z
```

When viewed from C#, both methods appear in standard C# style (i.e. with the parameters bracketed together):

```
public int TupleStyle(int x, int y);
public int CurriedStyle(int x, int y);
```

Specifying abstract members in interfaces and classes is slightly more complicated because you have a few more options. The following example demonstrates this:

```
namespace Strangelights

type IDemoInterface =
    // method in the curried style
    abstract CurriedStyle: int -> int -> int
    // method in the C# style
    abstract CSharpStyle: int * int -> int
    // method in the C# style with named arguments
    abstract CSharpNamedStyle: x : int * y : int -> int
    // method in the tupled style
    abstract TupleStyle: (int * int) -> int
```

When you implement these members in C#, the subtle differences between the implementations become apparent:

```
class CSharpClass : Strangelights.IDemoInterface
{
    public int CurriedStyle(int value1, int value2)
    {
        return value1 + value2;
    }

    public int CSharpStyle(int value1, int value2)
    {
        return value1 + value2;
    }

    public int CSharpNamedStyle(int x, int y)
    {
        return x + y;
    }
```

```
    public int TupleStyle(Tuple<int, int> value)
    {
        return value.Item1 + value.Item2;
    }
}
```

Note that the difference between C# style and curried style is disguised by the F# compiler, so you can call from C# in the same way in these two cases. C# named style is the most caller-friendly because the IDE can know the names of the interface parameters and hence can name the arguments meaningfully when generating code. Tuple style, where you explicitly require that the caller used an F# tuple at the call site, is the least caller-friendly.

Calling Using COM Objects

■ **Note** The need to interact with COM objects, or with unmanaged code, is now something of a rarity in the .NET world. However, we've decided to leave this and the following sections in this edition of *Beginning F#* to help get you started in those very few cases where you may find yourself having to do so.

Most programmers who work with the Windows platform will be familiar with the Component Object Model (COM). To a certain extent the .NET Framework was meant to replace COM, but you will still encounter COM-based systems from time to time.

The .NET Framework was designed to interoperate well with COM, and calling COM components is generally quite straightforward. Calling COM components is always done through a managed wrapper that takes care of calling the unmanaged code for you. You can produce these wrappers using a tool called TlbImp.exe, the Type Library Importer, that ships with the .NET SDK.

■ **Note** You can find more information about the TlbImp.exe tool at http://msdn.microsoft.com/en-us/library/tt0cf3sx(v=vs.110).aspx .

However, despite the existence of TlbImp.exe, if you find yourself in a situation where you need to use a COM component, first check whether the vendor provides a managed wrapper for it, called *primary interop assemblies*. For more information on primary interop assemblies, see the next section, "Using COM-Style APIs."

However, sometimes it is necessary to use TlbImp.exe directly. Fortunately, this is very straightforward. Normally all that is necessary is to pass TlbImp.exe the location of the .dll that contains the COM component, and the managed wrapper will be placed in the current directory. If you want to create a managed wrapper for the Microsoft Speech API, you use the following command line:

```
tlbimp "C:\Program Files\Common Files\Microsoft Shared\Speech\sapi.dll"
```

■ **Note** There are two command-line switches that I find useful with TlbImp.exe. These are /out:, which controls the name and location of the resulting manage wrapper, and /keyfile:, which can provide a key to sign the output assembly.

The resulting .dll is a .NET assembly and can be used just like any .NET assembly, by referencing it via the fsc.exe command line switch -r. A useful side effect of this is if the API is not well documented, you can use an assembly browser, such as .NET Reflector (available via the Visual Studio Gallery), to find out more about the structure of the API.

After that, the worst thing I can say about using managed wrappers is you might find the structure of these assemblies a little unusual since the COM model dictates structure and therefore they do not share the same naming conventions as most .NET assemblies. You will notice that all classes in the assembly are postfixed with the word Class and each one is provided with a separate interface: this is just a requirement of COM objects. The following example shows the wrapper for the Microsoft Speech API that you created in the previous example being used:

```
open SpeechLib

let main() =
    // create an new instance of a com class
    // (these almost always end with "Class")
    let voice = new SpVoiceClass()
    // call a method Speak, ignoring the result
    voice.Speak("Hello world", SpeechVoiceSpeakFlags.SVSFDefault) |> ignore

do main()
```

Using COM-Style APIs

Rather than using COM libraries directly, creating your own wrappers, it's more likely you'll have to use COM-style API's. This is because many vendors now distribute their applications with primary interop assemblies. These are precreated COM wrappers, so generally you won't need to bother creating wrappers with TlbImp.exe yourself.

■ **Note**   More information about primary interop assemblies can be found on MSDN at https://msdn.microsoft.com/en-us/library/aa302338.aspx.

Although primary interop assemblies are just ordinary .NET assemblies, there are typically a few quirks you have to watch out for, such as the following:

- Some arrays and collections often start at one rather than zero.

- There are often methods that are composed of large numbers of optional arguments. Fortunately, F# supports optional and named arguments to make interacting with these more natural and easier to understand.

- Many properties and methods have a return type of object. The resulting object needs to be cast to its true type.

- COM classes contain unmanaged resources that need to be disposed of. However, these classes do not implement the standard .NET IDisposable interface, meaning they cannot be used in an F# use binding. Fortunately, you can use F# object expressions to easily implement IDisposable.

A key difference when interacting with COM in F# as opposed to C# is that you must always create instances of objects, not interfaces. This may sound strange, but in COM libraries each object typically has an interface and a class that implements it. In C#, if you try to create an instance of a COM interface using the new keyword in C#, the compiler will automatically redirect the call to the appropriate class, but this is not the case in F#.

Interacting with Microsoft Office is probably the most common reason for interacting with COM-style libraries. Here is code that reads information from an Excel spreadsheet:

```
open System
open Microsoft.Office.Interop.Excel

let main() =
    // initalize an excel application
    let app = new ApplicationClass()

    // load a excel work book
    let workBook = app.Workbooks.Open(@"Book1.xls", ReadOnly = true)
    // ensure work book is closed corectly
    use bookCloser = { new IDisposable with
                           member x.Dispose() = workBook.Close() }

    // open the first worksheet
    let worksheet = workBook.Worksheets.[1] :?> _Worksheet

    // get the A1 cell and all surrounding cells
    let a1Cell = worksheet.Range("A1")
    let allCells = a1Cell.CurrentRegion
    // load all cells into a list of lists
    let matrix =
        [ for row in allCells.Rows ->
            let row = row :?> Range
            [ for cell in row.Columns ->
                let cell = cell :?> Range
                cell.Value2 ] ]

    // close the workbook
    workBook.Close()

    // print the matrix
    printfn "%A" matrix

do main()
```

Notice how this sample deals with some of the quirks I mentioned earlier. You implement IDisposable and bind it to bookCloser to ensure the workbook is closed, even in the case of an error. The Open method actually has 15 arguments, though you only use two: .Open(@"Book1.xls", ReadOnly = true). The first worksheet is an index one: workBook.Worksheets.[1]. Finally, each row must be upcast in order to use it: let row = row :?> Range.

Using P/Invoke

P/Invoke, or *platform invoke* to give its full name, is used to call unmanaged flat APIs implemented in DLLs and is called using the C or C++ calling conventions. The most famous example of this is the Win32 API, a vast library that exposes all the functionality built into Windows.

To call a flat unmanaged API, you must first define the function you want to call; you can do this in two parts. First, you use the DllImport attribute from the System.Runtime.InteropServices namespace, which allows you to define which .dll contains the function you want to import, along with some other optional attributes. Then you use the keyword extern; followed by the signature of the function to be called in the C style, meaning you give the return type, the F# type, the name of the function, and finally the types and names of the parameters surrounded by parentheses. The resulting function can then be called as if it were an external .NET method.

The following example shows how to import the Windows function MessageBeep and then call it:

```
open System.Runtime.InteropServices

// declare a function found in an external dll
[<DllImport("User32.dll")>]
extern bool MessageBeep(uint32 beepType)

// call this method ignoring the result
MessageBeep(0ul) |> ignore
```

■ **Note**   The trickiest part of using P/Invoke can often be working out what signature to use to call the function. The web site http://pinvoke.net contains a list of signatures for common APIs in C# and VB .NET, which are similar to the required signature in F#. The site is a wiki, so feel free to add F# signatures as you find them.

The following code shows how to use P/Invoke when the target function expects a pointer. You need to note several points about setting up the pointer. When defining the function, you need to put an asterisk (*) after the type name to show that you are passing a pointer. You need to define a mutable identifier before the function call to represent the area of memory that is pointed to. This may not be global, in the top level, but it must be part of a function definition. This is why you define the function main, so the identifier status can be part of the definition of this. Finally, you must use the address of operator (&&) to ensure the pointer is passed to the function rather than the value itself.

■ **Tip**   This compiled code will always result in a warning because of the use of the address of operator (&&). This can be suppressed by using the compiler flag --nowarn 51 or the command #nowarn 51.

```
open System.Runtime.InteropServices

// declare a function found in an external dll
[<DllImport("Advapi32.dll")>]
extern bool FileEncryptionStatus(string filename, uint32* status)
```

```
let main() =
    // declare a mutable idenifier to be passed to the function
    let mutable status = 0ul
    // call the function, using the address of operator with the
    // second parameter
    FileEncryptionStatus(@"C:\test.txt", && status) |> ignore
    // print the status to check it has be altered
    printfn "%d" status

main()
```

The result of this example, when compiled and executed (assuming you have a file at the root of your C: drive called test.txt that is encrypted), is as follows:

```
1ul
```

■ **Note** P/Invoke also works on Mono, and in F# the syntax is exactly the same. The tricky bit is ensuring the library you are invoking is available on all the platforms you're targeting and following the different naming conventions of libraries on all the different platforms. For a more detailed explanation, see the article at www.mono-project.com/docs/advanced/pinvoke/.

The DllImport attribute has some useful functions that can be set to control how the unmanaged function is called. I summarize them in Table 12-1.

Table 12-1. *Useful Attributes on the DllImport Attribute*

Attribute Name	Description
CharSet	This defines the character set to be used when marshaling string data. It can be CharSet.Auto, CharSet.Ansi, or CharSet.Unicode.
EntryPoint	This allows you to set the name of the function to be called. If no name is given, then it defaults to the name of the function as defined after the extern keyword.
SetLastError	This is a Boolean value that allows you to specify whether any error that occurs should be marshaled and therefore available by calling the Marshal.GetLastWin32Error() method.

■ **Note** As with COM components, the number of flat unmanaged APIs that have no .NET equivalent is decreasing all the time. Always check whether a managed equivalent of the function you are calling is available, which will generally save you lots of time.

Using F# from Native Code via COM

Although it is more likely that you will want to call native code from F# code, there may be some times when you want to call F# library functions from native code. For example, suppose you have a large application written in C++, and perhaps you are happy for the user interface to remain in C++ but want to migrate some logic that performs complicated mathematical calculations to F# for easier maintenance. In this case, you want to call F# from native code. The easiest way to do this is to use the tools provided with .NET to create a COM wrapper for your F# assembly. You can then use the COM runtime to call the F# functions from C++.

To expose functions though COM, you need to develop them in a certain way. First, you must define an interface that will specify the contract for your functions. The members of the interface must be written using named arguments (see the section on "Calling F# Libraries from C#" earlier in the chapter), and the interface itself must be marked with the System.Runtime.InteropServices.Guid attribute. Then you must provide a class that implements the interface. This too must be marked the System.Runtime.InteropServices.Guid attribute and also the System.Runtime.InteropServices.ClassInterface, and you should always pass the ClassInterfaceType.None enumeration member to the ClassInterface attribute constructor to say that no interface should be automatically generated.

Let's look at an example of doing this. Suppose you want to expose two functions to your unmanaged client called Add and Sub. Create an interface named IMath in the namespace Strangelights, and then create a class named Math to implement this interface. Now you need to ensure that both the class and the interface are marked with the appropriate attributes. The resulting code is as follows:

```
namespace Strangelights
open System
open System.Runtime.InteropServices

// define an interface (since all COM classes must
// have a seperate interface)
// mark it with a freshly generated Guid
[<Guid("6180B9DF-2BA7-4a9f-8B67-AD43D4EE0563")>]
type IMath =
    abstract Add : x: int * y: int -> int
    abstract Sub : x: int * y: int -> int

// implement the interface, the class must:
// - have an empty constuctor
// - be marked with its own guid
// - be marked with the ClassInterface attribute
[<Guid("B040B134-734B-4a57-8B46-9090B41F0D62");
ClassInterface(ClassInterfaceType.None)>]
type Math() =
    interface IMath with
        member this.Add(x, y) = x + y
        member this.Sub(x, y) = x - y
```

The functions Add and Sub are of course simple, so there is no problem implementing them directly in the body of the Math class. If you need to break them down into other helper functions outside of the class, this is not a problem. It is fine to implement your class members any way you see fit. You simply need to provide the interface and the class so the COM runtime has an entry point into your code.

Now comes arguably the most complicated part of the process: registering the assembly so the COM runtime can find it. To do this, you need to use a tool called RegAsm.exe. Suppose you compiled the previous sample code into a .NET .dll called ComLibrary.dll. Now you need to call RegAsm.exe twice using the following command lines:

```
regasm comlibrary.dll /tlb:comlibrary.tlb
regasm comlibrary.dll
```

The first time is to create a type library file, a .tlb file, which you can use in your C++ project to develop against. The second registers the assembly itself so the COM runtime can find it. You will also need to perform these two steps on any machine to which you deploy your assembly.

The C++ to call the Add function is as follows. The development environment and how you set up the C++ compiler will also play a large part in getting this code to compile. In this case, I created a Visual Studio project, choosing a console application template, and activated ATL. Notice the following about this source code:

- The #import command tells the compiler to import your type library. You may need to use the full path to its location. The compiler will also automatically generate a header file, in this case comlibrary.tlh, located in the debug or release directory. This is useful because it lets you know the functions and identifiers that are available as a result of your type library.

- You then need to initialize the COM runtime. You do this by calling the CoInitialize function.

- You then need to declare a pointer to the IMath interface you created. You do this via the code comlibrary::IMathPtr pDotNetCOMPtr;. Note how the namespace comes from the library name rather than the .NET namespace.

- Next, you need to create an instance of your Math class. You achieve this by calling the CreateInstance method, passing it the GUID of the Math class. Fortunately, there is a constant defined for this purpose.

- If this was successful, you can call the Add function. Note how the result of the function is actually an HRESULT, a value that will tell you whether the call was successful. The actual result of the function is passed out via an out parameter.

```cpp
// !!! C++ Source !!!
#include "stdafx.h"
// import the meta data about out .NET/COM library
#import "..\ComLibrary\ComLibrary.tlb" named_guids raw_interfaces_only

// the applications main entry point
int _tmain(int argc, _TCHAR* argv[])
{
        // initialize the COM runtime
        CoInitialize(NULL);
        // a pointer to our COM class
    comlibrary::IMathPtr pDotNetCOMPtr;
```

```
// create a new instance of the Math class
HRESULT hRes = pDotNetCOMPtr.CreateInstance(comlibrary::CLSID_Math);
// check it was created okay
if (hRes == S_OK)
{
        // define a local to hold the result
long res = 0L;
        // call the Add function
        hRes = pDotNetCOMPtr->Add(1, 2, &res);
        // check Add was called okay
    if (hRes == S_OK)
    {
                // print the result
    printf("The result was: %ld", res);
}

        // release the pointer to the math COM class
pDotNetCOMPtr.Release();
}

// uninitialise the COM runtime
CoUninitialize ();
}
```

This example, when executed, returns the following:

```
The result was: 3
```

When you execute the resulting executable, you must ensure that ComLibrary.dll is in the same directory as the executable or the COM runtime will not be able to find it. If you intend that the library be used by several clients, then I strongly recommend that you sign the assembly and place it in the GAC. This will allow all clients to be able to find it without having to keep a copy in the directory with them.

Summary

In this chapter, you saw some advanced techniques in F# for compatibility and interoperation. Although these techniques are definitely some of the most difficult to master, they also add a huge degree of flexibility to your F# programming.

CHAPTER 13

Type Providers

In this chapter, you will learn about F# *type providers*. Type providers let you bridge the gap between language and data—a gap you may not even have realized existed until you give type providers a try. You'll learn to apply type providers to CSV files, HTML sources, and SQL Server databases. You'll learn a bit about the potential pitfalls of type providers and how to mitigate them. Finally, you'll learn how to use a query expression to combine the results of two type providers.

What Are Type Providers?

Type providers are a feature that is more or less unique to the F# language, and this fact makes them a little hard to explain in the abstract. Instead, let's start by looking at a concrete example. Figure 13-1 shows the CSV type provider in action, allowing you to access the data fields in a CSV file about London Underground stations. See how the columns from the CSV file are available in IntelliSense, just as if you'd written a whole infrastructure of classes and methods to read the CSV file, parsed it into fields, and exposed the fields in objects? But you never had to write this infrastructure!

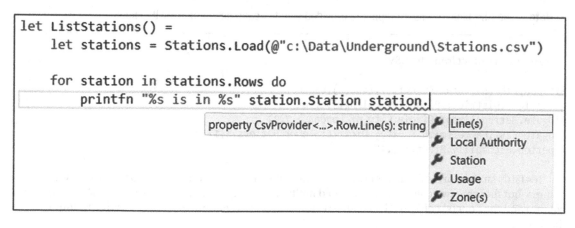

Figure 13-1. *Using the CSV type provider*

© Robert Pickering and Kit Eason 2016

R. Pickering and K. Eason, *Beginning F# 4.0*, DOI 10.1007/978-1-4842-1374-2_13

You'll go on to replicate this example yourself in the next section, but take a moment first to appreciate the elements in play here:

- An external data source that has some kind of implicit or explicit schema. In this case, the data source is CSV, but given the appropriate type provider it could be XML, JSON, HTML, a SQL database, or even another language. (Yes, you can use type providers to access other languages! This is too advanced a topic for this book, but if you are interested you should look at the type provider for the R statistical programming language at http://bluemountaincapital.github.io/FSharpRProvider/).

- A type provider for the kind of data source being used. Someone needs to have written that type provider; fortunately the open source community has produced type providers for most common scenarios. If there isn't one in existence, you can actually write your own type provider. This is beyond the scope of this book but is a well-documented process.

- Your own code, as shown in Figure 13-1. Here you can access fields (and sometimes methods) from the data source as if the data source had been encapsulated in classes.

You really only need to make an effort in the last of these steps, although that effort often amounts to simply pressing the period (.) key.

Using the CSV Type Provider

In this section, you use the CSV type provider to access data about the London Underground train system's stations.

■ **Note** The CSV files for this example are provided with the code downloads for this book.

Here's an extract from the CSV:

```
Station,Line(s),Local Authority,Zone(s),Usage
Acton Town,District; Picadilly,Ealing,3,6.06
Aldgate,Metropolitan; Circle,City of London,1,7.22
Aldgate East,Hammersmith & City; Dictrict,Tower Hamlets,1,12.25
Alperton,Piccadilly,Brent,4,3.17
```

It's fairly straightforward but there are also some subtleties. The column separator is obviously a comma, but there are two columns that can hold multiple values separated by semicolons: the Line(s) column and the Zone(s) column. The good news is that there is a column headers line at the beginning of the file.

It's time to apply the CSV type provider to this dataset. Place the CSV file in a suitable location, such as c:\Data\Underground\Stations.csv. (If you use the data from this book's code downloads, use the version in the file Stations_short.csv to begin with.)

Create a new F# library project, and use NuGet or your favorite package manager to add the package FSharp.Data to your project. You will then see the warning dialog in Figure 13-2. (The example shown is for Visual Studio but other environments will show similar dialogs.)

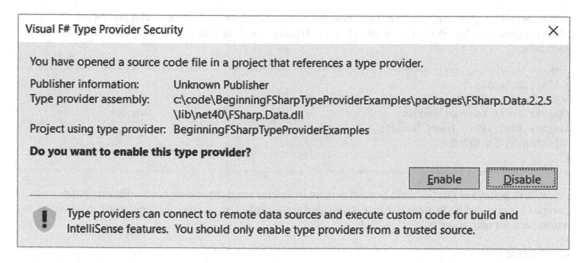

Figure 13-2. Type provider security warning

This dialog is shown because type providers are powerful beasts, so, as indicated in the dialog, you should only download them from trustworthy sources. FSharp.Data from NuGet is trustworthy, so click the Enable button.

Rename Library1.fs to UndergroundCSV.fs and edit it so that it looks like the code in Listing 13-1.

Listing 13-1. Listing London Underground Stations from a CSV File

```
#if INTERACTIVE
// You may have to alter this path depending on the version
// of FSharp.Data downloaded and on you project structure
#r @"..\packages\FSharp.Data.2.2.5\lib\net40\FSharp.Data.dll"
#else
module UndergroundCSV
#endif

open FSharp.Data

type Stations = CsvProvider< @"c:\Data\Underground\Stations.csv",
                HasHeaders=true>

let ListStations() =
    let stations = Stations.Load(@"c:\Data\Underground\Stations.csv")

    for station in stations.Rows do
        printfn "%s is in %s" station.Station station.``Local Authority``
```

Select all the code and send it to F# Interactive. Switch to the F# Interactive screen and type `ListStations();;`. You should see a list of London Underground stations and the Local Authority in which each falls.

```
> ListStations();;
Acton Town is in Ealing
Aldgate is in City of London
Aldgate East is in Tower Hamlets
Alperton is in Brent
>
```

What's going on? First is a little section that, for F# Interactive only, references the FSharp.Data library. (In compiled code, this reference is provided at the project level.) You also open the FSharp.Data namespace for convenience.

```
#if INTERACTIVE
// You may have to alter this path depending on the version
// of FSharp.Data downloaded and on you project structure
#r @"..\packages\FSharp.Data.2.2.5\lib\net40\FSharp.Data.dll"
#else
module UndergroundCSV
#endif

open FSharp.Data
```

Then you create a new type called `Stations`, which looks like a type abbreviation for the `CsvProvider` type from `FSharp.Data`:

```
type Stations = CsvProvider< @"c:\Data\Underground\Stations.csv",
                 HasHeaders=true>
```

Note how you must give the path of a sample of the CSV data you want to read. You give this as a static generic parameter, hence the angle brackets, `<>`. Note also the space between the opening angle bracket and the following `@`. The `@` is needed so that the backslashes in the following literal string aren't interpreted as escape characters, but `<@` in the F# syntax means "open code quotation." So you use a space to separate the angle bracket and the `@` sign, and thus prevent this misinterpretation.

Also in the angle brackets is `HasHeaders=true`. This tells the type provider that the CSV sample file you are providing has a header line giving column names.

Next is some code to actually use the data:

```
let ListStations() =
    let stations = Stations.Load(@"c:\Data\Underground\Stations.csv")
```

You call the `Load` method in your `Stations` type, providing the path of a CSV file as an ordinary function parameter value, and binding the result to a label called `stations`. In this case you use the same file for the sample and for the data, but in a production scenario you would likely use a small but representative sample at the earlier declaration stage and a larger but identically structured file when getting the actual data. The sample file will need to be available at compile time, so in cases where you are using a non-local build pipeline, it has to be checked in.

Then you iterate over the rows, printing out two of the properties:

```
for station in stations.Rows do
    printfn "%s is in %s" station.Station station.``Local Authority``
```

See how the type provider is clever enough to enclose property names in back-quotes in cases, such as `` Local Authority``, where the column name from the CSV file wouldn't constitute a valid F# identifier, typically because it includes spaces.

To get a feel for how type providers interact with IntelliSense, try deleting the text `Station` in `station.Station` and pressing `Ctrl+Spacebar` (or whatever shortcut activates IntelliSense in your environment). You should see a list of properties, as shown in Figure 13-3. This list was derived from the column names in the first line of the sample CSV file you specified.

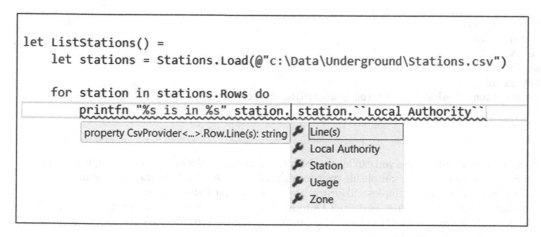

Figure 13-3. *IntelliSense from the CSV header*

Now let's look at some of the real-world complications you might encounter with the CSV type provider and how to deal with them. I mentioned earlier that some of the columns in the CSV contain potentially multiple values. One of these is the Zone column, because some Underground stations are in more than one ticketing zone. This isn't apparent in the preceding examples because the stations used in the sample and the actual data all happened to have a single zone. Let's see what happens when that isn't the case. To set this up, make a copy of the `Stations.csv` file and call the copy `StationsSample.csv`. Edit the `Stations.csv` file (but not `StationsSample.csv`) to include the following additional station:

```
Archway,Northern,Islington,2;3,8.94
```

As you can see, Archway is in zones 2 and 3. Now edit your F# source so that it uses the sample file (`StationsSample.csv`) when setting up the type provider and the file including Archway (`Stations.csv`) as the data file. Also, change it to print out Zone as an integer (Listing 13-2).

Listing 13-2. Printing Out Zone Using Separate Sample and Data Files

```
open FSharp.Data

type Stations = CsvProvider< @"c:\Data\Underground\StationsSample.csv",
                HasHeaders=true>
```

```
let ListStations() =
    let stations = Stations.Load(@"c:\Data\Underground\Stations.csv")

    for station in stations.Rows do
        printfn "%s is in %i" station.Station station.Zone
```

This compiles absolutely fine. The type provider inferred that Zone is an integer because all the values in the sample were integers. (Actually, if you're super observant, you might notice that it infers that the Zone is an integer with a unit-of-measure of seconds. This is because the column title was Zone(s), and the type provider assumed that (s) meant "seconds.") Now try sending the amended code to F# Interactive and running ListStations().

As you might expect, you get an error trying to print out the new station:

```
> ListStations();;
Acton Town is in 3
Aldgate is in 1
Aldgate East is in 1
Alperton is in 4
System.Exception: Couldn't parse row 5 according to schema: Expecting Int32 in Zone,
got 2;3
>
```

There are several approaches you can take to fix this. One is to add "Archway" to the sample file, and more generally to ensure that the sample file contains examples of every kind of data item that might be in the data at runtime. (These examples will have to appear in the first 1000 rows because that is the size of sample that the type provider uses by default.) Another is to coerce the types of any columns that might cause problems. To force the type of the Zone(s) column, simply edit your Stations declaration to include a Schema assignment, as shown in Listing 13-3.

Listing 13-3. Forcing the Type of a Column

```
type Stations = CsvProvider< @"c:\Data\Underground\StationsSample.csv",
                            HasHeaders=true,
                            Schema="Zone(s)=string">
```

As soon as you do this, you should get an error in your printfn statement because the format string you used was treating Zone as a string. (And also because the column is now called Zone(s) because there is no longer an assumption that (s) stands for seconds.) Edit the print statement to fix this, and you should find that the ListStations() function runs reliably:

```
for station in stations.Rows do
    printfn "%s is in %s" station.Station station.``Zone(s)``
```

```
> ListStations();;
Acton Town is in 3
Aldgate is in 1
Aldgate East is in 1
Alperton is in 4
Archway is in 2;3
>
```

■ **Note** The CSV type provider contains an incredibly rich set of features for specifying the types and optionality of columns, for the treatment of missing data, and so on. You can also override the separator so, for example, files with tab or | separators can be treated in the same way as comma-separated files. These settings are documented on the type provider's GitHub page at `https://fsharp.github.io/FSharp.Data/library/CsvProvider.html`.

Using the HTML Type Provider

In this section, you'll learn how to use the HTML type provider. You'll return to the London Underground stations example, but this time you'll get the data from a Wikipedia page, which means accessing HTML. If you visit the Wikipedia page called "List of London Underground Stations" at `https://en.wikipedia.org/wiki/List_of_London_Underground_stations`, you'll see that it contains a nicely-curated list of stations with all sorts of useful information. But how easy is it to access this information programmatically, so that you can rank the stations by traffic, find all the stations on the Northern line, or answer trivia questions like which station has the most distinct letters in its name?

Once again, start by creating an F# Library project and adding `FSharp.Data`. Then add the code in Listing 13-4.

Listing 13-4. Accessing Wikipedia Information on London Underground Stations

```
#if INTERACTIVE
// You may have to alter this path depending on the version
// of FSharp.Data downloaded and on you project structure
#r @"..\packages\FSharp.Data.2.2.5\lib\net40\FSharp.Data.dll"
#else
module UndergroundHTML
#endif

open FSharp.Data

type Stations = HtmlProvider< @"https://en.wikipedia.org/wiki/List_of_London_Underground_stations">

let ListStations() =
    let stations = Stations.Load(@"https://en.wikipedia.org/wiki/List_of_London_Underground_stations")

    let list = stations.Tables.Stations
    for station in list.Rows do
        printfn "%s is in %s" station.Station station.``Zone(s)[†]``
```

Note how close in structure this version is to the CSV example in Listing 13-1. Generally, F# type provider usage always follows this pattern: a setup phase that looks like a type alias, but with a static parameter indicating some location where a sample or schema information can be obtained (and maybe other static parameters specifying options); then the runtime initialization with real data; and finally the use of that data. So similar is this to the CSV example that you really only need to pull out one line for further examination:

```
let list = stations.Tables.Stations
```

This is where you specify the specific table that you want from the HTML: the table named `Stations`. Once again you see how a type provider can blur the distinction between data and code: you didn't have to say something like `stations.Tables("Stations")`. The `Stations` property is right there in IntelliSense.

You'd better check that the example works! Send all the code to F# Interactive and run `ListStations()`:

```
> ListStations();;
Acton Town is in 3
Aldgate is in 1
Aldgate East is in 1
Alperton is in 4
Amersham is in 9
Angel is in 1
Archway is in 2.1 !2&3
...
Woodford is in 4
Woodside Park is in 4
>
```

That was pretty successful! However, if you look at the entry for Archway, you'll see that the Zones value is shown as `2.1 !2&3`. This is because the table in Wikipedia contains two elements in this cell: a sort key to facilitate correct sorting by zone (this is where the `2.1 !` comes from), and the actual zone information. Fortunately, with a little extra code you can tidy this up (see Listing 13-5).

Listing 13-5. Tidying Up the Zones Column

```
for station in list.Rows do

    let zones =
        match station.``Zone(s)[†]`` |> Seq.tryFindIndex ((=) '!') with
        | Some(idx) -> station.``Zone(s)[†]``.[idx+1 ..]
        | None -> station.``Zone(s)[†]``

    printfn "%s is in %s" station.Station zones
```

■ **Note**   I am indebted to Evelina Gabasova for the code in Listing 13-5. Her blog at `http://evelinag.com/` is a must for all students of F#.

Here you are binding a new value called zones. To make a value for zones, you start by treating the raw value from the table as a sequence of characters, and trying to find an exclamation point. If one is found, you get all the characters after the index position of the exclamation point. If no exclamation point is found, you use the original string. Then you use your cleaned-up zones value in the `printfn` statement. This produces a nicer value for Archway and other station's zones:

```
Archway is in 2&3
```

In real life, you might go further and parse the &-separated values into a little array.

Answering Some Questions with the HTML Type Provider

So how about those challenges we mentioned at the beginning of this section? Once you have the data from the CSV type provider, it's just a matter of using the appropriate F# language constructs to select and manipulate the data as required.

Rank the Stations by Traffic

To rank the stations by passenger traffic (the Usage column) you need to get the usage as a floating point value. Unfortunately, you hit the same problem as earlier for ticketing zones: the Wikipedia table has some additional hidden information in that column, which appears in the text retrieved by the type provider. This time you have both sorting information (in the form 7001523100000000000♠), and for some columns, a note in square brackets. For example, the usage column for Bank Station contains the string 7001523100000000000♠52.31 [note 3]. This means you have to beef up your clean-up code to get the substring *after* any heart symbol and *before* any [symbol, and then try to convert that to a floating point value. Then you sort by the resulting value. This code is shown in Listing 13-6.

Listing 13-6. Stations by Usage

```
let StationsByUsage() =
    let getAfter (c : char) (s : string) =
        match s |> Seq.tryFindIndex ((=) c) with
            | Some(idx) -> s.[idx+1 ..]
            | None -> s

    let getBefore (c : char) (s : string) =
        match s |> Seq.tryFindIndex ((=) c) with
            | Some(idx) -> s.[.. idx-1]
            | None -> s

    let floatOrZero (s : string) =
        let ok, f = System.Double.TryParse(s)
        if ok then f else 0.

    let usageAsFloat (s : string) =
        s |> getAfter '♠' |> getBefore '[' |> floatOrZero

    let stations =
        Stations.Load(@"https://en.wikipedia.org/wiki/List_of_London_Underground_stations")

    let list = stations.Tables.Stations

    let ranked =
        list.Rows
        |> Array.map (fun s -> s.Station, s.``Usage[5]`` |> usageAsFloat)
        |> Array.sortByDescending snd

    for station, usage in ranked do
        printfn "%s, %f" station usage
```

Finding All of the Stations on the Northern Line

Finding all the stations on a particular line is a bit easier. You just need to filter for stations whose Line(s) column contains the name in question (see Listing 13-7). If you want perfect safety, you need to be a bit more careful about parsing the Line(s) column into separate lines, but the code works in practice.

Listing 13-7. Stations on a Specific Underground Line

```
let StationsOnLine (lineName : string) =
    let stations =
        Stations.Load( @"https://en.wikipedia.org/wiki/List_of_London_Underground_stations")

    let list = stations.Tables.Stations

    let ranked =
        list.Rows
        |> Array.filter (fun s -> s.``Line(s)[*]``.Contains lineName)

    for station in ranked do
        printfn "%s, %s" station.Station station.``Line(s)[*]``
```

Which Station Has the Most Distinct Letters in Its Name?

This is a matter of performing a descending sort by a count of the distinct letters in the station name, and getting the first resulting value. In F#, strings can be treated as sequences of characters, so you can directly call functions in the Seq module to do the work. See Listing 13-8.

Listing 13-8. The Station with the Most Distinct Letters

```
let StationWithMostLetters() =
    let stations =
        Stations.Load( @"https://en.wikipedia.org/wiki/List_of_London_Underground_stations")

    let list = stations.Tables.Stations

    let byChars =
        list.Rows
        |> Array.sortByDescending
            (fun s -> s.Station |> Seq.distinct |> Seq.length)

    byChars.[0]
```

Using the SQL Client Type Provider

In this section, you'll learn how to use the SQL Client type provider, which gives you frictionless, strongly typed access to SQL Server databases. In many scenarios, this type provider is a great alternative to heavyweight solutions like Entity Framework.

■ **Note** To use this example, you need to install SQL Server (the Express edition is suitable, but you can also use the full versions) or have access to SQL Server on another machine. You'll also need the AdventureWorks sample database or some other interesting dataset. You can readily adapt the code in this example to your own data.

If you need the AdventureWorks sample, you can find it at http://msftdbprodsamples.codeplex.com/.

To get started, create a new F# Library project, and add a reference to System.Data. Use NuGet or your favorite package manager to install the package FSharp.Data.SqlClient. Rename Library.fs to AdventureWorks.fs and add the code in Listing 13-9. Edit the connectionString value to reflect the requirements of the SQL Server installation to which you are connecting.

Listing 13-9. Using the SQL Client Type Provider

```
#if INTERACTIVE
// You may have to alter this path depending on the version
// of FSharp.Data.SqlClient downloaded and on your project structure
#r @"..\packages\FSharp.Data.SqlClient.1.8\lib\net40\FSharp.Data.SqlClient.dll"
#else
module AdventureWorks
#endif

open FSharp.Data

[<Literal>]
let connectionString =
    @"Data Source=.\SQLEXPRESS;Initial Catalog=AdventureWorks2014;Integrated Security=True"

let FindPeople surnameWildCard =
    use cmd = new SqlCommandProvider<"""
        SELECT
            BusinessEntityId,
            Title,
            FirstName,
            LastName
        FROM
            Person.Person
        WHERE
            Person.LastName LIKE @surnameWildCard
        ORDER BY
            LastName,
            FirstName
    """ , connectionString>()

    cmd.Execute(surnameWildCard = surnameWildCard)
```

Try the code by selecting all and sending to F# Interactive. Then switch to the F# Interactive window and run the function by typing FindPeople "%sen";; in the window, like so:

```
> FindPeople "%sen";;
val it :
  System.Collections.Generic.IEnumerable<SqlCommandProvider<...>.Record> =
  seq
    [{ BusinessEntityId = 12548; Title = None; FirstName = "Alejandro";
    LastName = "Andersen" }
      {Item = ?;};
    { BusinessEntityId = 19795; Title = None; FirstName = "Alicia"; LastName = "Andersen" }
      {Item = ?;};
    { BusinessEntityId = 12018; Title = None; FirstName = "Alisha"; LastName = "Andersen" }
      {Item = ?;};
    { BusinessEntityId = 16657; Title = None; FirstName = "Alison"; LastName = "Andersen" }
      {Item = ?;}; ...]
>
```

As you can see, the function returns a sequence of records, and each record has a field that comes straight from the corresponding database column. Also note how the optional field Title is mapped as an option type, so it gets the value None when the underlying database row contains a database NULL value for that row.

There are some other points to note about this particular type provider. It doesn't provide you with direct IntelliSense-style support while you write your SQL. Nor does it try to "abstract away" SQL. The benefit of this is that you get the full richness of the SQL language in all its raw power. Also, you are free to write the most efficient queries possible, something which is always compromised to some extent when SQL is abstracted away.

Having said this, you do get feedback about whether your SQL is valid as you type, provided that you are using an environment like Visual Studio, which offers "red wiggly line" support for language syntax errors. Prove this by editing the SQL from Listing 13-9 to introduce a deliberate error. After a short delay you'll see a red wiggly line below all your SQL code (Figure 13-4). If you hover the cursor above any of the highlighted code, you'll see details of the error.

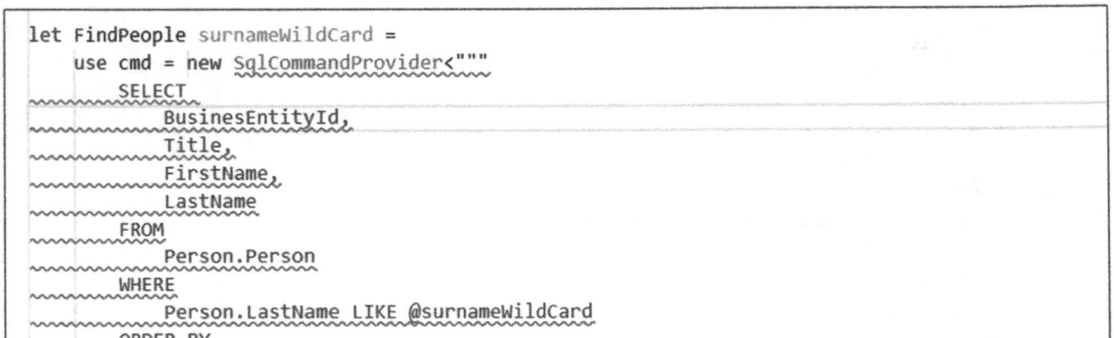

```
let FindPeople surnameWildCard =
    use cmd = new SqlCommandProvider<"""
        SELECT
            BusinesEntityId,
            Title,
            FirstName,
            LastName
        FROM
            Person.Person
        WHERE
            Person.LastName LIKE @surnameWildCard
        ORDER BY
            LastName,
            FirstName
        """, connectionString>()

        cmd.Execute(
```
The type provider 'FSharp.Data.SqlCommandProvider' reported an error: Invalid column name 'BusinesEntityId'. The batch could not be analyzed because of compile errors.

Figure 13-4. *Errors in SQL are highlighted*

This is usually enough information to home in on the mistake.

Another thing to note is that any SQL variables you include (such as @surnameWildCard in this example) are automatically picked up by the type provider and become required parameters of the Execute method:

```
cmd.Execute(surnameWildCard = surnameWildCard)
```

If you activate IntelliSense for Execute in this code (in Visual Studio, place the cursor just after the opening bracket and press Ctrl+Shift+Space), you'll see a tool tip indicating that Execute takes a string parameter called surnameWildCard (Figure 13-5). The parameter list will update every time you add, rename, or remove SQL @ variables in your SQL code. Amazing!

```
cmd.Execute(surnameWildCard = surnameWildCard)
Execute(surnameWildCard: string) : System.Collections.Generic.IEnumerable<SqlCommandProvider<...>.Record>
```

Figure 13-5. *A parameter automatically generated from an SQL variable*

Now take a moment to explore the implications of the fact that nullable database columns are exposed by the type provider as option types. Add the code from Listing 13-10 below your existing code.

Listing 13-10. Attempting to List People Separated by Tabs

```
let ShowPeople =
    FindPeople
    >> Seq.iter (fun person ->
        printfn "%s\t%s\t%s"
            person.Title person.FirstName person.LastName)
```

Here you are attempting to write a function that calls FindPeople and then lists out some fields from the result in a tab-separated form. (Incidentally, you partially apply FindPeople and use function composition via the >> operator, meaning that you don't have to repeat the surnameWildCard parameter in this function.) As soon as you paste this code, you should get an error because the format string is expecting person.Title to be a string when in fact it is an Option<string>. This doesn't happen for the FirstName and LastName fields because these are mandatory in the database, and so can be mapped directly to strings.

You can fix this by providing a little function that maps from an Option<string> to either the underlying string if the input is Some, or to an empty string if it is None. Listing 13-11 shows such a function, named as an operator (~~) so that it appears super-lightweight at the call site.

Listing 13-11. Dealing with Optional Strings

```
let (~~) (s : string option) =
    match s with
    | Some s -> s
    | None -> ""
```

Paste this into your code above ShowPeople, and amend ShowPeople so that it uses the ~~ operator for the person.Title field:

```
printfn "%s\t%s\t%s"
    ~~person.Title person.FirstName person.LastName
```

Send all your code to F# Interactive and try it out by calling ShowPeople:

```
> ShowPeople("%sen");;
        Alejandro       Andersen
        Alicia          Andersen
        Alisha          Andersen
        Alison          Andersen
        Alvin           Andersen
        ...
Ms.     Dorothy         Wollesen
>
```

Joining Datasets from Differing Data Sources

A common scenario, particularly in reporting and data cleansing situations, is the need to combine datasets from completely different sources. You can use F# type providers and F# query expressions to do this simply and effectively.

Let's imagine you are doing a data cleansing exercise on the data in the AdventureWorks2014 database. You need to see any country names in Person.CountryRegion where the country names don't match up with a reference list, and take a look at any notes that might indicate that a country code has been reassigned or is otherwise unusual. You can do this using the HTML type provider to get the country code's reference information from Wikipedia, the SQL Client type provider to get the data to be checked from the database, and an F# query expression to combine them.

Start by creating a new F# library project; rename Library1.fs to VerifyCountryCodes.fs. Use NuGet or your favorite package manager to add the FSharp.Data and FSharp.Data.SqlClient packages. Then add setup information for your Wikipedia and SQL connections, much like you did in the preceding exercises for the HTML and SQL Client type providers (Listing 13-12).

Listing 13-12. Setting up the HTML and SQL Client Type Providers

```
#if INTERACTIVE
// You may have to alter this path depending on the version
// of FSharp.Data downloaded and on you project structure
#r @"..\packages\FSharp.Data.2.2.5\lib\net40\FSharp.Data.dll"
#r @"..\packages\FSharp.Data.SqlClient.1.8\lib\net40\FSharp.Data.SqlClient.dll"
#else
module VerifyCountryCodes
#endif

open FSharp.Data

[<Literal>]
let url = "https://en.wikipedia.org/wiki/ISO_3166-1_alpha-2"
[<Literal>]
let connectionString =
    @"Data Source=.\SQLEXPRESS;Initial Catalog=AdventureWorks2014;Integrated Security=True"

type WikipediaPage =
    HtmlProvider<url>
```

Now make some record types to hold the fields that you want to get from each source and the fields you want in the final report (Listing 13-13).

Listing 13-13. Record Types for Data Sources and the Final Report

```
type WikiCode =
    {
        Code : string
        Name : string
        Notes : string
    }

type DbCode =
    {
        Code : string
        Name : string
    }

type ReportItem =
    {
        Code : string
        WikiName : string
        DBName : string
        Notes : string
    }
```

Now you need a function that will get the list of codes from the relevant Wikipedia page (Listing 13-14). Note how, as before, you use `page.Tables.<Table Name>` to get all the rows from a named table within the page. Then you iterate over the rows, creating a `WikiCode` instance for each row and returning the results as an F# list.

Listing 13-14. Getting County Codes from Wikipedia

```
let CountryCodesWikipedia() =
    let page = WikipediaPage.Load(url)

    let codes = page.Tables.``Officially assigned code elements``

    [ for row in codes.Rows ->
        { WikiCode.Code = row.Code
          Name = row.``Country name``
          Notes = row.Notes } ]
```

If you like, you can now send this code to F# Interactive and check that the `CountryCodesWikipedia` function works as expected.

```
> CountryCodesWikipedia();;
val it : WikiCode list =
  [{Code = "AD";
    Name = "Andorra";
    Notes = "";};
...
```

Now you need a function to get country codes and names from the database. This is very similar to CountryCodesWikipedia except that you use the SQL Client type provider (Listing 13-15).

Listing 13-15. Getting Country Codes from the Database

```
let CountryCodesDatabase() =
    use cmd = new SqlCommandProvider<"""
        SELECT
                CountryRegionCode,
                Name
        FROM
                Person.CountryRegion
        ORDER BY
                CountryRegionCode
        """ , connectionString>()

    let data = cmd.Execute()

    [ for row in data ->
        { DbCode.Code = row.CountryRegionCode
          Name = row.Name } ]
```

Once again you can send this to F# Interactive and give it a try:

```
> CountryCodesDatabase();;
val it : DbCode list =
  [{Code = "AD";
    Name = "Andorra";};
...
```

Now you need to tie these two data sources together, and filter for suspicious results, which in this scenario are any codes with notes on Wikipedia and any codes whose country names differ between Wikipedia and the AdventureWorks2014 database. A good way of joining IEnumerable datasets is F#'s query expression syntax, as shown in Listing 13-16.

Listing 13-16. Using a Query Expression to Join Two Datasets

```
let Report() =
    query {
        for dbc in CountryCodesDatabase() do
        join wkc in CountryCodesWikipedia() on
            (dbc.Code = wkc.Code)
        where (wkc.Notes <> "" || wkc.Name <> dbc.Name)
        sortBy (wkc.Code)
        select
            {
                ReportItem.Code = wkc.Code
                WikiName = wkc.Name
```

```
            DBName = dbc.Name
            Notes = wkc.Notes
        }
    }
    |> Array.ofSeq
```

The main logic is enclosed in query {}, which is a computation expression like seq {} in which certain keywords and constructs have a special meaning. In the case of query {}, these are keywords that let you get, join, filter, and project data from IEnumerables. You start by calling CountryCodesDatabase and defining a label dbc for items from IEnumerable:

```
for dbc in CountryCodesDatabase() do
```

Then you call CountryCodesWikipedia(), stating that you want to join the Wikipedia results to the database results where the two match on code:

```
join wkc in CountryCodesWikipedia() on
    (dbc.Code = wkc.Code)
```

Next, you filter the results for items that are suspicious according to the required logic: different country codes or notes in Wikipedia. You also sort the results by code:

```
where (wkc.Notes <> "" || wkc.Name <> dbc.Name)
sortBy (wkc.Code)
```

Finally, within the query expression you project the results into instances of your ReportItem record type:

```
select
    {
        ReportItem.Code = wkc.Code
        WikiName = wkc.Name
        DBName = dbc.Name
        Notes = wkc.Notes
    }
```

All that remains is to convert the results from an F# sequence to an array. The advantages of doing this are that it prevents any laziness from leaking into the wider scope, it's friendlier to other calling languages, and it also makes it easier to see the full results in F# Interactive.

Send all your code to F# Interactive and run it by calling Report(). You get a nice dataset that can be used as a great basis for reviewing the validity of the country codes and names in the database.

```
> Report();;
val it : ReportItem [] =
  [|{Code = "AI";
    WikiName = "Anguilla";
    DBName = "Anguilla";
    Notes = "AI previously represented French Afar and Issas";};
    {Code = "AQ";
    WikiName = "Antarctica";
    DBName = "Antarctica";
```

```
    Notes =
     "Covers the territories south of 60° south latitude Code taken from name in French:
     Antarctique";};
...
   {Code = "VN";
    WikiName = "Viet Nam";
    DBName = "Vietnam";
    Notes = "ISO country name follows UN designation (common name: Vietnam)";};
...
```

Summary

In this chapter, you learned about the concept of type providers, and how that concept plays out in the CSV type provider, the HTML type provider, and the SQL Client type provider. Type providers yield an amazing productivity gain in a wide variety of situations where you are required to access external, structured data.

You also learned about F# query expressions, and how to apply them to join datasets coming from two different type providers into a single stream of data.

Index

■ A

Abstract syntax tree (AST), 246
    compilation
        Command Line Input, 259
        DynamicMethod, 257
        vs. interpretation, 263–264
        vs. interpretation test harness, 261
        native code generation, 257
        .NET Code-Generation technologies, 258
        .NET framework, 257
    construction, 255
    interpretation
        Command-Line Input, 256
        outcomes, 255
        value, 255
    languages, 255
    types, 255
Active patterns
    complete (*see* Complete active patterns)
    partial (*see* Partial active patterns)
ADO.NET
    AdventureWorks sample database and SQL
        Server 2014 Express Edition, 177
    classes in, 189
    database providers, 190
    Dispose method, 179
    getString() function, 179–180
    preceding codes, 178
    printRows() function, 181
    read()function, 180, 182
    system.data and system.configuration, 177
Anonymous functions
    defined, 21
    lambda, 21
Apple OS X, 10–11
Arithmetic-language implementation
    AST (*see* Abstract syntax tree (AST))
    compiler/interpreter, 254
    design, 254
    NuGet package, 254

■ B

Bitwise "Or" and "And" operators, 152

■ C

cast function, 154, 160
Casting
    description, 120
    downcasting, 121
    upcasting, 120
choose function, 154, 158
Class
    abstract classes, 118–119
    ChangePassword method, 106–107
    description, 104
    and inheritance, 112
    let bindings, 105–106
    logon message, 105
    method, 104
    and static methods, 119–120

Arithmetic operators

Arithmetic operators
    basic arithmetic operations, 147
    operators module, 148
    PhysicalEquality function, 149
    record, struct and discriminated
        union types, 148
    structural comparison, 149
Array.Parallel module, 207, 209
Asynchronous programming
    async keyword, 210
    Async.RunSynchronously function, 210
    Begin/End, 210
    Beginning and Ending file, 213
    blocked threads, 209
    execution flow, 211
    version of, 211–212
    workflow/"computation
        expression" syntax, 210
Autoproperties, 117–118

© Robert Pickering and Kit Eason 2016
R. Pickering and K. Eason, *Beginning F# 4.0*, DOI 10.1007/978-1-4842-1374-2

Comments
  cross-compilation, 140
  doc comments, 138–140
  multiple-line comments, 138
  single-line, 138
Compatibility and advanced interoperation
  COM Objects, 276–277
  COM-style API's, 277–278
  F# from native code, 281–283
  F# libraries (*see* F# libraries)
  platform invoke, 279–280
  techniques, 283
Complete active patterns
  banana brackets, 56
  description, 56
  parsing input string data, 56
  TryParse method, 57
Component Object Model (COM)
  COM-Style APIs, 277–278
  F# from native code, 281–283
  Microsoft Office, 278
  .NET assembly, 277
  .NET Framework, 276
concat Function, 154–155
Control flow
  if … then … else … expression, 37
  uninitialized identifiers, 38
Conversion functions, 151
CSV type provider
  access data, 286
  Archway data file, 289
  column names, 289
  column separator, 286
  dataset, 286
  features, 291
  F# library project, 286
  FSharp.Data library, 288
  header columns, 288–289
  security warning, 287
  undergroundCSV.fs, 287
  zones, 289–290
Custom attributes
  obsolete attributes, 141–142
  unrestricted property, 141

■ D

Data binding process
  App.config, 182–184
  data-bound combo box, 184
  DataSource property, 185
  and DataGridView Control, 185–188
  peopleTable row collection, 184
  user interface control,
      mapping of, 182

Data parallelism
  Array.Parallel module, 207, 209
  data collection in parallel, 207
  description, 207
  FSharp.Collections.ParallelSeq module, 209
  multicore systems, 207
Data structures
  language implementation
    AST, 246
    combinator library, 247, 249–250, 252
    CompositeShape, 246, 248
    2D images, 245
    DSL library, 245
    F# Console Application, 247
    lines function, 246–247
    Polygon, 248
    WinForm, 248
  little languages
    Argu, 242, 244
    ArgumentParser.Create, 244
    creating functions/modules, 241
    CSV-Friendly Style, 242
    default value, 244
    Directory.EnumerateFiles, 243
    DSL, 242, 245
    F# expressions, 241
    ListFiles function, 243–244
    parameter values, 244
    simple exploratory test, 243
    string type's IndexOf, 245
    substring methods, 245
Delegate, 122–123
Discriminated unions, 50–53
Distributed applications
  client-server applications, 223
  description, 223
  fault tolerance, 223
  HTTP (*see* Hypertext Transfer Protocol (HTTP))
  peer-to-peer applications, 223
  scalability, 223
  security, 224
  web services, 224
Distributed applications. Suave.io
Doc comments, 138–140
Domain-specific languages (DSLs), 5, 241
DSLs . *See* Domain-specific languages (DSLs)

■ E

Enums, 123–124
Exceptions
  finally keyword, 61
  raise keyword, 60
  WrongSecond, 60
exists and forall Functions, 154, 156–157

■ F, G

filter, find and tryFind Functions, 154, 157
filter Function, 164
F# libraries
    C# list, 273
    defining classes and interfaces, 274, 276
    defining types, namespace, 273
    design, 265
    expose functions, 267–268
    F# list, 272
    FSharp.Collections.Seq module
        (*see* FSharp.Collections.Seq module)
    FSharp.Control.Event module
        (*see* FSharp.Control.Event module)
    FSharp.Core.Operators module
        (*see* FSharp.Core.Operators module)
    FSharp.Core.Printf module
        (*see* FSharp.Core.Printf module)
    FSharp.Reflection module
        (*see* FSharp.Reflection module)
    .NET languages, 265
    returning tuples, 266
    rules, 265–266
    union types
        C# code, 269
        Discrete/Continuous, 270
        pattern matching, 271–272
        quantity, 269
        series of properties, 270
Floating-point arithmetic functions, 147, 149–150
fold function, 154, 156
F# programming
    Apple OS X, 10–11
    DLLs, 15
    F# interactive
        creation, new project, 15
        running, function, 18
        sending code, 17
    interactive, 14
    Linux, 12, 14
    microsoft windows, 7–8, 10
    Windows/Mono platforms, 15
FSharp.Collections.ParallelSeq module, 209
FSharp.Collections.Seq module
    cast Function, 160
    choose Function, 158
    concat Function, 155
    exists and forall Functions, 156–157
    filter, find and tryFind Functions, 157
    fold Function, 156
    IEnumerable interface, 147, 154
    init and initInfinite Functions, 158–159
    map and iter Functions, 154–155
    unfold Function, 159–160

FSharp.Control.Event module
    creating and handling events, 163–164
    description, 147
    filter Function, 164
    map Function, 165
    partition Function, 164
    trigger function, 163
FSharp.Core.Operators module
    arithmetic, 148–149
    bitwise "Or" and "And" operators, 152
    conversion functions, 151
    floating-point arithmetic
        functions, 147, 149–150
    language's operators, 147
    mathematical operators, 147
    tuple functions, 151
FSharp.Reflection module
    .NET Framework's reflection, 147
    reflection over types, 152–153
    reflection over values, 153–154
    System.Reflection
        namespace, 152
FSharp.Text.Printf module
    error type, 162
    formatting strings, 147
    numeric types, 162–163
    placeholders and flags, 161
Functional programming (FP)
    advantages, 2
    COBOL, 1
    F#, 2–5
    FORTRAN, 1
    imperative languages, 1
    object-oriented languages, 1
    real-world applications, 1
Function application
    add function, 31
    function calling with arguments, 31
    to partial application, 32–33
    pipe-forward operator (|>), 32
    System.Math.Cos, 32

■ H

HTML type provider
    Archway, 292
    data and code, 292
    FSharp.Data, 291
    Station, Distinct Letters, 294
    Stations rank, traffic, 293–294
    Stations, underground line, 294
    Tidying up Zones column, 292
    value for zones, 292
    Wikipedia information, 291
    Wikipedia page, 291

Hypertext Transfer Protocol (HTTP)
coding using, 224–225
description, 224
with Google Spreadsheets, 226–228
System.Net.WebResponse class, 224

■ I

Identifiers
add function, 22
calculatePrefixFunction, 27
description, 21
names, 23
scope of, 23–26
string/integer literals, 22
use binding, 28
values and functions, 22
Imperative programming
arrays, 73–77
control flow, 77–80
definition, mutable records, 69–70
mutable keyword, 67–69
NET libraries
calling static methods and properties, 80–82
events, 85–88
indexers, 85
objects and instance members, 82–84
|> operator, 90–91
pattern matching, 88–89
reference type, 70–73
unit type, 65–67
init and initInfinite Functions, 154, 158

■ J, K

Java Virtual Machine (JVM), 252

■ L

Lambda functions, 21
Language-Integrated Query (LINQ)
classes, to XML, 193
codes, 191–192, 194
Enumerable.Select, 191
Enumerable.Where, 191
methods, 191
System.Xml.Linq namespace, 193
useful.NET data access technology, 190
XElement's ToString method, 193
Language-oriented programming
arithmetic-language implementation
(see Arithmetic-language implementation)
data structures (see Data structures)
DSL, 241

F#, 264
features and techniques, 264
techniques, 241
Lazy evaluation
code, 62
computation, 62
Fibonacci numbers, 63–64
functional programming, 62
IEnumerable type. seq values, 62
lazyList identifier, 63
unfold function, 63
Linux, 12, 14
List comprehensions
comprehension syntax, 42
positive integers, 43
squarePoints, 44
step size, incrementing numbers, 43
yield keyword, 44
Lists
comprehensions, 42–44
empty list, 38
immutable, 39
List.rev function, 40
pattern matching against, 40–42
syntax to, 38
System.Object code, 38
Literals
building blocks for computations, 19
F#, 19–20
printf function, 20–21
string literals, 20

■ M

map and iter functions, 154–155
map Function, 165
Message passing
AddValue union case, 221
agents/actors, 213
Closed event, 222
Collector<'a>, 220
Console.ReadLine(), 214
F# Interactive, 214–219
GetValues member
method implementation, 221
GUIs, 214
List.length function, 216
MailboxProcessor class, 213
pattern matching, 220
Post method, 216
printPoints function, 217
runInGuiContext function, 221
Stop union case, 221
Updates event, 221

Metaprogramming with quotations
    F# code, 252
    integer-based arithmetic expressions, 253
    JVM, 252
    .NET languages, 254
    SpecificCall, 253
    stack-based evaluation, 253
Modules
    aliases, 130
    execution, 134–135
    identifiers, 125–126
    keyword, 125
    scope, 132–133
    submodules, 126

■ **N**

Namespaces, 273–274
    module names, 127
    opening, 128–130
    organizing code, 127
    submodule names, 127

■ **O**

Object expressions
    description, 100
    IComparer interface, 101, 103
    makeNumberControl function, 103
    override methods, 103
    sorted, custom-drawn controls, 104
    sorted text box controls, 103
Object-oriented programming
    additional constructor, 108–109
    base class, 114–115
    casting, 120–121
    class, 104–107
    delegate, 122–123
    encapsulation, 93
    enums, 123–124
    F# types with members
        overriding, 100
        Point record type, 98
        Swap function, 98–99
        union type, 99
    implementation inheritance, 93
    interfaces
        defining, 109
        implementation, 110–111
    methods and inheritance, 112–114
    object expressions (*see* Object expressions)
    optional parameters, 107–108
    overriding methods, non-F# libraries, 118
    polymorphism, 93
    property, 115–117
    records as objects
        drawing shapes, 95–97
        makeShape function, 94
        reposition function, 94–95
    structs, 123
    tenets, 93
    type tests, 122
Operators
    consequences, 30
    defined, 29
    NET library, 30
    prefix and infix, 29, 31
    user-defined (*custom*) operators, 30
Optional compilation
    DEBUG and TRACE switches, 137
    description, 136
    MonoDevelop's compiler
        configuration dialog, 137
    visual studio's build configuration dialog, 136

■ **P**

Parallel programming
    asynchronous (*see* Asynchronous
        programming)
    context switch, 198
    critical section, 199
    functional, 197
    locking, 201
    lockObj and lock function, 200
    makeSafeThread, 199–200
    message passing (*see* Message passing)
    monitor section, 199
    multicore processors, 197
    threads, 198
    parallel programming (*see* Data parallelism)
Partial active patterns
    description, 56
    .NET regular expression, 57–58
    option type, 57
Partition Function, 164
Pattern matching
    Boolean expression, 34
    compiler, 34
    fundamental building blocks of F#, 37
    input data analysis, 33
    Lucas sequence, 33
    myOr function, 36
    over tuples, 35
    stringToBoolean, 35
    syntax for, 34
    types and values, 33
    wildcard, 34
pipe-forward operator (|>), 32
Private and internal let bindings, 131–132

Property
 abstract properties, 116
 definition, 115
 description, 115
 indexers, 116–117
 single property, 115

■ Q

Quoted Code, 143–146

■ R

Reactive programming
 calculation on threads, 203–204
 data grid view, 205–206
 DoWork and RunWorker
  Completed events, 204–205
 Fibonacci calculation algorithm, 201
 GUI for Fibonacci numbers, 203
 GUI programming, 201
 multi-threaded programming, 207
 runWorker(), 205
 System.ComponentModel namespace, 201
 WinForms, 202
Record types
 description, 48
 field values, 50
 findDavid function, 49
 syntax for, 48
 type definition organizationl, 48
 wayneManor, 49
Recursion
 base case, 29
 defined, 28
 n^{th} term in Fibonacci sequence, 29
 recursive case, 29

■ S

Signature files
 creation, 131
 Visual Studio, 131
SQL client type provider
 access, 294
 direct IntelliSense-style support, 296
 errors, 296
 F# Library project, 295–296
 List People Separated by Tabs, 297
 Optional Strings, 297
 parameter, 297
Structs, 123
Suave.io
 ConcurrentDictionary instances, 233
 description, 229

Fiddler setting up, to send POST, 231
 limitations, 229
 longToShort dictionary, 234
 NET random
  number generator, 232
 response in Fiddler, 232
 shortToLong dictionary, 233
 url, defined, 231
 URL Shortener, 229–230
 WebPart instances, 234
Suave.io (*see* Web services)
Sum types, 50–53
System.Configuration namespace
 App.config and
  MyApp.exe.config, 167
 ConfigurationManager's
  static AppSettings property, 168
 configuration values, access of, 167
 ConnectionStrings property, 168
 machine.config, 169
 "MyConnectionString", 168
 System.IO namespace, 170
System.IO namespace
 FileInfo and DirectoryInfo
  objects, 170
 File.ReadAllLines method, 171
 memory and network
  streams, 170
 sequences with, 172–173
System.Xml namespace
 AppendChild method, 174
 classes, 176
 description, 173
 fruitsDoc, 174
 fruits.xml, 174

■ T

ToUpperInvariant() method, 25
Tuple functions, 151
Tuples
 description, 47
 user-defined types in F#, 47
Type annotation, 47
Type parameterization, 46
Type providers
 CSV (*see* CSV type provider)
 CSV file, 285
 datasets
  AdventureWorks2014 database, 298
  CountryCodesdatabase, 300–301
  County Codes from Wikipedia, 299
  data sources and
   final report, 299, 301
  elements, 286

expressions, 298
  HTML and SQL client, 298
  query expression, 300
features, 285
HTML (*see* F# type providers:HTML type provider)
language and data, 285
query expressions, 302
SQL client (*see* SQL client type provider)
structured data, 302
Type system
  annotation, 47
  defined, 44
  div1 and div2 functions, 45
  doNothingToAnInt function, 46
  identifiers, 45
  makeMessage function, 45
  parameterization, 46
  recursive, 55
  stringList list, 46
  tuple and record types, 47–50
  type parameters, 53–55
  union and sum types, 50–53
  Visual Studio users, 45
Type tests, 122

■ U, V

unfold Function, 154, 159–160
Union types, 50–53
Units of measure
  F# type system, 58
  sprintf, printf/printtfn, 60
  syntax, 59
  type float<liter/pint>, 59
User-defined operators, 30

■ W, X, Y, Z

Web services
  ASP.NET Web API 2.0 project, 235
  F# ASP.NET MVC 5/Web API 2 template, 236
  Fiddler to send post with query string, 239
  IHttpActionResult, 239
  project type selection, 236
  response in Fiddler, 240
  RoutePrefix attribute, 238
  URL Shortener, 237–239
Windows Presentation Foundation (WPF) graphics, 142

Get the eBook for only $5!

Why limit yourself?

Now you can take the weightless companion with you wherever you go and access your content on your PC, phone, tablet, or reader.

Since you've purchased this print book, we're happy to offer you the eBook in all 3 formats for just $5.

Convenient and fully searchable, the PDF version enables you to easily find and copy code—or perform examples by quickly toggling between instructions and applications. The MOBI format is ideal for your Kindle, while the ePUB can be utilized on a variety of mobile devices.

To learn more, go to www.apress.com/companion or contact support@apress.com.

Printed in the United States
By Bookmasters